Releases From My Soul

Releases From My Soul
Gina Iafrate

Published by Gina Iafrate
Hollywood FL

© Copyright - Gina Iafrate. All rights reserved.
First Paperback Printing August 2019

As this is a product of fiction, any names or coincidental connections contained in this novel are totally fictional and not based on any real people or events. All names, characters, businesses, places, events, locales and incidents are the product of the author's imagination and are used in a fictitious manner. No part of this publication may be reproduced in any form, or by any means, electronic or mechanical, including photocopying, recording, or any information browsing, or retrieval system, without permission in writing from Gina Iafrate or the established publisher.

Publisher: Gina Iafrate

ISBN: 978-1-7752407-4-7

Cover Design: Gina Iafrate

Back Cover Design: Gina Iafrate

Originally published in the USA by Gina Iafrate
Hollywood FL

In Gratitude

This book is dedicated to my loving parents who have passed on. They loved literature and so believed in education to be the best ammunition one could possess. I know they would be ever so proud as they couldn't stress enough my desire to keep learning. Once more, my husband Mario for his love, patience, and support as my passion for writing diverted me in my own world of solitude.

My precious grandson Carl Trivieri for inviting me to California where I had great opportunities to enhance my research and to observe numerous homeless first-hand. It gave me the chance to share my contribution to them, which gave me great fulfillment.

CONTENTS

Chapter	Page
The Sealed Envelope	1
He Healed her "Broken Heart"	29
The Stranger on My Path	43
The Forbidden Love Affair	49
Dad's Last Celebration	61
The Divorce	67
A Coincidental Encounter	77
To Mother with Love	89
Across the Ocean	95
The Glorious Game of Golf	103
The Forest Adventure: Melbourne	109
Bring Out the Best in People	117
A Passion for Learning	119
The War in Memory	123
Living In Memories	127
With Love in Her Heart	133

A Poem: Shadows of the Night	151
A Poem: August. My Weeping Soul	153
An Interesting Job	155
Two Souls come together	161
The Marriage Vows	185
Nature on Planet Earth	199
Rise Above the Tide	203
Finding Serenity	207
My Heavenly Gift	221
A poem: Lady Cheek Performance	233
A Pebble on the Beach	235
Our Terrestrial Journey	281
We Seek Happiness	283
Mi Amour Just Vanished	285
Let's Spread our Love	297
Come into My World	299

Also by Gina Iafrate

The English Professor

The Girl from The Corn Field

Bestowed by Love and Splendour

Novel No.1

THE SEALED ENVELOPE

Bianca Rosa's anxiety level was off the charts this morning. Her hands were trembling and her heart raced as she held the brown envelope. She never dreamed that from this day forward, the contents were going to change her life forever.

Her shoulder-length blonde hair adorned her round facial features. A petite young woman with captivating sparkling eyes, she had inherited a turned-up nose with a vibrant and intelligent face. Her polished and professional appearance gave her the look of an intellect, yet deep in her heart the humbleness surfaced, manifesting her insecurities.

Her professional demeanour combined with her credentials had impressed and influenced the law firm of Lowell and Cohen to include her with their selected staff. Bianca Rosa Tempesta, a young attorney, had chosen her career path specializing in family law.

From her highly disciplined childhood, her daily routine was to arrive early at the office. Grandmother's preaching had been repeatedly ingrained in her: "It takes dedication, my girl. Immerse yourself totally in hard work, and success will automatically follow." This morning was no different, that was why she had come in early: to get ahead of the game. None of the other employees had arrived yet. Oh, how she cherished the quietness; the solitude gave her a chance to properly plan her day's work. *How right you were, Grandma!* she thought, though lately, the overload was getting unbearable. As much as she loved her work, in the past, her resentment had been building up. Wiping the perspiration from her forehead, she took a deep breath and whispered to herself, God, please give me a break.

The office was located in the heart of downtown Miami by the Bayside District, on the twenty-first floor. This was the place where Bianca had been spending most of her waking hours, with the exclusion of court appearances. Lowell and Cohen employed one hundred-eighteen lawyers to serve the different needs of their clients. She had not reached the partnership rank yet. The unfairness of the office politics these days was getting on her nerves. The work seemed to pile up by the day, with difficult clients, more and more families splitting up. Why, she couldn't understand. The anger of the spouses, from either gender was flouting in the air and reigned on the four walls of her office. It was renewed by one client after another; these were the people she dealt with all day in war. The children were the rubber strings pulled between their fingers to snap, broken, anytime. Bianca took a deep breath, and in quick steps made her way to the window to open it and to allow some fresh air in. The sun's rays filtered through the large window, warmer than ever this morning. This is why the room felt unbearably hot and the air stuffy. She took a few moments to look out. The ocean was calm and the beach not yet invaded by beach lovers. A strong desire flowed through her veins to run freely, barefoot on that white sand out there. She pictured herself running with her arms outstretched and the morning breeze gently refreshing her tired body. She brushed a hand through her forehead "That would be so nice, but I need to pull myself away from this enticing scenery and get to work." She had gotten to the habit of talking to herself lately.

Her eyes glanced at the stack of files on her desk; another big day of hard work lay ahead. She reluctantly sat on her swivel chair and glanced once more at her L-shaped cherrywood desk. A heavy rock seemed to be sitting right on top her head, pressuring, swirling into a migraine. In the midst of the pain, her hands automatically raised gently to press against her temples; the circular motion worked to release the pressure. She opened the desk drawer, grabbed and swallowed a couple of Tylenol with a glass of water. Shook her head in a strong resolve and diligently began immersing herself into her files, one after another—the usual monotonous routine. One case after the other of troubled couples in family battles fueled by hatred and resentment. The children were the subject of her main concern. Many of them were being pulled like yo-yos into custody battles and parental quarrels.

She couldn't quite comprehend it. Disturbed she dipped her thoughts into her own soul and she often questioned why these people took family for granted and never realized how really lucky they were. Why are these couples throwing their families away? If I had only been given a chance with my siblings and, most of all, my parents. Even the one and only person I had has been taken from me. How cruel can life turn out to be!

Chapter Two.

As Bianca delved deeper into her work, a knock on the door interrupted her concentration.

"Yes," she responded. "Come in."

"Miss Tempesta," a paralegal called out. "Mr. Lowell would like to see you in his office."

"Oh, when?" she asked.

"As soon as you can," she replied. "He's in his office now."

"Fine, I will be there shortly."

Oh, this is all I need this morning; one of Mr. Gordon Lowell's 'ceremonies'. His favorite hobby as C.E.O. of the firm, she thought, anticipating one more of his lengthy lectures and complaints. Mr. Lowell intimidated her, therefore he was not one of her favorite people, and she dreaded any conversation with him. But he had summoned her and she had no choice but to oblige. She checked her appearance in the full-length mirror behind the closet door; the firm had implemented a professional dress code and this morning, while rushing to get to her overload, she had not paid much attention to her appearance. Mr. Lowell always stressed at the staff monthly meetings to dress professionally in the business world, you need to portray the part you represent. Therefore, your appearance is important.

When she had first been hired, she had no money to buy expensive suits, and one day, some dignitaries were visiting the office, but Mr. Lowell did not introduce her. He later confessed to her that she was not dressed appropriately to represent the firm of Cohen and Lowell.

Reluctantly, she now walked to Lowell's office. What could he want? she pondered. But to her surprise, Mr. Lowell seemed cheerful and pleasant as he welcomed her in this time.

"Bianca Rosa, good morning. How are you on this lovely bright day?" he cheerfully greeted her, extending his hand, gracefully inviting her to take a seat on the superb Italian leather chair in front of his huge desk. She didn't know what to make of his good humor since she had always known him as curt and unfriendly, which was the reason she never felt comfortable in his company.

"Thank you, Mr. Lowell, I'm fine," she said curtly, while willing her headache to go away.

As usual, presented himself well-groomed with his dark navy-blue suit and a crisp white shirt with a perfectly matching paisley tie. His attire indicated a look of authority. As she scrutinized him, his amicable facial expression had turned him into a likeable soul on this day. She felt somewhat encouraged.

With a big smile, Mr. Lowell picked up a brown envelope. "Bianca Rosa, I was given instructions by your grandmother to put this together for you. It is my obligation to proceed with my duty and hand this to you now. You have my permission to take a leave of absence."

"Mr. Lowell, what do you mean?" she gasped, puzzled.

"Please, open the envelope," he motioned, handing it to her.

She hesitated. A sealed envelope. She could not imagine what this was all about.

Grandma or Nonna, as she called her, was so far removed from her life that none of this made any sense. This was totally unexpected. Bianca had been so used to receiving bad news that she thought the contents of this envelope meant more of the same. Her grandmother's health was in decline, for sure.

Mr. Lowell repeated gently, "Go ahead, open it. It's all yours, and this is the right time for you to have it:" with much uncertainty, she was reluctant. But his smile and kindness helped reassure Bianca Rosa that something good was coming her way.

With shaking hands, she opened the large brown envelope. The first item was a birthday card along with a collection of all her past birthday cards; her grandmother had saved them all for her. They were nicely tucked one inside the other, including the paper one; which was once made by Nonna herself when she could not spare a penny to buy a real card. The cards were held together by a silky white ribbon, in a notebook format.

A handwritten message in gold ink was inscribed on the ribbon: "My love for you will never cease. You will always be close to my heart. Forever, Grandma, your Nonna."

Bianca Rose burst into tears. "Poor Grandma, so loving and intelligent at one time, now all she does is stare into empty space, she can't stand up anymore," she exclaimed.

"I understand how you feel, Bianca Rosa, life can be so cruel," he responded.

Tenderly, he put his arm around her shoulders, handed her some tissue paper to wipe her tears, and patiently stood by for her to regain her composure.

"Continue. There is much more," he coaxed. She looked at the front cover of a large illustrated card that pictured a renaissance, angelic young girl holding a beautiful bouquet of white roses. In her grandmother's handwriting were the words:

"Happy Thirtieth Birthday, my darling. Please, celebrate it to the fullest at a place where our ancestors lived. This is my delivered promise to you and my wish for you. Enjoy it, Bianca Rosa, with all my love, Grandma."

Bianca's hands trembled and her heart felt a sharp pain. She realised her grandmother must have prepared this for her when she was well. For the last few years, her grandmother had stopped recognizing her because of Alzheimer's had taken her over. Bianca Rosa had suffered along with her as it progressed to the point of no return. The ugly sickness of her grandmother had left the young attorney alone, heart-broken, distressed. She had no other family members except her eighty-eight-year-old grandmother, who now lived in a hospice like a vegetable.

Mr. Lowell said, "Check further, see what else is there for you."

Her smeared eye makeup with tears streaming down her cheeks had rendered her like a sad clown, with black paint smeared under her eyes, unfit for a professional look. Oh, how she missed her grandmother. For such a long time now, she had felt abandoned by God and the entire universe. Between tears, she asked Mr. Lowell, "Why has life been so unfair to me?"

He replied, "Bianca Rosa, my dear. I know it does not seem fair, but you have your youth, a brilliant career, and good health. Be grateful for the good things in your life."

Trying to console her, Mr. Lowell felt the need to assist with the envelope, so he helped her with the rest of the papers.

"Look here, my dear girl," he extracted and waved an airline ticket.

Bianca wiped her messy eyes, trying hard to clear her vision.

"Read it." She quickly glanced through it, holding her breath.

"It is an airline ticket to Salsa Maggiore, Italy with an option to stay from six months to a year? Oh my!"

"Bianca, you do know a pension is an all-inclusive accommodation at a private residence. I have planned and researched the trip with safety in mind at the request of Grandma Tempesta when she was well. This gift was to be delivered to you on your thirtieth birthday, which is coming up." He quoted with a stern look on his face. "I am delivering it to you, and fulfill my duties ordered by your grandmother."

Lowell was well aware of the family history and Bianca Rosa's past. Nonna had been their housekeeper. A hard-working loyal employee, for years. She had been allowed to take her little granddaughter with her to work when she was growing up as a preschool child, because Mrs. Tempesta couldn't afford a babysitter. When she was well, she had requested him to be the executor of her will.

The Lowell family of Jewish faith loved and appreciated the devotion of Mrs. Tempesta, with the little girl in her care.

This was the promise she had requested to deliver, and she had begged him if anything happened to her, for Mr. Lowell to continue to watch over her. Mrs. Lowell in her kindness had been good to them, and had encouraged her to become an attorney, although Bianca, from her childhood, had always felt intimidated by Mr. Lowell. Which was caused only by her own insecurities by not having had a father or mother figure around to love and reassure her.

Mr. Lowell was severe, with a genuine heart in every respect. He wished to execute and deliver his duty as instructed. But the rest was up to Bianca Rosa, whom he felt was mature enough to make sound decisions. She would soon reach her thirtieth birthday.

After Bianca Rosa regained her composure, she realized that she needed a break from her eighty hour a week job. Work was all she had known; her job was her only salvation to maintain her sanity. On second thought, Bianca questioned if she could be absent for such a long time, especially not being able to see her helpless grandmother. But before she could speak, Lowell seemed to sense her concerns.

"Bianca, I know you're concerned about your grandmother, but you must go. You must fulfill her wishes. There is nothing you can do for her, and she has professional, capable people looking after her."

She pensively nodded, not so sure in agreement. But she quickly added, "Mr. Lowell, what about my files? My cases? Who will be assigned to handle these battles I am dealing with?"

"It's all arranged, don't you worry," he said. "You only need to get yourself ready for the European adventure."

It took some convincing with Bianca's reluctance. Her co-workers, and mainly Mr. Lowell, had become sympathetic and kinder in her eyes. Her departure day arrived sooner than she realized. Mr. Lowell drove her to the Miami airport. It was May 5, 1988, the day of her thirtieth birthday. Bianca Rosa now took her very first plane trip and flew to Milan, with all expenses paid by her grandmother, and the blessings of Lowell and Cohen, she set off to a new horizon.

Bianca Rosa knew no one abroad and reluctantly set herself on this trip. She wondered if anyone would miss her in Miami. Alone with no family left, she was the only survivor after her family was swept away one stormy night during a devastating hurricane that hit South Florida in 1960. Fire rescuers called her the miracle child after they found her in a swamp, among branches covered in mud and debris. The strong winds had battered the area severely, and she had been in the swamp for several days and nights. How she survived was beyond their understanding. She must have been spared by the will of God. When rescuers found her, her little body was lifeless. They had wrapped her in a body bag, believing she was dead. But a sudden cry from the seemingly lifeless body made them take a second look. One man grabbed her tiny wrist and felt a faint pulse, which previously had gone undetected. Then they hustled her into the rescue van and sped away to Jackson Memorial Hospital's emergency room in Miami, where medical care immediately took over, and later intervened by notifying the authorities and the search began for the child's identity. She was only two years old. After a lengthy effort by the medical staff, she slowly recuperated; her body was frail and footsteps unsteady. The little girl had become the love of the nurses and doctors on staff. They were determined to fully rehabilitate her, while the authorities searched diligently for her identity. Once her identity was verified, they found she had a living paternal grandmother north of Florida, who was notified. Nonna was overwhelmed. When the two officers appeared at her door, she could not believe the news they offered. As she had been told that the entire family had been destroyed by the horrendous hurricane; a lot of the bodies had disappeared into the canals or had been swept away into the ocean and not been found. With sharks, crocodiles, snakes, and wild species, uprooted trees, and debris, the local area was in total chaos.

Mrs. Tempesta felt delighted. "A survivor from my destroyed family! A miracle!" she shouted. Overwhelmed, she couldn't wait to hold and see her one and only granddaughter left. Quickly, she assumed care and nurture of Bianca Rosa, the daughter of her only son, and sole survivor of her family. She moved to the South, where the climate in the winter was much better, and to Miami, a city with more opportunities. A couple years later, she had found employment at the Lowell's residence where she was in full charge of their household.

***

Thirty years later, here she was. How many stories had Nonna told her about her family, and Bianca often wondered how ironic it was, that her last name was Tempesta, the Italian word for storm.

Bianca Rosa could not remember any members of her family. She had been told of her parents and siblings by Grandma, who missed them immensely. She was way too young for recollection of them, but Nonna had shown her pictures, repeatedly reminding her of them, plus sharing the tragic stories. Nonna continued to raise her with sincere love and devotion. She also often talked to her about the relatives left back in the old country. Nonna was passionate about their Italian origin, and taught her about Italian customs and influence. Grandma made her promise that one day she would travel to Italy and look into her family ancestry. But Bianca never considered the possibility of going to Italy because she had no money and Nonna's money went for their necessities and her education. Unfortunately, poor Grandma Luisa Tempesta became sick before she graduated. Now, in turn, most of Bianca's salary went toward taking care of Nonna. The hospice was expensive, and Bianca lived modestly on her salary. Her savings was small. She could not understand how her grandmother had been able to pay for her trip. Now, her trip was a reality, but with a sorrowful heart, she was traveling alone.

After a long smooth flight, she landed at Milan Airport. The morning air was crisp when she stepped off the plane and walked into the terminal filled with people from all over the world, but not a familiar face in the crowd. Bianca spoke little Italian and understood only a few words but was not familiar with their musical tones.

How am I going to communicate? This seems so foreign, she thought. So, she decided to just listen and make gestures for any requests in the crowded airport. After collecting her luggage, she pushed her way through the people to the exit, and then headed to the train station to get to her destination. Her place to stay was a Pension, all inclusive. Yes, she needed to meet new people, but she was not looking forward to it.

Speaking in broken English, the porters offered their help and were courteous to Bianca Rosa, who felt relieved and followed them willingly. She took a taxi to the train station and held her breath while observing the traffic and erratic driving. The driver swerved right and left, trying to occupy a little space and she feared at any time they were going to crash, but somehow, she made it safely. She had never seen so many railroad tracks for so many destinations and people struggling to make their way, with trains zipping in and out so fast, leaving little time for anyone to board. She felt anxious and confused.

"Which is the right train to take for this destination?" she asked a stranger close by.

"No speak English," he nodded.

A conductor noticed her and came to her rescue. Gesturing and speaking in broken Italian, she held a piece of paper with the address and pointed to it to him. "Follow me, miss," he said and gestured with his arm. Then she was on board a train, but she was not sure if it was the right one. She had been told by Mr. Lowell someone was to meet her and lead her to the Pension.

The train ride was short, zipping along fast. She expected to see the countryside but was disappointed by the commercial route. Now, her concern was to get to her destination and meet the person who was waiting for her, if anyone. Being alone was a routine that had become a part of her life.

The controller punched her ticket, Bianca's mind swamped with doubt. To reassure herself, she hesitantly asked him, "Can you advise when to scendere? Or get off?"

"Not to worry, miss, I will signal you," he assured her. Bianca Rosa gave a sigh of relief. She had never travelled before; the trains here were overwhelming. Soon after the loud speaker announced, "Fermata Salsa Maggiore," and the controller signaled her to get off.

Many people were there, greeting each other with hugs and kisses, obviously joyful to see one another and knew each other. But who would be greeting her? she wondered. Her eyes searched for someone who may be interested in her, but her eyes only stared at total strangers.

After a few minutes, she noticed a young fellow standing beside an elderly lady, holding a sign which read: "Pensione Jolly, per Bianca Rosa Tempesta." A jolt of relief zipped through her spine; two people were indeed waiting for her. She ran to them, outstretching her hand, ready for a handshake. They greeted her enthusiastically with open arms and a long embrace. First, the lady spoke and introduced herself.

"Bianca Rosa," she said, "I am La Signora Gloriana Palladio, and this is my son Stefano. Ben venuto. Welcome, welcome to Italy! Please, let us take your belongings, e andiamo, let's go." They seemed loving, friendly, sincere with pleasant sounding voices. Bianca let out a big sigh of relief. Their affectionate welcome was helping to calm her shattered nerves and anxiety. Gloriana, in her gentile manner, asked, "Tell me, amore, did you have a good flight?"

"Oh! Yes. It was smooth. I managed to sleep a little."

"I am glad; of course, once at home you can have a good rest."

She was genuinely interested about her wellbeing, which made Bianca Rosa feel good. Stefano, although polite and courteous, was quieter. Bianca noticed that he did not resemble his mother. He was tall and lean with black, straggly hair covering his forehead and partly shadowing his eyes. His unshaven short beard made him appear older than he was, but his dark brown eyes, darted in kindness. She noticed his skin complexion was a little darker than his mother's. He looked more like an ordinary Italian fellow, but handsome in his own way. On the contrary, his mother was a distinguished blonde, her hair pulled up in a chignon. She was heavy set with fair skin, good features, and blue eyes. Her words resonated pleasurably in her ears, which made Bianca Rosa wonder why her grandmother did not speak like that. After a short drive, Stefano announced, "Here we are at Park Jolly, our

Pension."

A strange name for an Italian villa, she thought.

"This is our place," Gloriana said. "Scende, su, come."

The tone of her voice energized Bianca Rosa. At the door step of the front entrance, ready to greet her was an older gentleman with three smiling children. They all embraced her warmly. After taking a good look, Bianca realized Stefano resembled the gentleman.

"You must be Signor Palladio," she asked with a soft smile.

"Si, Sicuro." He nodded. "The children, Rosella, ten, is the eldest; Milena, eight years old; and Carlo, the youngest, four, are our grandchildren — Stefano's children."

Bianca Rosa waited for an additional, the mother of the children or Stefano's wife to appear.

No one else came . . . After the cheerful introductions, Bianca Rosa, escorted by all her new acquaintances, toured her new residence, a modest but well-kept place. The two-story building was painted in white stucco with a tiered rooftop covered with terra cotta shingles. Large windows were covered with green Persian side panels, caressed by fuchsia bougainvilleas in full bloom.

These gregarious strangers made Bianca Rosa feel warm, welcomed, and at home. The aroma coming from the kitchen, combined with the smell of freshly baked bread, feverishly stimulated the juices of her taste buds. Her nostrils took in and recognized the smell of simmering tomato salsa, like Nonna's Italian cooking.

Stefano, in his fine manners, took her baggage to her assigned bedroom, while Gloriana continued her chitchat about pensione Jolly. Then she put her arm at Bianca Rosa's waist and gently led her toward her room. "This is your room, Bianca Rosa — the south side of the house. It's much quieter for you to rest."

The room was bright and inviting and the bed set with a Venetian headboard and foot board, white linen, and organza bedcover with an abundance of cozy cushions. A sparkling clean window provided a beautiful view of the outdoors and the vibrant fuchsia bougainvilleas. A lovely blue chaise with fluffy silver cushions was waiting invitingly, with a matching silver lamp lined up behind, hanging over for comfort reading. A fresh, clean breeze from the open window kept gently blowing, caressing her flushed cheeks. As she turned to face the opposite wall, her eyes caught a well stacked bookshelf, so she could relax and read with pleasure. The rest of the room was picture perfect. Bianca Rosa could not have asked for a better place to live.

"Amore, Love, il bagno, the powder room, is right here," as she opened a tinted glass door. "You might want to freshen up, then we will have lunch when you are ready."

"Thank you, Signora Palladio. You are so accommodating; everything is more than I expected."

It didn't take long for Bianca to get herself together, although she felt a bit intimidated. She was anxious to join her new landlords with their family. They all gathered around the table with their added guest of honor. The children were in a little uproar, shoving and bickering among themselves, when Mr. Palladio, with a high tone called them to order. "I will assign the place for la Signorina Bianca, you will take turns in seating beside her, okay?" He turned to Bianca and announced to her, "Signorina Bianca, since they heard of your arrival, they have been fighting amongst themselves as to who was going to sit beside you."

"Oh! I am flattered. They are so sweet, and I certainly feel privileged that they want to sit close to me." She bent over and patted them.

After a short commotion about the seating assignments, everyone settled down to enjoy the homemade delicacies prepared by Signor Palladio. They feasted on an endless selection of food, followed by espresso coffee with the famous la torta cake Milanese, a special welcome cake for Bianca, centered between Milena and Carlo, the youngest.

Bianca Rosa was delighted. These people seemed wonderful and genuine, and their kindness touched her heart.

In a motherly tone, Gloriana advised her to take a day's rest from the travel. "Once rested, you will feel ready to visit the sites of this northern part of Italy," she said.

How right she was. Since Bianca Rosa had not slept much on the plane during the long flight, she was extremely exhausted and jet lagged. After all, she thought, If I am booked to stay here for six months, with a one-year option if I so desire, there is no need to hurry. This place was her base and the excursions would take off from here. May was a great time to travel and see the beautiful country. The weather was warm and the crowds were manageable. But Bianca Rosa was overwhelmed just to be with these loving people. Of course, she had come to explore this fascinating country and maybe search for her ancestors, if she cared to. But the task seemed difficult because she didn't know the language. With Nonna not functioning anymore, what was the use when she could not see the sparkle in her eyes when she would relate everything to her?

On the third day during breakfast, Gloriana announced that Stefano was on holidays with his children, and if Bianca agreed, he could be her tour guide, accompanied by his youngsters. She was not used to children and therefore had some reservations, but was willing to give it a try.

While chatting with Bianca, Gloriana revealed that Stefano was an art director in the film industry; he set the stages for the proper seen according to the era and the specific requirements for shooting movies. Specializing in that department required him to work long hours, lots of travel. He had designed and supervised big projects in New York and Miami, as well as in Spain and London. He had worked on some major projects in Dubai for quite some time and his work was precise and distinguished. People in the movie industry quickly recognized his style and signature and he had been highly sought. However, she said, "He has refused to take on any new projects for the time being. He wants to spend as much time as possible with his children, for now."

A few days later, Bianca Rosa, Stefano, and his three children all jumped into an Italian Fiat and headed for le Cinque Terre or, The Five Lands. Bianca Rosa was full of joy and did not seem to mind the children at all. Their chattering actually made her feel more at ease with their dad. Rosella was a pretty blonde girl with her grandmother's features, her voice pleasurably resonated with the Milanese accent. Stefano served as their translator. Milena, the middle child, was impeccably dressed: embroidered socks with fine leather white shoes, complimented her lovely white lace outfit. In contrast to her sister, she had brown hair and big brown eyes. Bianca was incredibly impressed with their manners. She wanted to be like them, and with a big smile on her lips, she asked, "May I slightly open the window? I love to feel the warm breeze on my face."

"As you please, Bianca," they cheerfully replied.

Surrounded by the loveliness all around her, she wanted to make sure this trip was for real, not just in her imagination. Bianca Rosa could not believe the beauty before her eyes. The evolving sceneries were magical. The islands stretched across the deep blue waters of the Mediterranean Sea, the rocky hills pointed toward the blue sky, and the pathways were romantic and mysterious. Nature here was unspoiled. No wonder the place was called, "The path of the poets," she thought. The setting of the entire place was absolutely mesmerizing.

"This is for real?" Bianca Rosa asked, turning to Stefano.

Stefano tried hard to explain in English. He wanted to make sure she understood him; even with his strong accent she did understand. His voice was pleasant as he led the way in front. They walked La strada dell'amore, the path of the lovers; there was an aura of comfort being with the children and this person. "What a dream," she whispered to herself.

Afterwards, they took the vaporetto, a small vessel, to view the islands from the sea, and the bilingual tour guide gave the full history of the amazing sites.

Bianca Rosa was speechless as the children held her hands as they went along, jumping jolly around. They appeared happy with their newfound friend. They were sweet, obedient to their dad, and showed respect and admiration toward Bianca.

What a spectacular journey: the sites, the company, and the food. Everything was incredible; Bianca Rosa was immensely grateful. She found it not too difficult to adjust to her new life in this new part of the world.

She had imprisoned herself in her own office for too long, listening every day to her clients' troubles, which left her drained of energy and mentally low in spirits. This trip was making such a difference. As time passed, she felt much calmer in the present atmosphere of peacefulness.

The next day, they headed for Pisa. Finally, she was getting to see the famous leaning Tower of Pisa. She had heard so much about it from her grandmother. The day began with a visit to the city, its churches, and the famous cathedral. And once more, the children were willing participants. They walked everywhere, enjoying all the walking, taking it all in without complaints. Gloriana and her husband would anxiously wait and greet them every night upon their return from the day's sightseeing, ready to serve her succulent meals, and listen to the review of the day. Bianca Rosa fell more and more in love with these people, and it gave her a sense of belonging here with this family.

She found she was also becoming fonder of Stefano and was looking forward to each new day. She enjoyed his company.

Stefano, who she figured was in his late thirties or early forties with a touch of gray on his sideburns, was handsome and courteous, polite, but seemed distant and removed. A cloud of sadness seemed to hang over him at times. Once, she had caught him with his hands holding his temples as if he was in pain.

What was troubling him? she wondered. He was well informed on history and the sites and was an excellent tour guide. He would explain everything to her, and the sound of his voice was awakening her inner being. The stimuli, the churning in the pit of her stomach, made her feel like a young teenager in love for the first time. She had never dated much back home, her experience with young men was nil.

"What on earth is happening to me?" she said to herself. Stefano's interest was solely based on showing her his beautiful country. He never looked into her eyes. He was a perfect gentleman. Not a sign of interest for her on his part. She was astounded about her inner feelings. Was it Italy, or being with such pleasant company? Her mood had changed since arriving here. She now felt open to absorb the good things around her. Bianca was sure that if Stefano would look into her eyes, he would have seen her admiration and, yes, lust for him.

Shame on me, she thought. She tried hard to conceal her feelings and keep focused on exploring and sightseeing. But the curiosity was nagging her at the pit of her stomach. She had to know why Stefano looked so sad and what happened to the mother of his children, that no one ever mentioned. She wondered…what's the mystery?

One day, Stefano politely announced that he wanted her to see the Amalfi Coast, which would require more time. They would need to stay overnight, and he suggested maybe all the family should go, including the parents.

"Only with your permission," he had asked politely. While questioning her, he took her hand and held it for a moment, almost apologetically, as if he was imposing on her with his parents. Bianca Rosa felt a shiver down her spine. She knew that Italian families were always in unity, a tradition her grandmother had preached about through the years for when she would return to Italy. She would never be lonely because families stayed together. Bianca Rosa was willing to go along with any suggestion. She was falling in love with this untouchable person and his family, so she had no objection about the plans.

"Oh, Stefano, it is perfectly fine with me, you don't even have to ask," she responded.

A couple of days later, seven of them piled into an SUV like one big happy family. They headed down to the Amalfi Coast and drove through Umbria. The countryside was splendid, lush in greenery, trees in full bloom with flowering fruits in a rainbow of colours. The climate was warm and comfortable, with direct sunlight adding lustre to the Earth. At the end of May, Italy was well into spring, and delightful.

Bianca Rosa observed the different towns scattered on hill tops, some situated in spectacular valleys. But once they reached the Amalfi Coast, she was breathless from its beauty.

The Mediterranean Sea was calm and serene, gently rocking, and the waves caressed the shore. Some homes looked as if they hung on the cliffs above the sea. Terraced landscapes were filled with yellow lemon trees. Now, she knew why the Italian lemoncella was made here. She had been introduced to the lemoncella after her fabulous meals at the Pension. They called it the finale digestive, the liqueur to digest. The children were comfortably singing folkloric songs and playing games with their grandparents. The family had made bookings at a hotel in Positano, which hung over rocky terrain. From their room, the balcony extended, leading to a magnificent view of the sea, with music to be heard from everywhere. Neapolitan music seems to have a unique tone: romantic, poetic, and nostalgic. Bianca thought, The writers of these lyrics must have been inspired by the sea and their magnificent surroundings.

Stefano stood beside her on the balcony, and in his usual polite tone, pointed out the different residences of American actors and Sophia Lauren, and most of the notorious people from different parts of the world.

Her heart was aching for affection. The vibration in the air was that of love. With handsome Stefano at her side, she often found herself daydreaming. She secretly willed for Stefano to show some interest in her. This is all she needed to feel more delighted and complete. But she saw no sign on his part. She was getting restless and could not sleep well.

One more sleepless night hit her restless feverish body. She stepped out onto the balcony. There, a full moon glared up above, and with the moon and the gentle waves of the sea splashing on the shore beneath her, she closed her eyes, let the fresh breeze of the sea caress her face while allowing her brain to carry her in fantasy. Her imagination transported her to a world of love and affection. She was young and starving for love and her body craved to be touched — the missing component to her life, she desperately felt.

The following evening, they dined outdoors on the terraced hotel Baglione. Stefano seemed more relaxed after his father insisted he drink a glass of Merlot wine. He was talking not only with the children and his parents, but also referring more to Bianca Rosa. He mentioned about his meetings with Mr. Lowell in Miami and dinners at some of the great restaurants in downtown Miami by the bay.

Surprised, Bianca cried, "Stefano, you know Mr. Lowell?"

"Yes. I have had dealings with Mr. Lowell. He was acting in some contracts, closing for my clients."

"Wow!" she said, beginning to fit the pieces of the puzzle together. But then the children interrupted and wanted to move on to the piazza for their gelato ice cream. So, they completed the evening with a stroll and ice cream cones. The city was alive with people, well into the night, and the music was inspiring. She would have loved to continue talking with Stefano, but once he turned his attention to his children, the evening was over for her.

Selfishly, she wished that she could have Stefano to herself, but she knew that he was focused on his children as a good devoted daddy. She admired that in him; he was a good parent. She was now part of a family and living in a country filled with kindness and beauty. She had become more aware of her appearance and had changed her looks from a simple intellect to an attractive young woman with a European flair. She had no problem wearing chiffon dresses and mid-heel shoes, which made her look more attractive, and she felt more feminine. She chose colours to enhance her eyes, often blue and yellow combinations that made her feel alive and happy. She wondered why she never felt motivated to focus on these things before. Her thoughts went to her grandma. If only she could have confided in her. She would have the answer for her.

Did she want to go back to America? No, she had no one there except her grandmother, and she was in her own world, which tore her heart apart every time she visited her. Mr. Lowell had become her friend, and she wrote to him from time to time. She felt obliged to update him and thank him for his part in this great adventure.

In the meantime, she did not want to come out of this spell. She wondered if it was fate that she had found these people or if someone had sent them her way. Mr. Lowell had done his research well. Nonna must have expressed her real concern in details before she got sick; it's the only thing that made sense. This trip was like a miracle sent from heaven.

The bond with the Palladio family was becoming stronger with each passing day. She wondered how she was going to return to her previous life. Her heart was beating faster and faster each time she looked at Stefano. No doubt, she was madly in love, hopelessly in love. Stefano continued with his duties in a serious professional manner, distant and removed, in a world of Stefano and his own dream. Never did he show a sign of interest toward her other than attending to the task at hand. His uniqueness only made him more desirable, and Bianca Rosa thought, If I could only reach out to him, but I don't know how. She was not experienced in the romance department. Her life had been dedicated to her studies, a career, hard work, caring for her grandmother. Now, she had developed this restless ache in her heart and it was out of control. It gave her no peace.

Their voyage continued. Next, they would head for Rome, the eternal city. Three days in Rome, so much to learn and see of the rich history. The Romans had so much to offer. She visited the Vatican City, the Colosseum, Piazza di Spagna, each seeming more spectacular than the other. In the evening when the children retired for the night, they had gotten in the habit of taking turns reading to Bianca in Italian, competing with one another in teaching her. Carl had really taken to her and sweetly took her by the hand, leading her to his room for the good night closure. Bianca loved to interact with them. They had taught her to play scopa, a card game with Italian cards. She was a fast learner and the children were praising her with encouragement for her accomplishments. Then one evening as they sat around the table having supper, Carl with his sweet innocent voice, asked, surprising everyone, "Bianca, can we play a game after supper?"

"Yes, of course, Carl, my darling," she responded with true, genuine love for him.

"I would like all of us to write on a piece of paper who is our little friend from the heart, l'amichetta del cuore, and pass it on to one another," he said this in his own language.

"Carl! What a splendid idea; we shall."

The children hurried through supper to get to the game.

They all revealed their person of choice. Carl's number one was no surprise; Bianca Rosa was his choice. She received the most votes.

"Congratulations, Bianca Rosa, I see you have really made a hit with our grandchildren. Fantastic!" said Gloriana.

Rosella, one morning, stretched herself to whisper in her ear, "Bianca, will you go shopping with me? The two of us alone will tour the outdoor market. I want to get a Saint Day gift for my grandfather."

"Oh, I have never heard of a Saint Day gift, but I would love to go with you."

"Yes, here we celebrate, L'onomastico, the anniversary of the saint's name which Grandpa has been named after. We will take the tram; I don't want dad or grandpa to drive us."

"That sounds like fun, as long as you lead the way, Rosella."

Rosella spoke broken English, but she was understandable. She was taking English as her second language at school and trying hard to communicate.

Bianca wished the clock would stop and the time would stand still. But the clock was ticking. Soon, days turned into weeks and months had flown by and her departure day had arrived.

Everyone was sad. Gloriana was in tears, and so were the children. Bianca Rosa had never felt so much love, hospitality, and celebration with total strangers. What a priceless experience. The entire family seemed to possess the same Italian mannerisms, kindness, love, and passion. She was sad that she would have to leave them and return to her empty family life.

When Stefano came close to her, her body felt electrified. She so desired him. But so far, her feelings had not been reciprocated. She did not care anymore if her pleading eyes were going to give her away. She made it obvious that she did not want to leave. Silently, she prayed for him to ask her to stay. How was she going to continue to live with the secret love that was buried deep in her heart?

Then something wonderful happened. She was in her room packing when she heard a knock on the door.

"Yes, come in," she said.

"Bianca Rosa," Stefano said, hesitating. "May I disturb you for few minutes?"

"Yes, of course, Stefano," she responded with a shaky voice.

He walked toward her slowly and sheepishly. Speaking softly, he said, "Bianca Rosa, if you are willing to return, we can continue the tour. I would like to show you the south of Italy. Perhaps Sicily."

Bianca Rosa held her breath. She was ready to scream and reveal her longing for him. But instead, she scolded him. "Stefano is this all you can say? What about us?"

He just stood there, staring at her, trying to choose words, not feeling sure of himself. Reluctantly, he finally spoke, "Bianca Rosa, I'm fond of you." He hesitated for a moment, then let out a big sigh and continued to walk away. She turned and grabbed his arms, ready to burst out crying. "Stefano! I hate to leave."

To her shock, he replied, "I think I have fallen in love with you, too." As a matter of fact, and continued "I didn't have the courage to tell you before, out of respect. You are a gifted and beautiful woman. I'm a father of three children, and I am a widower. I have much admiration for you and a strong desire to take you in my arms and never let you go. But how can I claim you?"

She looked at him, perplexed, as he spoke. "Bianca Rosa, the custom in Italy requires for me to be responsible for my parents, along with my children, who are all part of my household. You, Bianca Rosa, are a single girl. A free-spirited individual with a career. You could not accept the burden of a widower, three children, and older parents."

"Stefano, did you ever ask me what I think or prefer? Or what are my needs and wants?"

"Bianca Rosa, I am already riddled by guilt from my previous marriage, which has ended in failure, and I blame myself for being away so much and spending more time on projects than with my family. That's why I have taken a long leave of absence so I can be with my children."

"Stefano, you and your family are a Godsend to me," she pitifully said. "Now that I know you love me, I think together we can overcome any obstacle." Then throwing her arms around him, she offered him her lips. He hesitated and looked deep in her eyes. She could not conceal her hidden love for him. "Please, forgive me, Stefano. I think I fell in love with you the minute I saw you," she confessed.

He took a deep breath, and with lucid eyes, pulled her body closer to him. He whispered breathing in her ear, "How could I be so lucky?"

He pulled her back, to look at her with the same strong devotion, then hugged her tightly. He gave her a long passionate kiss, taking her breath away.

Bianca was speechless. She broke in tears. The rest of the clan knew Stefano was in Bianca's room. They were all standing in the hallway, anxiously praying for them to make some kind of connection. Gloriana had been vigilant as a mother, and sensed Bianca's love for her son.

Holding hands, Bianca and Stefano emerged radiant out of the room to join the rest of the family. The Palladio family, as soon as they saw the two holding hands, the smiles on their faces, joined hands and formed a circle around them.

Bianca Rosa knew that Gloriana would make a wonderful mother and coach her, as for Mr. Palladio , he was equally kind. The children, with their innocence and laughter, were ready to love her unconditionally.

Stefano knew he was running out of time. He stepped forward, looked into Bianca's eyes, and said, "Bianca, if you are willing, I want you in my life. Will you be my wife?"

Bianca was speechless, but the big smile on her face gave her away. Stefano quickly grabbed her and led her back to her room. He held her tenderly, afraid to let go. He kissed her again and again. His inhibitions had vanished. Dispirited he confessed, "There's something you must know. Olivia was beautiful wife, young and restless due to my absence. . . Long ago, she took a lover. She abandoned us and broke my heart, along with my self-esteem."

She could tell it hurt him to talk about it, but he continued, "You see, one Sunday afternoon, she dropped off the children at my parents' and went on a mountain joy ride with her lover. Driving on mount St. Angelo along the Mediterranean coast, where the road is extremely narrow and dangerous, overlooking the cliffs, the twosome missed a narrow curve and the convertible Lamborghini rolled down the embankment and split into pieces. Two mangled bodies were found and later identified by their dental x-rays. I was in Dubai at the time on a filming project when I was notified by the authorities of the mishap."

He was fighting tears back, and the unpleasantness showed in his sorrowful face.

"That was such a shock, I will never forget," said Stefano. "I was devastated, and ever since then, I have been greatly disappointed in life, tormented by my wife's ending, her actions, and my own guilt. I lost trust and interest in women, although I am also to blame." He shook his head and said, "My poor children without a mother, they have been my only reason for living and giving me courage to go on."

He continued relating to her that his parents' love and support kept him from going insane. But his remorse for being away from his children and his wife for so long placed blame of failing the family.

Pulling her closer to him, in a shaky voice, he said, "Bianca, my dear girl, when you appeared in my world, you seemed as lost as I was when I first saw you. By spending time with you, I have grown to love and admire your courage and your stamina. You are a caring and gentle human being. The children are crazy about you; that is important to me and the rest of the family."

"Oh! Stefano." She reached out to lock her arms around his neck. She needed to feel his body close to her.

"Bianca, there is more. After my wife died, my son Carl, then four years old, had a difficult time accepting his mother's disappearance; we had a hard time pacifying him, especially at night. He cried hysterically and wanted his mother, which broke our hearts. But I must confess, ever since you came into their lives, I have never seen my children happier," he confessed, inclining in his sincere gratitude.

"You have become their new ideal, and you have restored hope in me and laughter in them. My parents adore you, Bianca Rosa," he declared. "How lucky can we be?"

"I must tell you also," Stefano revealed, "that before you arrived Bianca Rosa Tempesta, I had received a registered letter from Mr. Lowell. At first, I assumed it was another work offer from one of his client. But after opening it, I found . . . and noticed Mr. Lowell's handwritten letter, requesting me personally to take care of a grandmother's prodigy, and a special member of his firm. He had also penned a brief biography of Bianca Rosa Tempesta.

"As time went on, I wondered if fate sent you to us," said Stefano, holding back his emotions "You have certainly been a blessing for me and my family."

Bianca Rosa loved his voice and listened attentively to his every word. She had traveled to Italy feeling intimidated, fearing the unknown, with the intention to look for her ancestors and explore the countryside. The ancestor part did not happen at this time, but maybe in the future. Instead, she had found these wonderful people. Italy was no longer a foreign country to her. She knew in time she would restore the passion in Stefano's heart. Most of all, the big void of emptiness in her life would be filled because now she had regained a family, and especially the children — they were an added bonus. As for her grandmother and Gordon Lowell, she would be forever grateful to them.

When she said her goodbyes and the plane raised off in the sky, Bianca Rosa felt she was raising in heaven, blessed in the universe. She had made a promise: "Stefano, mio amore, my love, I shall return. This is where I belong, with all of you, my beloved family. Together, we will meet our challenges and overcome our obstacles. Where there is love, there is always hope."

Novel No. 2 Narreted

HE HEALED HER BROKEN HEART

What would lay ahead with the unknown, Angelica wondered. She was devastated and broken-hearted as she boarded the ship at the port of Naples in Italy. The Christmas holidays were just over; the New Year had rolled around. A new chapter was beginning in her life. It was a cold and misty January morning in the 1950s. Young Angelica accompanied by her mother, Gloria, and younger sister, Stefania. They were bound for New York City, then on to their destination in Canada. Her dad was eagerly awaiting their arrival and the family would be reunited after a long separation, ready to start a new life there.

Angelica's mom wanted a father figure for her two daughters, especially for Angelica a teen ager. She was a petite girl, of medium stature, with light brown hair and brown eyes. She was born with an oval sculptured face and good features. Her demeanor was docile and approachable; the boys at school were showing much interest in her. This was the main reason Gloria, her mother, was concerned and wanted the family together to share the responsibility of raising a family with her husband. Gloria herself was, by nature, shy, but she had no trouble enforcing her rules. She would put a lot of responsibility on the fifteen-year-old Angelica, including looking after her younger sister Stefania. In the meantime, when it came to stronger discipline, this was for her husband to implement.

As much as Angelica wanted to be reunited with her dad and be with her family, this transition in her life was devastating. She was madly in love. Mother's decision was putting an enormous distance between her and the young man she had a crush on, that was her first love. She had left behind a seventeen-year-old classmate, without letting him know of her whereabouts or knowledge of her new address. Communication between the two had been forbidden by her mother, which did not bode well for the relationship. As a result, Angelica had been traveling with great sadness in her heart, and a somber soul. She had been taken away from the love of her life by her imposing mother. Her friends had been left behind, plus the love she nurtured for this young man would, in time, had to be erased forever. She figured her life would be more difficult by living her native land. But even if she had continued to live in Italy, her professed love had to end.

She was not excited by what was taking place. In her mind, there was little desire to settle in Canada. Knowing this voyage and emigration was sure to be a temporary move, she intended to be here a short period of time and then return to her city. There she would reunite with her Joseph and spend the rest of her life with the young man she had left behind. Although this had all been forbidden, her dream was to find a way to return and search for her lost love.

Once the family was settled in Canada, Angelica continued to nurture her melancholy feelings. She rarely laughed or took part in family occasions, because the craving in her heart was incessant. Her passion was reading and going to school and learning. She had quickly been enrolled in a private school run by the nuns and began hibernating in her room with her books. That was how she spent her free time. The person she longed for and wanted to be with was across the ocean. Therefore, she was spending a lot of time dreaming of the impossible dream that someday she would find herself in the arms of her beloved Joseph, and life for them would be happy ever after.

In the '50s, there were no computers, or easy communication

like today. Money was scarce, as her family barely made enough to buy their necessities and pay the bills. There were no plans to return to Italy any time soon, and the only people that were left there were her grandparents. But they had both passed on not long after the family's departure. The two elderly people missed the family so much; they could not cope with the void that was left by the grandchildren's departure and an empty nest. A cardiac arrest had taken her grandfather, Angelo, and a month later her grandmother, Nina, gave in to the same fate. Angelica knew they had died of a broken heart. Their love had had a strong presence in her heart, because they were her protectors and saviors, but now they were gone. The other relatives had their own children to worry about, no room for other siblings with young, silly intentions, especially looking for a young boy who was not accepted by her mother.

Angelica's dream was only an unrealistic reverie. The Atlantic Ocean dividing the two continents was an immense body of water. A trip by air was expensive, not even possible. It was not permissible for a sixteen-year-old girl to go anywhere alone in those days. Besides, her dad would never permit it. Angelica belonged to a strict Catholic Italian family. You obeyed and lived by their rules. She felt trapped with no hope. Angelica's social life was limited, consisting of attending school and church services, and the Sunday afternoon family sightseeing excursions. She could only resign herself to her fate and make the best of the situation.

It was at one of the church functions that life changed for Angelica. The Catholic group was putting together some plays to entertain the members of the congregation. Angelica became a member and started to participate on stage; this was allowed by her dad and it was something the entire family could enjoy.

These plays were well-attended, because a lot of young people were in the cast and it attracted a crowd of all ages, including some of the city's available bachelors who found their way into the church auditorium when they weren't working or going to school.

Angelica was exposed on the stage, both heard and seen. This was a small community, it did not take long to be known and she was well received. This is where it all began. The performances and her participation in the Catholic group brought some relief to Angelica, plus she made new friends. These friends helped to change her mood and gave her some motivation in her newfound interest in Canada. She started to venture out of her room more often, and left the dreaming and the longing for what she had across the sea in a sealed off place in her heart.

Some young fellows that were among the group were showing Angelica their interest and good intentions, looking at her with admiration, desperately seeking her attention. She was showing no emotion or response. She was asking herself if she would ever get over this aching pain in her heart from the love she had left behind, across the ocean, without hope. He was always on her mind. The priests and the nuns from school had asked her if she would consider enrolling in the convent to become one of them and serve the house of God. Because of her disinterest, not wanting to get involved with male company, they thought it would be a good place for Angelica to serve a life in the mission. She suited her name well, because she possessed a loving face, showed profuse kindness in her eyes, and her demeanor portrayed the image of an angel. She had no desire to dress up or groom herself with cosmetics, like the other girls in her class; she just presented herself in a very natural way. The teachers and the priests had already taken steps to send her to school in one of the local hospital, where she could start her nursing career. She was going along with this since she had not much interest in anything else uplifting, but she liked to help people in need, and she would give of herself in any way she could. This might have not been a bad idea, because it would put her where she could be dedicated to the wellbeing of others.

But call it fate or what was meant to be a new turn to take place in Angelica's life. One Sunday afternoon after the church gathering, one of the boys invited a group of friends to his home for an afternoon of music and dancing and included Angelica. She gracefully accepted, unlike other times when she would refuse, only to run home to her books and solitude. Two young men arrived at this gathering; they were not part of their group but they were invited. They introduced themselves as John and Luca as they were welcomed to participate in the festivities. Angelica loved music and hoped it would lift her spirits. The songs played were sentimental and romantic, placid and soothing. In some instances, her mind would drift away as the words from the songs would make her feel sad and bring tears to her eyes. To hear some of the lyrics brought back memories that intensified her sorrow. She loved to dance back in her homeland with her cousins and friends, but here she had not allowed herself that pleasure.

She seemed to have escalated to this sad zone and often questioned if her heart would ever open up and allow her to love another, since she had been so fixed on her old forbidden young lover.

But this particular Sunday afternoon, since this new young man had arrived, he seemed to have eyes only for Angelica. Strangely she also felt intrigued by him. She asked herself, what is my interest in this person? Before she had a chance for a second thought, the music started to play a lovely, slow, but striking melody called "Red Roses for You," a romantic song that awakens the heart. This new young man, Luca, had crossed the room and was right beside her, tapping on her shoulder and asking her to dance, and to her surprise, she accepted gladly. When dancing, she found she enjoyed being in this stranger's arms; it felt warm and comfortable. She started to relax and let herself open to his friendship, while noting he was well dressed, well spoken, had beautiful big brown eyes with long lashes, his black hair slicked back, and he was of a medium stature, and well-polished. In the little conversation they had while dancing, she also noticed that he spoke with good grammar, which was gratifying to hear. Most of all, he had awakened an interest and some feelings in her deadened body. To her surprise dancing with him simply felt good. She could sense, that the feeling was mutual, because if someone else asked her to dance, he would simply sit and wait. He chose to dance only with her. To her amazement, the young man had left an impression on her that lingered for the rest of the evening.

Finally, a little spark of fire and some happiness seemed to have struck a nerve. She sincerely wanted to talk to her mother now to tell her all about her new experience and her new acquaintance. Although her mom had caused her misery, she still respected her and loved her. Deep down, she figured that her mom wanted only the best for her, because she always praised her and boosted her self-esteem. She constantly reminded Angelica how both she and her dad were proud of her. She felt their love was sincere, and therefore she could not hate her mother or resent her for what she had done. She went to sleep that night thinking of this fellow, that she would not mind seeing again, to spend some time with him, and get to know him.

When her mom questioned her the next morning. "Angelica, how was your gathering yesterday?" Smiling tilting her head she responded, "Mom, I think. . . I have met the fellow I am going to marry." This was so strange, she thought, why would I even consider or make such a statement? I do not want or desire anyone other than my Joseph. A spell seemed to be cast over Angelica.

To her surprise, Luca did not call, and although he had not asked for her phone number, he knew her name and could have looked it up in the phone book. Months passed and Angelica put this young Luca at the back of her mind with not much care or value to that encounter. *I guess I was wrong*, she thought, and continued her life with the church outings. The old misery resumed its home in her heart. Several months later at one of the church feast celebrations, totally unexpected, she ran into this young man again, her affect was carefree and nonchalant, and by now, whatever had taken place months earlier had dissipated. She had settled back into her old pattern of sadness and was comfortable there. The very next day the phone rang. To her surprise, he was at the other end of the phone, imploring her to please see him. Angelica still had to run such things by her family as she was not at liberty to come and go as she pleased. She needed permission, but this young man was insistent in his demands. Although she did not care one way or the other, again she questioned why he had not called since they had met. How could she have been wrong? Almost indignant, or curiosity, Angelica was motivated to meet this fellow to find out what had caused his delay in calling her. A force stronger than her seemed to guide her toward his direction. A date was set for a Sunday afternoon. Poor Angelica, she did not possess a large wardrobe and only had two pairs of shoes: one for everyday wear, and one pair of white summer sandals to dress up with. On her way walking to church that morning, one of the heels had broken, and here she was to go on a date with broken shoes. Her little spark of desire to look good turned this into another dilemma.

A nice English lady, Mrs. Smith, lived next door. She liked Angelica and they often chatted. She was a petite, pretty woman with a great sense of humor, and often sympathized with Angelica's lack of wardrobe or other necessary needs. Mrs. Smith every now and then would offer her some of her surplus. She decided that she needed to go pay a visit to the neighbor and explain her problem. Mrs. Smith happily came to her aid with a big smile on her face; she had no trouble finding a white pair of sandals for Angelica to wear since they wore the same size. Her only Sunday dress came together in perfect completion with the borrowed shoes. Usually, Angelica managed to get herself together with her few possessions, pulling her golden-brown hair back in a ponytail, the curled bangs adorning her forehead, her big brown eyes sparkling with radiance. She was a kind-hearted girl by nature, so with a smile on her face, she went to meet the new young man that had found his way into her life.

A new beginning had appeared in her horizon. Luca had come along to heal her broken heart. This Sunday afternoon meeting consisted of a pleasant sightseeing drive. They stopped for an ice cream cone and a soft drink, and then decided to take a stroll by the Lake, on the pier. The sky was without a cloud, a mantle of blue up above, the sun was creating a golden glow all around them, a gentle warm breeze caressing their faces. The lake on each side of the pier was peaceful and filled with Canada geese floating harmoniously. At the extension on the northern part, where the pier ended, they stood watching the sail boats peacefully floating the lake connected to Toronto. It was a picture-perfect scene in early July. There, the two-young people slowly strolled the pier, holding hands and absorbed in their surroundings of water and nature immersed in pleasant conversation. They seemed to be the only ones on the planet, and they felt complete. Luca, was remarkably pleasant; he was well spoken, mature, most of all humble in his revelations, with the appearance of a serious demeanor. He related to her all his great plans; she listened attentively because he had captured her attention. Some of his plans seemed unrealistic, but she had observed that he believed in himself with sincerity in his heart. She thought, Good for him, it's admirable to think big and reach for the sky. He seemed so honest that Angelica felt a sense of security and protection being with him. She was not a spoiled girl, her demands were few, therefore natural simple offerings were more than she needed to fulfill her wants.

It would soon be time to return home and bring the lovely outing to an end. Angelica had always been a lover of nature and water, and the company of this newfound friend had been most pleasurable.

The car had been parked alongside a row of pine trees, and the scent was invigorating. As they made their way back to the car, Luca put his arm around her waist and she found herself wanting to do the same; this all seemed to come on like a guiding force for Angelica, feeling warm and comfortable. When they sat in the car, he asked her permission to kiss her, and because of the gentleness in his voice and the sincerity in his eyes Angelica took one look at his lips and welcomed him to meet hers. They engaged in a passionate kiss that sent shivers all through her body. The chemistry among them placed both in a state of ecstasy. The spell of pleasure captured, was upon them. They looked at each other surprised; neither of them wanted the magic to come to an end. With this awakened emotion, Angelica returned home with the resolution that this young man was the one to heal her broken heart. Just to be in his company brought her great comfort and pleasure.

The relationship continued and Luca wanted to be with Angelica every moment he could spare. The feeling of unity between them was captivating. Slowly, this universal bliss seemed to erase all her past misery. As she told herself that maybe her mom was right all along to have forbidden her previous mad love. This new found love with Luca was waiting for her.

Angelica could not help but fall in love with this young man because being together made their world seem so serene. She could hardly believe what was taking place in her heart and in her soul. She was a religious girl and believed that Luca in her life was a Godsend; he was meant to be on her path, as if by fate. Her past despair for the love that had been taken away from her seemed to dissipate. This new young love had transformed her existence. Now she was eager to live, to have a life here and even plan for a future. But most of all, the abyss of her stirred emotions that Luca was able to provoke in her was an awakening.

He became her best friend and her soul mate as their love grew, and they became inseparable. Although Angelica was young, she was also mature for her age from her upbringing and the responsibilities she had been given by her parents. The grandparents had played a big role in her life also. Luca, being a little older, related well with her; he recognized her good qualities.

***

Not too long after their relationship had begun, Luca was stricken with serious health problems which led to financial problems, since he could not work and had no insurance coverage and found himself in a crucial situation. Angelica was his consolation, the place he found refuge and sincere support.

One evening, he arrived at her home somber, troubled, and despondent. He gently took her hands In his, inhaled a deep breath; with sincerity in his eyes said to her, "I am penniless, and sick, with no job and lots of bills to pay. I do not know how I am going to survive." He looked so troubled and in despair , Angelica listened to him attentively and allowed him to pour out all his troubles.

After he was finished, Angelica, being the caring girl that she was, with a sincere look on her face, reassured him, stating, "I will be here for you and I will never abandon you. Whatever obstacles may appear, we will overcome them together." With this encouragement, she put her arms around him in a tender embrace and with her imploring eyes said, "You have reason to succeed now because you are not alone. You have to give it all that life demands, because it is not only for you, but also for me. I will be here for you." Her reassurance was meaningful to Luca, as he felt the true love and friendship of this lovely creature that by luck had been placed on his path. He did not want to fail her, she had become the center of his universe, therefore he needed to pull himself together and try his utmost to overcome this bad period in his life.

As much as Luca wanted to pretend that things were going to change in what was only a matter of time, life for him was getting worse, not better. He was struck with a severe pain on his side that brought on a high fever. The family doctor did not know what to make of his symptoms when the fever started to persist and not break. He was unable to get out of bed and became delirious. Luca was admitted to the local Hospital for further investigation to research what had struck his body to become powerless and dysfunctional. In the meantime, he was sinking deeper and deeper into sickness every day that passed. The doctors kept saying it was a virus that had taken over all the muscles in his body. They had no medication to combat it, hoping the fever would break, and the immune system itself would be able to fight off this virus so he would survive. Otherwise, there was nothing they could do and eventually he would succumb with heart failure once this ugly virus had found its way into his internal organs. Lucas heart beat was erratic, and he was drifting in and out of conciouseness, having near death experience.

Angelica, who had been at his side daily. Whenever he came to lucidity, her image gave him hope strength and desire to fight whatever had taken over his body to reduce him to this lifeless state.

Angelica's outlook now had also changed. Since this precious man had come into her life, and there was a strong possibility that he would be taken away from her by some strange malady that no one could control. This person had become most important to her, mainly because she cared so much about his well-being and desperately hoped to help him get back on his feet. She always believed in her prayers, so she turned to her faith with all her might.

Luca kept fighting with his strong will also in him to be with his beloved Angelica, who had been at his side daily. Her image gave him hope and a desire to fight whatever had taken over his body to reduce him to this lifeless state.

The financial crisis was accumulating. Those days there was no OHP coverage, he had no private insurance for his healthcare, plus he could not afford a private policy. Regardless, he was seriously sick and he needed medical intervention more than anything else to save his life. After in and out of his near-death experience, Luca experienced a boost of energy, that gave him a strong bust to keep fighting. Yes, he needed to be with his beloved Angelica. Her image gave him hope and a desire to fight whatever had taken over his body to reduce him to this lifeless state.

Angelica had forgiven her mother for the pain she had caused her in the past; her great sadness had been alleviated by finding

Luca. Now, this could not be happening again to her; losing him to some strange virus that would eventually destroy his main artery, his heart, and he would be gone. Luca's heart was meant to love her; she could feel it by the blood running through her veins. She knew from the first time he had laid eyes on her that he was sent to her by some divine force for a reason. No, she could not lose him, he needed her. She needed him!

She was not going to accept the doctors' verdict, she would be there at his side with her own strength; will it on to him to destroy whatever had taken over. But most of all her prayers, yes, she believed her prayers were going to be answered and this ordeal would turn around, because she willed it to be. He was only twenty-three years old, his life could not be cut so short. Her beloved young man had so many plans, and such a powerful brain to do and create on this earth. It could not happen. Angelica knew in her heart that if she continued to pray hard, eventually, God would listen to her. It took a long time and continuous perseverance, but Luca started to come around; he was winning, and she was right there to cheer him on, and he wanted to live for her also. After many months of fighting and rehabilitation, his feeble body started to regain strength. The fever had given up battering his body. Luca started to regain strength. Finally, to everyone's surprise, including the doctors and the nurses, he was dismissed from the hospital. On his dismissal, a friend of his had gone to pick him up, and Luca insisted he drive him straight to Angelica's home. After arriving at her door, although her parents were not really in favor of her having a serious relationship because she was still young, they could not help, but embrace this young man and accept him with kindness.

Luca did manage to pull himself together. He slowly got his health back, and found himself two jobs. His work, allowed him to pay all his debts that had accumulated. He had said to Angelica. "As soon as you help me save some money we would get married. I want you with me at all times." Promising he would conquer the world for her. He kept stating his goals and promises, all for his beloved Angelica.

She really didn't care, as long as she had this wonderful human being to share her life with, her world would be happy.

Their first goal was soon reached. The two were united in matrimony, and their love blossomed with two lovely sons . When Angelica had met Luca, he was just coming out of a small haberdashery business where he worked alone with no support. This had robbed him of his small savings plus had brought him his ill health from contracting some strange bacteria, due to the unsanitary premises he had occupied. This was when Angelica had appeared in his life either by fate or because it was meant to be. He was at the lowest point of his life. When he first laid eyes on Angelica that Sunday afternoon, she had struck him like an angel. But he had reservations because of his troubled status at this time in his life. Once he saw her again, he had decided that come hell or high water, he was not going to miss out on this chance of a lifetime.

He cherished her from that moment on. He often stated his desire to wanting to reach the sky for her; as he wanted to enjoy together all the beautiful things this planet could offer. He kept saying that. Angelica smiling gently would lock him in an embrace "Honey I have you. We are together that is all I want" Although they were poor, for Angelica, it did not matter, because their hearts were full of love, and she was grateful to God for sparing her Luca.

***

In time Luca's dreams and goals all materialized, but Angelica had fallen madly in love with this precious soul, that really nothing else mattered as long as they had each other. They would have small disagreements, but Luca, in order to always keep peace, would patiently explain his position, and should Angelica insist, he would acquiesce to her wants. Their motto in life was togetherness. They indulged in simple pleasures like going for nature walks. Their favorite place was by the roaring falls. The theater was another of their favorite pastimes. They worked together, they grew together, and they cried together as they overcame the many obstacles that life presented to them. As long as they had one another, nothing else mattered.

They would separate for a little while, but when reuniting, it was just like the first time they discovered each other.

Luca and Angelica have been blessed with their marriage and their partnership in life. Angelica once stated that, "There are two kinds of mates, one created by people, one created by God." She always felt that hers and Luca's was arranged in Heaven. They will soon celebrate sixty- one years of marriage. They still walk side-by-side, holding hands. They still go dancing. Luca always requests the band play the song that brought Angelica into his arms, "Red Roses for You," so long ago. Angelica smiles at him with loving eyes, and with a strong embrace she looks up at him and whispers in his ear, to tell him that, with each day that goes by, she loves him more and more. A silent prayer is in her heart: "Please, God, let me keep my friend for ever."

Novel No. 3

THE STRANGER ON MY PATH

There I was, in the Los Angeles airport waiting to connect with my daughter, son-in-law, and my three grandchildren. I left Toronto on American Airlines. I had a three-hour waiting period before reuniting with my family and proceeding to Melbourne, Australia. My mental state was in turmoil. I had been totally taciturn and in a world of my own. I did not care to speak or even notice anybody around me. During my previous flight, I had been immersed in deep thoughts, re-evaluating my life at this point and time.

Which, to my analyzation, was not desirable. My addicted husband, obsessed in his forever ongoing projects, was not with me. Therefore, a strong resentment had taken over my well-being. Once in Los Angeles, all I wanted was to be reunited with my young family. The airport was crowded, people seemed to be rushing in every direction, but as far as I was concerned, the world was empty. As soon as I arrived, I immediately made my way to one of the shops to purchase a couple of magazines for interest. As usual, once immersed in my reading, the time would fly. In the meantime, I needed to remain vigilant, checking my watch every now and then to make sure I did not miss my family.

A vacant bench at a far corner seemed to attract me. No sooner had I settled in my comfort zone then a lovely red-headed lady, with tons of durable silver luggage, plumped herself beside me. I glanced at her from the corner of my eye. She was well dressed, portraying an aura of elegance. She was wearing a peach-colored suit with an organza blue-flowered shawl adorning her shoulders. Her reddish hair was swept away in an asymmetrical style.

Defensive of my space, I barely acknowledged her presence. "Don't you know I want to be alone?" I mumbled between my teeth. Then with my head down, I lowered my eyes and went back to the sanctuary of my magazine. She seemed restless, trying hard to get my attention. Her noises and movement were so annoying. I took a deep sigh of exasperation, put my magazine down and glanced at her again, disturbed.

This character's face responded with the sweetest smile; her eyes imploring like a puppy. My, she is swishy. She must be an actress. But I still wish she would leave me alone. Whoever you are, I am in no mood for conversation, or to meet new people. These were my sinister thoughts.

I retracted further in my corner to put more distance between us. A few minutes later, she mumbled words I could not comprehend. The stranger seemed adamant to get my attention. Finally, I gave in; she wanted to talk. I closed my magazine and turned to her.

"Yes, miss?" I said. "What is the matter? What is troubling you?"

In broken English, she responded, "My husband! He went to return the car long ago and he is not coming. I am worried and nervous."

"Oh! I see," I exclaimed "I am sure he will be here soon. The line of customers in L.A. is astronomic. It is quite a task to return a rental car. It can take long! Do not worry!" I reassured her. By now guilt churned at the pit of my stomach for my snobbishness. "You speak with a pleasant accent. Where are you from?" I continued.

"Belgium," she responded. "How about you?"

"I am from Niagara, Canada." With that, I felt compelled to introduce myself with a handshake. A graceful smile brightened her face. She mumbled her name, but my brain did not retain it.

Once she heard me mention Canada, she quickly replied, "We visited Toronto long ago. We got a cold reception, bad experience. Therefore, we never went back."

I was not pleased to hear that. But then I thought, Well! Bitter winter and cold reception can leave one with a bad impression. Look at how I had behaved. What was wrong with me? I always loved people and I was a people's person, but in my poor spirit, I was drowning in self-pity. The injustice I was doing to myself and others was the result of not absorbing the positive energy of the universe around me. I scolded myself. It's a shame for anyone to indulge in such behavior. But here I was… doing it. Had I not learned self-pity is a sin? I needed to shake myself out of the miserable state.

From there on, the chitchat began. Before we both knew it, we were in deep conversation. She was Mary Joe Milken, the kindest soul one could ever come across: sweet, gentle, classy, and most of all, with a heart full of love. I informed her of my destination. I noticed her facial expression of worry transformed in delight. Had that happened by simply engaging in conversation? I questioned myself. We repeated our names to be set in our memory bank. We quickly started to relate each other's lives. As we knew, we only had so much time. We were there for two and half hours when her husband arrived; they were catching a flight to Brussels. She was exuberant when she saw him. With liveliness, she introduced me to him. There was pride in her voice. She made me feel I was her newly discovered treasure. Her husband's name was Jack. He was an extremely tall fellow; well mannered.

"Please," she said, "Jack! Give Lora our address! I want her to keep in touch with us."

By now I knew her life story. We made a promise to reconnect and write to each other. She could not write in English, but her husband would do it for her. He was a professor of physics and familiar with English. They left before my connection. We embraced, and Mary Joe had tears in her eyes.

"What a pity to leave you behind," she said. Her husband nodded in accordance, he seemed to share her feelings.

These people were unexpectedly on my path. Was it a coincidence, or the will of God? Were these people sent my way for a purpose, or to serve a need? I couldn't help questioning. After they had left, the bench was empty and all mine again, but my sadness returned, stronger than before. She had managed to change my state of misery while I engaged with her. Once alone, strangely, I felt the loss of my newfound friend. She had forced herself into my life and vanished in a short time.

Once in Melbourne, I kept my promise and sent her cards. I narrated in them my experiences and my discoveries. Jack's letters for Mary Joe were a pleasure to read. She vowed that her vision of me was with her. "I will never forget you," she dictated to Jack, these were her words on paper. In the winter, I live in the south of the U.S.A. Mary Joe and Jack usually traveled abroad before Christmas. My husband and I made plans for them to visit. Once the fellows met, they got along well. Scheduling seemed to always be a problem: when they were arriving, we would be leaving to fly north for the Holidays. However, we managed to visit, and lived to the fullest in those short precious hours we had. This continued for few years.

Jack adored his Mary Joe. Oh, she was always so elegant: the perfect European noble lady. Often on our outings, strangers would come up to her with admiration.

"Mui Limpido, Seniora." You sparkle Mrs, One exclaimed.

She always responded gracefully and proud. She said one time, "This is the way Jack likes me to be."

Amused, I said, "Funny, my husband is the same."

Jack reluctantly said one day, "I think we are destined to always meet between flights."

That is exactly what was taking place. Many times, they extended invitations to us for Spain, Belgium, or France, but we never made it due to a lack of time. We became good friends. Mary Joe was precious; I looked forward to the letters she and Jack wrote. I invited them to Canada. "I want to take you for a tour of Niagara," I said many times. "Mary Joe, once you see our area, you will restore your thoughts about Canada and its people."

"Lora!" she said. "Now that I got to know you, if you are there, I know Niagara is beautiful."

Only nice words she spoke; her outlook of life was positive and complimentary.

Mary Joe never made it to Canada. She wanted to and had promised to. We never made it to their invite, places in Europe either. Lack of time...

One day, a letter came from Jack on an early December morning: "We will not be coming abroad this time. Mary Joe is not too well. We both are sad that we will miss our get together. We promise we will see you soon."

The following year, even though I had not heard from them, they were on my mind. On my return flight home for Christmas, my plane landed in New York; we were to continue to Buffalo. There, while seated on the plane, I thought, it would be funny if Mary Joe and Jack would be at the same airport, connecting to Florida. I was puzzled because I had not received their special card. No sooner had I arrived home, among my mail a very elite envelope stood out in my mail box. I immediately recognized the writing to be Jack's! The postmark was from New York. Anxiously, I opened it, confirming it was Jack's. The letter was written the same day I was at the New York airport.

Dear Lora,

I am writing to you from New York. I am in my hotel room,

alone...

Immediately a fearful grip grabbed my throat. As feared, the news was very sad.

"Mary Joe has passed away in my arms after battling colon cancer." he wrote. "She never wanted me to tell you of her illness because she loved you and did not want to cause you sorrow."

My eyes filled with tears and I sobbed uncontrollably. Our precious moments spent together were joyful; full of laughter and love. Mary Joe must have made some pre-arrangements because I received her picture Christmas card wishing me, "Merry Christmas, Happy New Year!" yearly. The greetings always caused a flood back of memories, from that chance encounter to our happy times together. She will always be remembered as my dear friend. When I question, Why do these people appear on my path at the very time that my soul was in despair? Like an angel, she turned the cloud of darkness into sunshine. And then, quickly she came and went.

In my heart, her kindness will live forever. We must remember: let's not ever close the door to whoever is placed in our path. The results of doing so are our great loss. When I analyze the meaning of these encounters, I know in my heart it is for a good reason.

Novel No.4

THE FORBIDDEN LOVE AFFAIR

When I noticed how pale Darleen was, I adhered to her request and remained behind. Our evening engagement was to tour Paris by night, following dinner and show at La Mona Ruschia. The rest of our friends went, including our husbands, but Darleen and I remained at the hotel. She had complained of a nasty migraine that rendered her terribly nauseous. I realized her need and felt duty bound.

We had taken a trip together, the four of us and some other acquaintances. Here, we were at the Hotel Nikko in Paris.

That afternoon, Darleen and I had gone to check the elite fruit market at the lower floor level of the hotel. I turned to comment on the marvelous display of fruits when I noticed my friend with teary eyes. "Darleen, what's wrong?"

Between tears, she blurted out, "Nora, I am not going anywhere tonight. Please stay with me this evening, I need to talk to you."

"Darleen, what about Roger? What will he say? Don't you prefer to have your husband with you?"

"No, not at all. I want him to go."

A bit confused, I replied, "Yes, of course, I'll stay with you. What are friends for? Especially, in a time of need." Body language told me she was relieved.

"Besides," I continued, "it's raining profusely out there. I'd rather remain at the hotel."

"I must admit, Nora, I feel guilty about depriving you of the outing: the dinner, the show…" she replied.

"Oh, sincerely, Darleen, I'm not missing anything. Paris by night: done that. La Mona Ruschia: I saw it in Toronto. I find repeats boring."

I knew in my heart that my husband did not appreciate my decision to stay behind with Darleen, but I was caught in a situation and would plead with him to understand.

When Roger came to call, David left with drooped eyebrows and a disturbed look on his face. He gave me a quick kiss and dashed out the door.

I needed to check on Darleen. If she hadn't been sixty, I would have suspected her of being pregnant. The way she had behaved all day was puzzling. Playing nurse, I walked next door with a bottle of extra-strength Tylenol and some Tums.

Once there, I found Darleen crying uncontrollably. Alarmed, I said, "Darleen, if you're so sick, maybe you should see a doctor?"

"Nora, yes, I am sick, not only physically, but mentally. I'm totally tormented by my conscience," she answered.

I need to tell someone. This secret and my sneaking are eating me up! I'm involved in a love affair, Nora. I have fallen out of love with my husband. I can't stand to be around Roger any longer. I'm happy when he's out of town on business, away from me. I thought taking this trip together would help, but it's making my life intolerable. It's a big effort to sleep with him, and I find him repulsive."

Am I hearing right? I thought.

"You're having an affair? With whom?" I responded. "Not you, Darleen, I cannot believe it!"

Then I caught myself. Nora, shut up and listen.

She brought her hands to her head and exclaimed with a trembling voice, "I'm losing my mind. I've fallen madly in love with a priest. What should I do?"

"What! A priest?" I exclaimed, giving her a disapproving glare. What on earth was she telling me? This love affair business was totally out of character for her, but I listened, in spite of my shock and surprise.

"Please, tell me what to do, Nora. You're the only one who can understand me," she pleaded.

"A priest is no ordinary person, Darleen. I thought you were happily married!" The expression on my face must have given me away. I did not want to make her feel worse, as her mental state was in jeopardy. I tried to conceal my judgment. The least I could do was listen to her outpouring. It was obvious she needed sympathy, not condemnation. No wonder her behavior had been bizarre.

"My love affair began innocently," she said. "Now I'm caught in a web. I can't get out of it."

She was trembling, her body showed signs of nervousness.

"My feelings for this man are so strong that my existence is meaningless without him."

Oh my God. I quietly brought a hand to my mouth. She was in trouble for sure. I thought, Darleen is a married woman, a mature adult, with three married sons. At the stage of becoming a grandmother. How could this be happening to her?

She continued, "He's fifteen years younger than I am and full of life."

I noticed a little joy when she mentioned her priest, as she wiped away her tears.

"Father Anthon is just as crazy about me as I am for him. What am I to do?"

I let her talk and I listened, stunned. This is real, not a story I read in a magazine or a movie. In the meantime, my concern reversed to her husband and her boys. I knew Roger as a hard worker, a good family man, a successful businessman, he had provided well for his family. He seemed devoted to Darleen and his boys. I noticed the little extra weight, but still an attractive man. Where had he gone wrong? This affair will hurt a lot of people. That was my concern.

Darleen is a pretty girl herself, with a bubbly personality. Her big blue eyes — radiant and captivating — always carried a contagious smile. She has always been a friendly soul; generously giving. I knew that smile of hers could be alluring to anyone, especially a priest. I made a comment in the past about her personality. Now, I reminded her, saying, "Darlene, people gravitate toward you. Why wouldn't Father Anthon find himself attracted to you? Especially as you are forbidden to him, and him to you. You know, Darleen, the forbidden fruit… it all goes back to that." I had her attention and she listened, while I tried reasoning.

She had calmed down somewhat, and in retrospect, tried to make me understand Father Anthon's behavior reasoning in defense.

"You know," she continued. "Their life with intimate female companionship is none existent. When he is in my company, I bring out the liveliness in him and his resistance is uncontrollable. We cherish our time together. I have become more spiritual and wait for the moment to be with him."

Any reasoning, in my mind, did not justify her actions. What could I do to shake Darleen out of her spell? She has so much to lose, I thought. She continued blabbering, like a teenager in love for the first time.

In my wits, I turned to her, put my hands on her shoulders, and gave her a gentle shake, trying to bring her back to reality, I said,

"Darleen, your husband, does he know or suspect anything?"

"Roger? No."

"Darleen, what will you do when he finds out? Are you prepared to lose him and the boys? Have you thought about the rest of the family, how they will be disgraced by you?"

"No! Of course not. Roger will not find out, and neither will the rest of them."

"Oh! What makes you so sure?"

"We are being very discreet."

"Discreet or not discreet, when you are engaged in deceit, sooner or later you will be discovered."

"I just pity him."

"But, Darleen, regardless, he will find out sooner or later. You cannot continue this affair. Darleen, you pity him because you love him. This thing with the priest is just a temporary fix of elevated dopamine."

"Nora, you don't understand how he makes me feel. I am alive with him."

"I understand perfectly well, any woman would be flattered, especially being sixty and showered with love and romance by a handsome young priest; it's tempting. But one needs to be realistic."

I was determined to talk some sense into Darleen. If she hated me, so be it.

"Your priest, Darleen, in retrospect, should control his emotions," I retorted. "You are another man's wife! For heaven's sake, remember the commandments."

Now, I knew I was scolding, but she needed to wake up. I refrained with a little guilt. Was that what Darleen wanted to hear? I knew they were two intelligent people who knew better, but I guess these things happen when you the least expect them to.

Father Anthon had been sworn to the priesthood. With that, he was committed to celibacy. A priest's life is dedicated to the service of God for the church and its people. He is not at liberty to do as he pleases, especially engaging in liaisons with another man's wife! He is supposed to renege his desires and pleasures. Indulging in sexual pleasures with a married woman, breaking a family, the commitment to his vows — Father Anthon knew the results: a big scandal for the church and the Catholic religion. Plus, he risked being expelled.

Darleen's matter was serious, and, of course, she was troubled. This is why her tormented soul made her search for answers. It seemed to me that good reasoning was puzzling her.

"How could this happen to me?" she asked. "What am I to do now?"

"You are seeking my advice, Darleen, and I will give you my honest opinion. Things should be stopped before they escalate. Can you keep it platonic at this point? If not, execute an end to it immediately, before it goes any further." I knew it to be the right instruction, but not for two people madly infatuated in forbidden love.

She answered, spaced out, "Before I knew it, I was in his arms. There is a force that draws us together. How can we keep it platonic?"

"Darleen," I said, "put a lid on it. Before you know it, the flame will die out."

"Nora," she responded, "how can I tell my heart what to do when my inner feelings are stronger than me?"

Darleen knew very well it was wrong. I questioned myself, trying to understand. She did not lack for anything, or did she? Is she just looking for a thrill? Is she bored with her family life? Is its temporary insanity, or a late midlife crisis? One never knows what triggers the mind. I could only guess and continue to wonder why.

It was obvious her eyes sparkled when she mentioned Father Anthon.

"He loves to be around me, I am the highlight of his life. I have his picture; do you want to see him?"

"Yes." With curiosity, I replied, "Show it to me."

"A good looking priest. What a shame they are not allowed to marry," I remarked. No sooner had I said that, her phone rang and interrupted our conversation. It was him. She signaled me. Darleen, all animated, walked away for privacy to greet him. The expression on her face had changed from worry to full of joy. She bounced from being curled up on her bed, promptly erect and full of energy, young, vibrant, and happy. In my observation, I knew for sure she was sick with love fever.

Darleen needed to unburden herself. She had chosen me for her disclosure. Would I keep this secret barred at the bottom of my soul, or would I intervene and save my friend? With those thoughts going through my mind, I gestured a goodbye with my right hand and reached for the door knob with my left to exit and return to my room. I knew she now preferred privacy to converse with her lover. I would not dare reveal my secret to my husband, although, we had made a promise no secrets between us. I knew he would not condone it, or even begin to understand.

Alone in my room, I began to plot and plan. I needed to stop this euphoria which had taken over my friend. Eventually, it would destroy her and her family. As for Father Anthon, I did not feel much sympathy for him.

We were to remain in France one week, and the following week to tour the northern European countries; two weeks total. This time away was good for distance between those two love birds, I contemplated in wishful thinking. Maybe Darleen's feelings would switch and rekindle with her husband. We went shopping the next day with our husbands. The boutiques were loaded with inventory, extravagant fall clothes were well displayed. The fashions were alluring; we could not resist buying. Darleen seemed to pick clothes too young and sexy for her age. She seemed excited and having a good time. Roger — obliging to her every request — made it clear that money was no object. We started out mid-morning, shopping until late afternoon. The boys were hungry. We took a taxi to the Avenue Des Champs Elysees district, and here at a small bistro we ordered a light, late lunch. Not enough food for our husbands, but as for Darleen and I, trying to fit into those fashionable dresses, we were okay with the small portions. Unconsciously, I kept vigilant of my two friends, mainly Darleen, as I so wished her to be kind to Roger. The aroma of coffee was inundating the restaurant and stimulating our taste buds. With our nostrils out of control, we ordered a cappuccino. It took longer than usual to be served. While we were waiting impatiently, a lovely song came on. A deep male voice. It was in French, but music is beautiful in any language. I could not understand the words, but the melody gave me goose bumps. I could tell it was profound and romantic. Darleen is fluent in French. I took one look at her and I knew in my heart that her mind was now floating far away with her lover in fantasy. I felt sorry for Roger. I noticed he had reached for his wife's hand in affection. Darleen, on the contrary, was in another world in deceit.

In observing that, I felt more compelled to take action. But it needed to wait for my return. Our days touring Germany, Austria, and Belgium were extremely interesting, the histories, the culture, sights, the food, and wine tasting made the time just fly by. Before we knew it, we were back at the Paris airport, and back to Canada.

We cordially parted with our friends. When I embraced Darleen, I whispered in her ear, "I worry about you. You know what you need to do."

Once in my domain, I could think clearly and concentrate better. I needed to do something. I regretted leaving my husband out of my plan, but I figured it was necessary. I needed to accomplish my mission on my own. I convinced myself that I would need to solve more than one problem: the devastating marriage breakup of my friends and Darleen's alienation from everyone, including our friendship. As a devoted Catholic, the bad publicity among the priesthood and the church was troublesome.

I did not waste time to place calls to the hierarchy of the church until I got to the bishop. Once I got him on the phone, I requested a meeting. Since they are holy men, it was granted with no problem. It was now October — a bright fall morning, the air was crisp and refreshing. Some of the leaves from our trees had started their transition. Nature would soon turn our area into a wonderland of fall colors.

It was time for a change. I wished the same spell for my dear friend. My husband had left for work. Alone I got in my car. I needed to travel a short distance and meet with his Highness. All the way I rehearsed. I thought about how I would plead with him. I tried hard to build my confidence. Yes, I prayed, "Oh! Please, God, let him listen to me and do what's right."

As I got to St. Michael's Cathedral, I made my way to the rectory. A modest lady answered the door bell. Of medium stature, her hair was pulled back in a knot. She was pleasant, but sternly businesslike. After introducing myself, she responded, "Yes, the bishop is expecting you, please come in."

I was escorted down an endless narrow hallway to a large library. On entering, the room felt musty and unpleasant to my nostrils. My eyes quickly shifted to the dark oak shelves from floor to ceiling which were loaded with books. An enormous antique desk set near a sketched multicoloured window. The bishop was sitting there, elevated on a high-back wing chair. His attire consisted of a long yellow tunic trimmed in mauve and the picked hat with all its gold-threaded embroidery. I was facing a celestial human figure, but not intimidated, as I knew him to be a man of God. I felt calm and at ease to speak. He presented himself to me gentle and kind. He got up to greet me, and with grace, invited me to sit facing him on a lower chair. He softly asked, "What brings you here, my child? Your request seemed urgent. I am here to listen; how can I be of assistance?"

I bowed to him and set down. I gathered my hands together in prayer.

"Your Highness, it's about a Father. I need your help. One of your priests has fallen out of grace. He is presently engaging in a love affair with a married woman — a dear friend that we need to save. My request to you is to please transfer this priest to the far away missions of South Africa for a long duration. The transfer must be done immediately, for everyone's concern, as well as the church and before the matter is spread out into the members of the congregation."

He listened attentively. Pain showed on his face, and in an amiable voice, he asked, "I need the name and the parish where one of our own has gone wrong. I will instruct Monsignor to take care of the matter promptly."

"Yes, Your Excellency. It is all here, documented on paper." I handed him the file with all the information. As a devoted human being, he did not question my credibility. He knew I was sincere and a concerned parishioner trying to help.

Father Anthon was sent away, though, he was overdue on his move, I was told. The archbishop sent me a letter of apology, with thanks. The priests are to be relocated every so often as a rule to preach the faith, therefore shifting is necessary.

Not much later, David's work had taken us away to the Far East. Eighteen months later, we came back to our country. There, we were attending a wedding in Toronto. I spotted Darleen, proudly standing beside Roger. I was overwhelmed with joy in seeing them together.

"David! David, look who is across the room!" We ran to greet them and we embraced them both affectionately. They appeared happy. Enthusiastically. they announced, "Eh! We are grandparents now." Before quickly fidgeting with an iPod for pictures to show us.

"Congratulations, he is adorable. A little boy!"

Darleen, first, "Oh, the biggest joy in our life."

"Oh, yes!" They echoed together.

Later, amiable open I accosted Darleen. "Can we have a little chat? Girl to girl? I need to ask you something." The guys reproached, especially my David. "You girls go ahead, sit together. Roger and I need to update ourselves."

I put my arm around Darleen's shoulder. Close to her ear, I asked, "Okay, my friend. Tell me, how is your love affair with Father Anthon going?"

She looked at me straight in the eyes. "He moved away, never heard from him since. I was sad. Nora, I am so sorry I burdened you. He is totally out of my life. I must have been temporarily insane. Oh, what a crazy infatuation I went through. I am so ashamed. Thank God I saved myself."

"Darleen, Roger... how you feel about him?"

"Poor Roger, I am so lucky to have him. How will I ever make it up to him?"

"Did you ever confess to him?"

"Oh! No! I cannot. I will have to live with my guilt, I guess."

Darleen's statements asserted my actions had brought good results. David and Roger barged into our conversation and the subject changed.

My husband, much animated, suggested, "Eh, Nora, it's time to plan another trip! Why don't you and Darleen decide on one?"

"Yes, we should," I answered.

Roger quickly replied, "How about joining us?"

"Yeah! Where are you going?"

"Hasn't Darleen mentioned it to you? She has convinced me to explore South Africa."

Novel No.5

DAD'S LAST CELEBRATION

It was Friday night, August 27, 2003. "What a perfect evening for a summer party!" I exclaimed to my husband.

"Yes, darling, it sure is!" He responded, putting an arm around my shoulder.

"We are so lucky, and it's time to rejoice with family and friends."

"Anything for you, darling. It's your special day."

The staff was busy fussing around with the final touches here and there for the festivity. We were to leave all our concerns behind and live it up in celebration. Those were our wishes when we initially planned my birthday party. It would be celebrated at Eagle Valley Golf Club in Canada, outdoors under the stars.

The balcony, which wrapped around the clubhouse, was filled with tables covered in pink and white linens. Two patios extended themselves into two levels, both featuring an outdoor bar, more tables and chairs and plenty of space for guests to socialize and enjoy.

The fantastic lighting outdoor was spectacular. The trees and surrounding shrubberies were all glittering with white and blue illuminations. A full moon in luster up above added to the setting. A gentle warm breeze cast a soothing spell to delight the glow on our faces.

Many of the arriving guests cheerfully commented, "Did you order this heavenly summer evening complimenting the festivities?"

"Yes, it is splendid, isn't it?" I responded.

Graciously, I welcomed and greeted every guest as I stood at the entrance way. Two large vases ornated with white roses released a fresh scent permeating the air. A soft music played in the background.

The first to arrive was my mom and dad; radiant as ever, with much love and pleasure glowing in their eyes. They were there that evening to celebrate my birthday with all their children and grandchildren. I knew how fulfilled they felt to be with the family.

The music was playing our favourite melodies. A cascading fountain at the corner was playing its magic. The tickling flow of water had captured some couples to gathering in a romantic mood. The atmosphere was exuberant and joyful, as dear friends and relatives mingled chatting away. Everyone helped themselves and enjoyed the abundance of the good food while wine and champagne flowed in crystal stemmed glasses. Laughter resonated throughout the clubhouse. Everyone had turned into a festive mood. My dad especially was the life of the party.

We took turns at the microphone, trying to outdo one another with funny jokes, clowning around, and dancing. The energy level was high, and my dad was having the time of his life. I had never seen him so happy. He twirled around the dance floor like a teenager, cherishing every moment. Admiringly, I watched him, my heart leaping joyfully, knowing he was happy.

The time went by fast. I guess that happens when you are having a good time. Before we realized, the time had slipped away. The celebration was over.

My mom kept calling dad, "It's time to go home. What has gotten into you tonight?" But Dad kept ignoring her pleas, continuing to dance and celebrating into the early hours of the morning.

"I'm having so much fun, loving every minute, and I don't ever want this night to end," Dad said.

I was happy for him and encouraged him on the glorious evening. "Good for you, Dad! Ignore Mom and keep dancing." My daughters were taking turns in twirling with him, according to the music. And he just kept up like a young teen full of energy. Oh! How he loved his granddaughters. I guess they gave him strength. He knew he was special for them also. It was four in the morning when he finally gave in into my mother's pleads. She was getting adamant.

I knew my dad had a doctor's appointment on the following Monday, but I was not concerned. Whenever he went to the doctor, he always bragged, saying, "Everything is perfect."

As I was driving home that Monday, I decided to detour to my parent's house. I contemplated kidding Dad about the party. But as I pulled up the driveway, I noticed my parents in the garage. Dad was sitting melancholic on a stool with Mom standing sympathetic by him.

I was in a cheerful mood and ready to joke with him about Friday night… But I noticed his teary eyes, his face, sombre and alarmed.

"Dad, what's the matter?" I asked. "What's happened?" No answer. "What did the doctor say?"

He was not responding. I kept insisting, "Dad, Dad, what's up?"

He could barely talk to answer me. A whisper finally came out of him. "The doctor… doctor… told me I'm… going to die."

"Dad, stop with the funny jokes," I replied. He had a habit of kidding around and liked to shock me, often with evasive answers. Then I looked up at my mother… "MOM! What's going on?"

With a puzzled expression, my mother simply said, "He has

come home with this statement. I really don't know!"

"Mom, did you go with him?"

"No. He went alone."

Dad had gone to the doctor by himself. The doctor had broken the news to him alone. After he arrived home, he fell into a silent state and would not talk to anyone.

Shocked by what I had heard, I called his doctor, who confirmed that dad had an advanced stage of cancer and his lungs and pancreas were totally invaded. The news vibrated through my body. There was nothing anyone could do for him, the doctor said.

I refused to accept the doctor's prognosis and later, kept yelling at my sister to get busy and find someone who could help him. I was not going to accept defeat. My world started to spin into an abyss, dark and ugly. The devastation was unbearable. But once the medical tour begin, the specialist showed us dad's x-rays and told us he may have only three weeks to live.

I was restless and desperate. I thought I would have my parents forever, especially my dad. I adored my dad because he was one of the best. He lived for his family, and I know how hard he had strived in his life to provide for us; he would sacrifice himself to benefit any one in need. As for myself, he was always ready to oblige to any of my requests.

"We're taking him to the U.S., where they will help him," I adamantly told my sister. "Forget these doctors here." We pay and we are going to see what they can do for him."

Dad continued to remain silent the rest of his days; lying on the sofa or on a lounge chair outdoors. He did not say a word. Mom was getting annoyed with his silence, but I can just imagine what was going through his mind. I hoped he was praying in silence, imploring for a miracle. Was he frightened of the unknown, was there life after death? He was a man of Faith, what was he wishing for? Whatever… I will never know… He had died in silence from the moment the news had been given to him. All I know is that he had fought through the war, often he related to me how some of his friends lay dead beside him. The agony he felt for his friends, was indescribable. Did he feel that same agony? I questioned myself.

Dad started to get jaundice and suffered immensely. He would not eat or drink. He totally gave up and looked sad. I could not get over the sight of my dad, once vibrant with so much personality, now wasting away to nothing.

The phone woke me up at four in the morning. My mom was frantic. She called to say that Dad was in bad shape and needed to go to the hospital. The ambulance whisked him to the St. Catharine's General where he was admitted. I stayed with him.

Offering encouraging words, I said, "Dad, maybe they are going to help you here."

He did not answer.

As I sat beside him, alone, funeral plans popped in my head. I tried to dismiss them, but I was cold, tired, sleepy, and in the worst mental state. I held his hand. He seemed serene.

My dad passed away the same day he was admitted. He died less than three weeks after being diagnosed. We never made it to the U.S. for his doctor's appointment.

Looking back on that last evening we celebrated together, I remembered that I had never seen my dad enjoy himself so much.

Was the universe working its magic on my dad to grab the moment? If he had known that he was going to die, would he have been able to celebrate the last joyful night of his life to the fullest as he did? I'll never know, but when fate stepped in, my dad stopped living.

What have I learned from this: Dad never wanted to let go of that glorious evening. Since we cannot control our life's destiny, we need to treasure every living moment, and choose only the beauty and learn to let go of the adversities. Let us go through this journey until the moment is taken away, hopefully in dignity.

Novel No. 6

THE DIVORCE

As always in time of despair, my belief is to turn to your faith. As the saying goes, "If you love something let it go, if it comes back, it is yours, if it doesn't, it never was."

There are times in our lives that whatever is presented to us by the will of God, or by some other natural force, or created by us as human beings, we do not have the capability to accept it as such and deal with it. We expect everything to be smooth and perfect and this is how we would prefer life to be.

Unfortunately, life is full of challenges and it is up to us to endure and cope with the hurdles that it brings. This is the story and my experience with my friend Martha and her husband Fred.

***

Sometime ago, Martha and Fred were reminiscing between themselves, chatting and counting their blessings. "What a perfect family we have! Everything is so good that it is almost scary. We all work together. Our married daughter and her husband are part of our business. They have given us four beautiful children, our grandchildren." She stated holding his hand sitting beside him.

"Yes, Dear we sure are." Responded Fred.

The first was a girl, Angela; the second a boy, Trenton; the third, Francis, Roger.

Fred couldn't stress enough, "A wonderful son-in-law that loves being with our family; to replace the son we never had."

They felt so blessed with the harmony in their home and in their workplace. One could detect the happiness in their well-being by the graciousness in their behaviour. When you are happy, the world smiles with you. You perform well, and it feels great to be alive.

This was good and went on for many years. For this particular family. The grandchildren did not know the difference between their home and their grandparent's, since they were strongly loved, and they felt the security of two homes with loving parents and grandparents to spoil them.

This was the spell that was upon them for a long while. How comfortable it was for everyone. But human beings are never satisfied. Once they settle in their comfort zone, they start to get bored and restless. It is easy to get used to a good life. They forget and the routinely daily life becomes monotonous; therefore, they start to search for stimulus to enhance their existence.

This is what took place in Martha's and Fred's young, beautiful family. The peace that once reigned in their household turned into a war zone, growing in hatred and resentment between the young couple at the expense of the children. The grandparents started to notice the love going sour, and the change in performance, and unpleasantness in their discord and behavior. Their concern was not only for the young couple, but mostly for the children. Martha's restlessness and stress from worry had reached its peak, especially when she couldn't help noticing the sadness showing gloom and doom evident on the children's faces and change in their appearance. She would bicker with Fred in tears, sick with worry, saying, "They are my jewels. I resent what they are being put through."

They were so young and could not understand, but they felt the impact of things not being right. Them, being grandparents tried to keep alert for their best interests of the family. But it was not always possible. They were all affected by what was taking place and feared for the horrible consequence — the divorce. Neither Fred or Martha were able to interfere with what was taking place. It was personal among the young couple and there was no reasoning with them. Before long, it had gone from bad to worse, out of control. Although they knew what was occurring among them... When Fred tried to address the matter to the adults to reverse the matter. All he heard "We have fallen out of love. Stay out of our affairs." Which older folks found difficult to understand.

On their visits, the sparkling eyes on their precious granddaughter were there no more. The sombre mood was written all over Angela's face. The boys could not understand as much, but they could feel the aura of confusion in the air. Angela, being the oldest at ten years of age, her forehead was crinkled in lines of worry and apprehension. When she would hear her grandparents talk some sense into her parents, she could not discern the reason for their discussions, and her reaction was against them. The karma in the household was one of discomfort and negativity in every direction.

Two years later, to everyone's dismay, the young family fell apart and separated. It was devastating in both homes, worse than death itself, but most of all, for the children. Angela was just about to start high school, a time of an exciting new chapter in her life with new friends, new location, new teachers, and a Catholic school with uniforms and discipline.

She did not like this new change. Her behavior was totally out of character from the good and sensible girl that she was. She rebelled against uniforms, she did not like her teachers, she hated religion, and she hated the school altogether. This got her into a lot of trouble. Her grades went down, often she got into fights at school, and her appearance totally changed.

Fred and Martha were used to seeing this well-rounded girl. Now, she had turned into a nasty young creature ready to put up a fight if you dared speak to her. No matter what anyone would say, it was all taken the wrong way. She was totally disturbed at this tender time of her life and one unhappy girl. She seemed to have slipped into a deep well, where she relinquished in boredom and misery. She did not know who to blame or who was really responsible for all this change in her life. Martha herself walked in a daze out of concern for her granddaughter. She was aware that at this time she had to deal with her body's hormonal changes, in addition to a new school, new house, a broken home, and the shuffling back and forth between her parents. That was enough to drive anyone off the deep end, especially a young child.

The mother had chosen to leave the household with the children. Angela's relationship with everyone started to deteriorate. Her resentment was one of hatred, including her grandparents. Often, she looked at her grandmother, unaware of how she was hurting also. On the contrary, she took her as her enemy.

Martha sympathized and understood exactly what she was going through, how her innocent mind had been filled with burden and muddle. The pillars of strength in her home had crumbled down, and she felt torn between the two parents, as she loved them both, regardless of who was at fault.

Since the majority of the girls seem to lean more towards their father, Angela felt the need to look after her dad because he was the one left alone, and she felt sorry for him. She became the sounding board mostly on the paternal side, and, of course, the curse from each of them complaining about the other. The nasty bursts of anger would snap out anytime unexpectedly.

One summer evening, the family was sitting at a sports complex watching a game for one of the boys. Angela turned extremely angry, and said to Martha, "If you were to move to Australia tomorrow, I would not care if I ever saw you again, and I would not miss you."

By now, as tolerant as she had tried to be with her, Martha

almost lost her calm and tried her patients. She looked straight into her eyes and said to her, "Angela, I have had enough of your behavior, and I will not allow it to go any further. Get a hold of yourself and smarten up."

She got harder and harder to cope with, and it seemed impossible for the grandparents to reach her. She was their main concern, therefore, on their mind constantly. Some of her outbursts would make them sick with worry as their hands seemed tied.

Martha and Fred did not know how to handle or refrain the anger that reigned in their strange granddaughter. Martha continued to walk around in total despair, and Angela was the thorn in her heart. She kept saying to her husband, "I do not give a darn about her parents, they are adults. But my angel, I really care what happens to her." Her eyes would shed tears until exhaustion would settle in.

For a long time, she knew she wasn't her granddaughter's favorite person; as her obnoxiousness conveyed those feelings. Her kindness was resented and abused. At one-point, poor Martha reached a decision. If she did not want to make herself sick, she had to leave her alone and let her be. In the meantime, she continued to have faith and prayed and beseeched God with all the strength in her heart. Martha confessed to me... She begged God to please send one of his guardian angels to put an arm around her Angela and guide her. In her prayers, she begged, "God, I cannot handle her anymore. I am leaving her in Your hands."

The older couple often traveled. During this particular time, they were in Avignone, France. Before they had left for their trip, things were not good with their granddaughter; this was troubling them immensely. Walking around the city of Avignone, they found themselves in front of a huge cathedral. It soared high into the blue sky in silver stones with different peaks reaching toward heaven with two sets of gold bells on each peak. They stared at the many steep steps they needed to climb in order to get to the mammoth front door.

After assessing the situation, Martha's aching body was exhausted from walking since early morning, and it was now late afternoon. But her own strong will was enticing her to go enter this immense church and say her prayers. She turned to her husband and said, "Honey, I need to go in there."

He asked, "Are you sure you will be able to make all those steps?"

She replied, "All I can do is try."

He stated, very obligingly, "Then let's try together."

She started to climb the stairs, forcing her tired feet and legs to take one step at the time. To her surprise, her tired body seemed to regain some strength, and she was able to continue. Finally, they reached the huge front doors. They stepped inside a vestibule where they were confronted by two other sets of doors! One could choose to enter to the right or left. They chose the left entrance. The minute Martha stepped inside the enormous sanctuary, the ambiance was heavenly. It had tinted glass facades and altars lined up on each side of the perimeter walls, plus a huge celestial altar in the centre. Candles were flickering in front of every altar with a special statue of a saint where people knelt to pray. After observing this scene, she recounted, "Where do I start?"

Surprisingly, her husband guided "Start from the right and work your way to the left."

She thought for a moment, and then said, "Fine, but first, let's light some candles for our deceased loved ones." She searched for change in her purse, got some euros, and dropped the donations in the brown wooden box slot and lit candles. Then moved forward, stopping and admiring the different altars, each honoring a different saint until they were almost at the end of the left wall, where she found herself in front of a beautiful white marble altar. She immediately recognized the statue of St. Ann with her arm around this young girl. "Oh, my God!" She exclaimed to Fred. "How could I have forgotten?" She grasped her husband's hand.

"This is where I need to pray." St. Ann had been in her prayers in her religious life as a young girl. How she had forgotten this patron saint, in her moments of despair?

Without thinking, she knelt down and started to pray deeply from her heart. Slowly, a soothing peace came over her soul, with a reassuring feeling that all her concerns about Angela would be taken care of, and things would be all right.

They slowly walked out of the church relieved. A renewed aura flowed around them. She was happy and ready to smile at the crowd of strangers outside in the piazza. They continued walking until they reached their hotel. She turned to her husband and said, "I want to call home and talk to my daughter. I need to know how Angela is doing. I want to hear her voice."

When her daughter answered, the first thing she uttered was, "Mom, everything is good with Angela."

The rest of the report was all positive. She told her, "I already knew it would be good, I felt it in my heart." And she related to her daughter what she had just experienced.

Martha said she didn't know if it was because she wished it so much, or if Angela felt her grandma's misery in her own heart. Often, she had lamented, to others. "Mamma does not approve of me." But little did she know of the profound love in her grandmother's heart.

Angela managed to finish high school and graduated. Although she kept informed, they left her free and did not pressure her with any request. Occasionally, the grandparents would get a phone call and that was such a treat just to hear her sweet voice. Whenever she decided to visit them, they assured her that the door at their home was always open for her. She would respond, "I know, Mamma." She would occasionally say, "I love you, Mom."

Of course, Martha rejoiced and would reply, "Likewise, my darling." Hugging her. Always with her heart filled with hope and gratefulness to God.

Angela slowly started to turn into their good little girl again, her appearance was changing, her behavior was improving, and her conversation intelligent and mature.

They hoped with patience, love, and kindness, goodness would surface. It took time... but they were pleased to think Angela was adjusting well. They realized, that she needed to deal with her own life and set her own goals. The grandparents later reported, "It is delightful to sit and talk with her. We almost see her daily now. If days go by when we do not see her, the phone rings quite often and there is Angela to say, 'Hello, Mom, I'm here.' I think she realizes how much she is loved, and she gives us strength to look forward to each day, knowing she will be fine. Serenity has returned with the smile on her face. I still pray to God every day and thank Him effervescently for having sent my precious angel back, guiding her along the way.

Angela has grown to be a young woman, graduated with honors, and received several merit awards. She became a care giver, and a counsellor one of the best in her field. She decided to spread her wings and started on a journey around the world. She stated "I want to explore this planet of ours mom. Before she left I gave her a St. Christopher medal to keep her safe."

"Great. That sounds all good, Martha," I said.

***

Much later, my last visit with my beloved Martha I asked her "How is your precious granddaughter?" I sat listening attentively.

"OH! Thanks for asking. You know she is away doing good deeds. But well! Really Well! As matter of fact". Her forehead creased and said "But I must admit; when she is visiting some parts of our troubled countries a temporary cloud comes over me. All we can do is continue to give her our unconditional love. With God's will and my prayers, she will be kept safe."

I got up walked over to her, gave her a loving deserving hug saying "Martha my dear, I am so proud of you. Your unconditional love works wonders not only for your granddaughter and your family. But also for the so many people you have touched with your kindness, by giving of yourself and asking nothing in return., including me. Thankyou." I just wanted to tell you that. I gently let go of her, as she looked at me perplexed.

"Come on, Rowina, I am nobody special. Thanks for the praises. Its only me no one special."

"This is why you are special, because of your humble existence. No false pretences."

She looked at me meek and shaking her head denying. "Rowina, come on."

My friend continued her daily life with her beloved Fred, always concerned about the well-being of others, neglecting herself. She was always busy, as she was needed by everyone. The phone rang one late evening startling me from my sleep. "Hello" I greeted disturbed, trying to clear my throat. "Rowina, sorry to call you at this hour it's Fred here. My Martha...my Martha is no longer with us."

"What Fred! What are you saying?" Strong sobs were the only answer and the phone dropped with a banging sound, then went dead.

"Yes," I later found out the terminal cancer was far advanced and she wanted no medical help, or intervention. She died peacefully at home. She never told anyone, jokingly, her sickness was fluffed off, according to Fred.

The pain and sorrow hit me like lightening. My dear friend was gone for ever. She is terribly missed, not a day goes by that I don't reminisce my dear Martha. How lucky have those people, including myself been to have had Martha touch our lives. As for her granddaughter I am told

She is modelling her grandmother's role.

Novel No. 7

A COINCIDENTAL ENCOUNTER

The shrill of the telephone interrupted their heated argument. Roxanne took a deep breath, trying to control her anger, and yanked up the receiver. "Hello," She said, greeting the caller much louder than usual.

A gentle voice responded, "Hello! Roxanne, this is Father Quinn."

"Yes, Father?" Roxanne responded, trying hard to calm down, to sound pleasant and polite, while hiding the irony caused by her husband, Julian.

"Roxanne, I'm sorry to bother you at this time on a Saturday evening. As you know, we are holding two seats for you and Julian, and the pilgrimage deposit for the upcoming trip is overdue. We need the money by tomorrow, otherwise, I'm instructed to release the seats to those on the waiting list."

"Yes, Father, I will be there in the morning," Roxanne promised, taking a deep breath. In the meantime, she knew she still needed to convince her husband.

"Okay. Roxanne, have a good evening and I will see you in the morning after the service."

"Yes, Father, I will be there," she promised.

Now Roxanne felt the pressure even more. She resented having to resume the battle with Julian.

The pilgrimage was planned by the church Roxanne attended, and was scheduled to commence on the 24th of July, 2016. The intention was to renew one's faith and replenish the soul. But Julian had remained in disagreement, protesting, "I have no desire to participate in yet another churchy journey."

He had been brought up in a different family environment, therefore, he didn't particularly fancy too much religion or priests in particular.

This had caused much concern for Roxanne right from the beginning of their relationship. As Julian originally refused to attend Sunday mass, but Roxanne had made it clear to him that if he wanted to be part of her life, he needed to oblige and attend church services. It took some convincing, but later he had complied. But every now and then his old stubbornness resurfaced.

Roxanne's childhood had been the opposite. She was placed in a convent with the nuns; in day care school since she was two years old, continuing on to attend a Catholic school. The nuns and priests were the only teachers she had known, therefore, she held great respect for them.

Here they were on the same subject once again. Roxanne insisted, "We are going, Julian, that's it, that's all. It's final." She slapped her dish cloth around irritated cleaning her kitchen counter.

She enjoyed the praying and the singing. Plus, it was a pleasure to be shifting the rosary beads between her fingers. The trip consisted of going by bus to Sainte-Anne-de-Beaupre in Montreal, Quebec. The religious journey would take off in the early morning from their church, and return to the Cathedral. But Julian adamantly continued with his refusal. This made her furious. She was determined to go with or without him. Why was he challenging her? She warned him, "I do not want to go without you, but should you insist... I can always contact my old flame in Montreal to meet me there." She was bluffing, of course. The old flame was an old boyfriend that she did not care about. But she had been told by her mother that he still had an old crush on her.

Of course, Roxanne would never bring such action to fruition, but thought her threats might motivate him. Lately, he was always against any travel or time for pleasure. His projects were a first priority, while Roxanne felt ignored and her wishes denied. For some time now, she had been breaking down in tears, wishing Julian would be more obliging toward her needs. Their marriage was on shaky grounds, this was the main reason she wanted to take him away.

Finally, after much arguing, Roxanne was able to convince him. Their journey began in harmony with the congregation. They were sitting on the steps of St. Joseph Cathedral in Montreal, waiting for the rest of the group to reunite, when Julian noticed a man struggling at a nearby public phone trying to make a call. The fellow lifted his head and looked around. From his facial expression, one could sense his imploration for help. Julian noticed the need, and spontaneously walked over to him and offered assistance.

"Are you trying to contact someone?" Julian asked the man.

"Yes," he replied, "but whatever I am doing, it's not working."

"Let me help you," Julian offered. "Who are you trying to call? May I ask?"

Humbly, the man replied, "My cousin asked me to call him when I arrived and he would come to meet me." The stranger looked pitiful, appearing lonely and lost.

Sitting close by, Roxanne could overhear the conversation. She was proud of her husband helping the old fellow. This was the main reason she liked pilgrimages. The kindness was starting to take effect in her husband's soul. Good, she thought smiling with pleasure.

Their traveling companions were emerging from the Cathedral. She waved at them to join her for their gathering. It was close to noon, and bus number one would soon pull up for them to move on.

Julian was still chatting with the man when Roxanne signaled him to rejoin the group. He returned with a grin on his face. Smiling, he said, "Roxanne, you are not going to believe this. The fellow I helped over there, his name is Robert. He is a cousin of your old flame. That is the person he called, and he is now driving up here to meet him."

Roxanne listened and burst into a big laugh. "Really? Oh, my goodness, this is crazy! I don't believe it." Roxanne retained no desire or interest to see this person from many years ago. But what a strange coincidence, she thought.

Julian was intrigued also. "Roxanne, I want to meet this guy. I hope our bus delays until he gets here. I just want to see him."

"Honey, don't be silly. I have not seen this person for so many years. He's probably changed so much that I won't recognize him."

"Regardless," Julian interrupted, kidding her, "your mother never stopped talking about him. Finally, I might get to see what you missed."

"Stop this nonsense, Julian. I did not miss anything. I chose you over him, didn't I? This is ridiculous. We are here to renew our faith, not to resume arguing," Roxanne exclaimed with a sigh of relief as their bus pulled up. "Thank God our Bus is here and hopefully we are going."

The rest of the group had returned and before they realized it, the bus driver whisked them away. Their next destination was the Sacre-Coeur Chapel in the Laurentian Mountains.

Roxanne's feelings shifted to a happy mood, glad to having gotten away. She had no desire to encounter old boyfriends, but Julian seemed disappointed. He became taciturn. When Roxanne nudged him to comply with the prayers, he defiantly responded, "No, I do not want to participate in recitation."

Silently, she prayed for him to switch his poor spirit. She liked him much better before the incident.

Roxanne was patient with compassion and understanding of her husband's health problem as a diabetic, but she couldn't help snapping at him sometimes. "Julian, I find your mood swings irritating," she exclaimed, perturbed.

He gave her a questionable look. She took a deep breath and let it go, but her inner feelings were churning. Roxanne often asked herself, Why was Julian so difficult at times?

The bus made its way to the Sacre-Coeur Chapel, arriving earlier than expected. But a priest from the parish was there to greet them. A lovely lady stood beside him. "This is Theresa," he introduced her to them. "She will take you on the journey of the stations of the Sacre-Coeur."

The group descended from the bus to follow Theresa. At first, Roxanne took her for a nun, although she wasn't dressed like one. The look and expression on her face was that of a saint image… the attire modest. She spoke softly; her eyes were placid, and docile. As the pilgrims followed the stations, they admired the perfect expressions on the sculpture of the statues. The combination of Theresa's narration and voice was soothing and captivating. At one station in particular, Roxanne looked at a statue in prayer. Theresa paused there also, and exclaimed, "Sometimes, we become disappointed in life. We ask and pray for things we wish and do not obtain. We need to be patient. When the time is right, our wishes will be granted." Her words flowed from her lips, soothing, capturing the group in a magical spell. The logic made so much sense. Everyone was listening in total silence.

Theresa's long skirt caught Roxanne's attention. It was scorching hot. The sandals on her feet are fine, but why she didn't wear a more appropriate skirt, she thought. She was leading them well and getting toward the end of the tour. That was when, finally, the mysterious lady announced she would tell them about herself — The reason she was there and doing what she was doing. "I am a volunteer," she explained. "I received a phone call one night and it changed my life. The only daughter of a friend of mine was killed in a car accident. I needed to go to her side for support. When I got there, my friend held my hand and would not let go... She was in total despair. I said, 'Oh, my God, do not let that ever happen to me. I wouldn't be able to cope.' Two weeks later, my own daughter succumbed to the same fate. I was angry; I rejected our faith, my husband abandoned me by choosing to move in with his secretary. I contemplated suicide as life sucked. 'Why?' I asked. 'This is hell!' I became deadly ill; I could not function anymore. Hospitalized, the doctors had given up on me and on my condition. My bowels were deteriorating and unless I was operated on, I would be gone in few days. A light came over me. My body seemed to take a peaceful journey. When the doctors arrived in the morning, I gave into them. 'Go ahead, do whatever you want with me,' I said. They operated on me. I was near death, but survived. They attached a bag which I have concealed under my skirt. That is how my life was spared. I had totally abandoned God. I was mad at Him. Then one day, in the total abyss, I drove up here to the mountain by myself. I knelt down and prayed in front of the Statue of the Sacre-Coeur in the church. My solitude was interrupted by the pilgrims entering. A stranger put an arm around me and said to me, 'May the Good Lord be your Sheppard.' Call it divine intervention or the will of God. I left the church to return the next day, and I offered my service. You and all the pilgrims I guide have helped me replace my anger with joy. Thank you for taking this journey of the Sacre-Coeur with me."

What a blissful experience! Roxanne thought. The celebration of the Mass followed. She noticed Julian had mellowed after listening to Theresa. He held her hand as they were ready for the next stop of their journey. Theresa's story seemed to have touched everyone, most people were kinder.

Their accommodation in Quebec was at the Three Rivers Hotel. Julian and Roxanne held hands as they strolled along the river in the evening. The cafes on Main Street were in full festivities; music and singers were alluring in their melodies. The streets were crowded with strolling tourists and locals. The air was warm and blissful. Julian extended his arm around Roxanne's waist, pulling her close to him. "Honey I am glad I came. Look at the stars sparkling in the sky; it's such a perfect romantic night, I would have missed it all." He sealed her lips in a passionate kiss.

After Roxanne caught her breath, she shook her head and said, "If I wasn't crazy in love with you, as I am, darling, I would not be able to endure your stubbornness." She hugged him affectionately, feeling his warm body against hers gave her strength.

"Sorry, dear. What do you say if we call it a night? The morning will soon be here. I must confess, I am looking forward to another of your holy experiences."

In prayer the next morning, they headed for Sainte-Anne-de-Beaupre. The Basilica was splendid with its heavenly colors. Many vendors set up around the area of the church, displaying numerous icons, figurines, and statues. In such an environment, most of the pilgrims were compelled to buy statues they offered for sale to create their own sanctuary at home.

After the evening mass finished, the procession of Saint-Anne was going to take place. It was dark by then. Everyone held a candle light, enabling them to join the rest of the pilgrims from every part of the world. The crowd was immense. It was hard to keep up with the group. Roxanne feared to become separated from Julian. She prompted to hold tight at Julian's arm. Toward the end, they needed to find their way back to the bus. They figured with this mess of human bodies, their fellow passengers and friends would probably be separated in the crowd. Julian was following the wide procession, holding his candle, when she noticed the light was fading away. Roxanne exclaimed, "Honey, you need to light it again, otherwise, it's not effective in sacrifice, and you need it also for lighting."

As soon as she said that, a man standing beside him offered assistance. "Julian, here let me relight you with my candle." Julian turned around puzzled. Who in this crowd knew his name? "Oh! Robert, it's you! Thanks. My goodness! With all these people here, imagine bumping into you again," Julian exclaimed. Robert was the man from the phone booth in Montreal. Their conversation continued in whispers, as they were not supposed to speak during the procession, especially when people were singing hymns. Roxanne, with one attentive ear, overheard Julian ask, "Your cousin, did he come?"

"Yes," the new acquaintance, Robert, responded.

Roxanne was sure Julian wanted to ask more and find out where Robert's cousin was, but she nudged him to be quiet. She knew his interest shifted from the spiritual to curiosity again. After a little silence, Julian resumed his whispers with Robert, while greeting someone else beside him.

"Hello, Julian."

Introductions were taking place in the middle of a procession and prayers, again, Roxanne was perturbed.

Julian leaned over to her, whispering in her ear, "Eh, your Mr. Lover boy is right here, beside us." And he chuckled.

"Are you joking?" she replied.

"No, I am serious. The fellow beside him, it's his cousin! Your old boyfriend."

Roxanne felt a jolt of anxiety, asking herself was this really happening?

She took a peek in the dark; the candle the man was holding illuminated his face bleakly. At first glance, he seemed an older man, a total stranger. Now, Roxanne scolded herself, as she was side tracking from the religious recital taking place. The devil seemed to switch her interest to scrutinize, a distinguished older gentleman tall and slim was on the other side of Julian, near them.

She searched her memory and forced herself to refresh. How did she remember him? He was a perfect candidate: handsome, wealthy, and older. That's what mother preached to her, but Roxanne was in love with her own young man of choice, despising her mother and him. Therefore, her chemistry was not with this fellow at that period in her life. She shook herself. "I need to get mentally back to my devotion and forget about this nonsense. Julian, you are like the devil in pursuit," she said to him.

"Take an accurate look," he whispered, teasing her.

"Julian, stop it. At least, he seems devoted; look and listen how he responds to the liturgy."

In all honesty, Roxanne could not help being intrigued. Once the procession ended, Robert introduced them officially, and with a laugh the four of them got acquainted. Anthony the cousin, was his name, pleasant and cordial from Montreal. Robert, a gentle older fellow, was a widower from their area. This is why Anthony joined him: after recently losing his wife, he was still grieving. His cousin had joined him for moral support. They were two friendly souls.

Robert said, "We always came here together, my wife and me, it was a yearly devotion." In saying that, tears ran down his cheeks.

Small world, thought Roxanne.

Julian was good with them. "Where are you guys staying?" he asked.

"At the Three Rivers," answered Anthony.

"Really?" answered Julian. "That is where we are staying"

"We can walk together until we find our buses."

They seemed happier and responded with gratitude. Anthony was polite, using his best manners, complimented Roxanne and her Julian with genuine pleasure.

He did say he was married with two adopted, grown sons, setting himself up in Montreal in some retail business and operating a sizeable haberdashery outlet.

On second thought, Roxanne asked herself, was her mother right by matching her up with this individual? Only by her own wishes... Julian gave her such a hard time at times, her endurance was sure tested. She had maintained a short relationship with Anthony at one time, but her heart was definitely not there then. She was young and foolish and dropped him. She knew it hurt him, but she did not care.

They went back to the hotel where they met for dinner. Afterwards, the group mingled around the hotel lobby, joking and socializing. Roxanne had dressed meticulously at Julian's request. He had selected a mauve dress, one perfectly shaping her body in the elegant way he always wanted her. Lots of laughter ensued and everyone seemed to be in a good mood, the champagne was flowing with Julian cracking jokes among the group. He was interacting well. She was happy to see her husband relaxed and having a good time.

A tap on her shoulder interrupted her thoughts. She turned to find Anthony facing her. "Oh! Anthony, hi!" She noticed he was well groomed and wearing an exquisite sport blazer, his salt and pepper hair accentuated his mature age in a distinguished attractive way. She hated to admit it, he was aging well; his polished demeanor was evident that, of a successful business man.

In the meantime, she kept her thoughts to herself so as not to boost his ego; this was her impression back in her youth. She had branded him as an egoist.

Her mother was on her case; she often fought with her in his regards. Her retort was, "Marry him yourself, Mother!"

Now, after so many years, here he was in her presence. He spoke gallantly, relating his life. Roxanne listened politely, not to be rude, and their conversation was going well. At one point, she excused herself to leave.

This is when Anthony reached gently for her arm to stop her. "Roxanne, please stay and talk to me longer," he pleaded, looking at her with lucid eyes. "You are as incredibly irresistible as ever. I cannot believe I found you again. For old time sake, can you slip away later, just the two of us. Let's make this night ours, Roxanne." Not believing what he had suggested... She stood there, stunned, with her mouth open. He proceeded, slipping his arm around her lower back.

She looked at him up and down with her sinister eyes. She snatched his arm away, in disgust. With a calm sweet voice, she said, "Anthony, you are a scum, I made the right choice when I dumped you. As young as I was, I knew then what you were like." She turned her back to him, relieved, and left him standing there to swallow his wounded pride, and walked away to claim her precious Julian a short distance away, chatting innocently in good humor.

Roxanne knew in her heart he was a hard worker, stubborn at times, but sincere and honest, definitely not a womanizer. In his own way, he loved her, and in return, she loved him, too, mostly for his humbleness.

The pilgrimage ended. Julian took Roxanne's bluffing for granted, but that coincidental encounter... what did it mean? The wrong state of mind was questionable? Theresa's speech had also sent a strong message. Roxanne wondered if Julian felt the Karma around them. He seemed to hold her arm tighter. Affectionately bent over to kiss her on the cheek, and apologetic, he said, "Honey, sorry I gave you such a hard time to come to this pilgrimage; so, glad I am here with you..." He squeezed her hand, and with lingering eyes, said, "I never want to lose you, my darling."

Roxanne questioned herself. Was it Theresa's spill? Was it the older Robert, the widower? Or Anthony's appearance? The combination of it all had affected them both immensely. She knew that encounter had put more value on her marriage. She vowed to herself, to accept her husband's moods with love and kindness.

To her surprise, once they got home, Julian was much more amiable. He hugged Roxanne, admitting, "Honey, you are right, the pilgrimage does affect you. I feel my soul is in peace, and my love for you renewed. Do you feel the same?"

"Julian, my darling," she responded, "as long as we can attend together, we will make pilgrimage part of our yearly devotion. Yes, likewise I feel blessed in my heart and my soul."

She locked her arms around his neck, kissing him repeatedly, totally devoted.

Novel No.8

TO MOTHER WITH LOVE

All Lila wanted was that particular afternoon a little time to herself. She knew in her heart that her want was not out of selfishness. It was their wedding anniversary. At breakfast that morning, she cheerfully called out to John, her husband, "Honey! My dearest," while walking over to him, and planted a quick kiss on his lips. "I made plans for us today, it's something we both love to do."

"Great! I am glad you took the time," he happily responded. "Let me guess… A musical, right? Looking forward to it." He pulled her to him in an affectionate hug.

"Honey, I'm glad you took care of it, because since you are so taken with your mom, I hesitated making any commitment," he responded.

It was an exception for Lila, to go out without her mother tagging along. As a devoted daughter, she had an abundance of love deep in her heart for her mom. But sometimes, regardless of her love, she would get resentful. As all human beings, Lila desperately sought for some space. It never occurred to her that she and John would soon have all the space, without her mother, and it would be forever. On this splendid afternoon, the plan was to go for a late lunch and take in a matinee at the Avalon Theater in Niagara Falls. They were on their way when her cell phone rang. She glanced at the I.D. It was Mother's. They were about to enter the tunnel when the ring went dead. She gulped a deep breath. I will call back once we reach the other side. She knew it couldn't be ignored. Before she had a chance, the phone was ringing again. She hesitated for a moment, then dutifully answered. Her house keeper was on the line. "Lila, it's Diane, your mother wants to talk to you."

"Oh, yes, Dianne put her on."

"Lila, where are you?" Mother demanded, the tone of her voice conveyed her annoyance.

"Mom, I'm on my way somewhere," she replied politely. "I'll be over later, okay?" she responded in guilt. "I'll pick you up later and take you to my place."

"I called you at home, many times; no answer. I don't know what has happened to me, but I am sick."

Lila took a deep breath before responding. The eternal complaints. Immediately, she went into details of all her aches and pains. She listened patiently. Her mother was a hypochondriac as far back as she could remember, and her illnesses had been always in existence. Her dad adored her and he catered to her every need. But now he was dead, therefore, the daughter had taken his place. Most times she sympathized with her and catered to her every need, but sometimes, especially if she was tired or not feeling well or up to par herself... It was painful for her also.

"Mom, get ready. I will pick you up later, okay?" she repeated.

"No, don't bother to come tonight," she said. "I want to go downstairs to play bingo. I'll see you tomorrow."

"Good," she said, relieved. She cannot be that sick if she still wants to go out to bingo, she thought, relieved, and tried to convince herself. "I'll check with you later, Mom." Lila knew how she worked — Mom often used her sickness for attention. She was used to her endless illnesses since her childhood. At times, out of desperation to have some freedom, nastiness would surface out of her. When that manifested, she didn't particularly like herself. On this particular day, she turned to her husband and said, "Is it possible that my mother has to continuously chase me and I cannot have a minute to myself; or peace? I'd anticipated a joyful afternoon to enjoy the play; now she put a doubt in my head of her well-being and I'm disturbed!" John, her husband being such an understanding person, never complained. He always obliged to any request, including Mother's. He felt she was a lonely widow and was lost without her husband.

At seven o'clock the next morning, the phone was ringing incessantly. They were awakened by Mother's call again. "I am ill and need to see a doctor. Come... here, and see what's going on with me." Immediately, Lila, much alarmed, pressed John and together rushed to her aid. She notified her younger sister and took her to the emergency at the hospital. Once there and admitted, they were given a death sentence.

"Mother had walked to the emergency. She had dressed herself meticulously; although she had some complaints, nothing out of the ordinary. I wondered how she could be dying." She could not believe it. She was beside herself, complaining to her sister and husband. The nurses, and later the doctor, quizzed them in decision making regarding her survival. She thought they were crazy. Her lungs were full of fluid and her heart would give up, they said. She was hospitalized and in one week she passed, leaving the daughter in total shock, but the loss never registered to the fullest in Lila. She went through the motions of the funeral service and later headed south for the winter. At first, a state of confusion invaded her heart and soul, but not devastation. Now, she was free, the time was her own, she could go as she pleased, and no one was hunting her down. Lots of space, no guilt, no call of duty to attend to her. But grief in the strangest way, eventually creeps up like the bad clover destroying the green lawn.

The effect on people is strange. The grieving took over and dominated Lila's emotions later in full spread and fury. A veil of sadness inundated Lila's heart and soul. The radiant joy she had often experienced being with her mother was not existent anymore. She missed her dearest friend. She knew in her heart how much she was always wanted. She often stated to her children and her husband, "No one is going to want me more than my mother! No one!" Her habit was to check the phone for messages every time she returned home. The urgency of the blinking red light wasn't there anymore. Mother's calls had ceased, along with her life. In the past, the voice mail was full of repeated messages. They were mostly from her mother. "Lila, where are you? I called; you are not home." This was the pattern when she was not with her. She was obsessed with her daughter. She called her many times a day and Lila wouldn't miss taking her on daily excursions, or her favorite places for lunches.

She loved shopping, but seldom got something for herself. She wanted all the beautiful things for her family. She loved to walk, smiling away on the long walks. She would say, "Just being with you, dear, makes me happy, funny, even my pains are alleviated." She lived two streets away from the family and she felt her daughter and husband were her security blanket. Lila had a younger sister. She knew Mother phoned her and demanded as much attention from her also. However, the eldest daughter was expected to assume more responsibility.

Lila stated, "My mother was the youngest of seven children. She came from an affluent family and was used to being catered to. By nature, she was a loving person, but the over-protectiveness she had received from her childhood and by my father had rendered her needy. Over-protectiveness is abuse; my mother could never fend for herself. She always relied on my father and my sister and I to do everything for her. The grandchildren loved her and she showered them with love. We knew she lived for her family and was so proud of us all. But oh! How she relied on me immensely. At the same time, she never ceased to praise me with compliments and encouragement to build my ego. Often, If I had a function to go to, she would say, 'Lila, make sure you stop by on your way. I want to see how beautiful you are.' I dressed for her; that gave her joy. I knew she was my one biggest admirer. I could detect the sparkle in her eyes in seeing me.

"One particular Thanksgiving we were coming back from a trip. I walked in to my daughter's place, and she said to me, 'Mom, Grandma stood by that window and would not move until you appeared in the driveway.' That was my mother. I often needed to travel. I knew she was sad when I would leave, counting the days for my return. My packing was done in her presence, and my wardrobe chosen with her approval. She loved every moment of togetherness. After she was gone, my life has continued, but I terribly miss my shadow. She was glued to me. My journey without her has become more and more difficult as time goes by. My missing her escalates as time goes on. The holidays are difficult because her chair is empty. My desire to dress is no longer there. I walk alone on shopping trips with no desire to buy anything. The stops at Tim Horton coffee shops are ignored because my dear friend is not there to share. I often sit idle and reminisce. Her memories keep me going, with her vision going back in time. In gratefulness, she is always on my mind. I know I have lost what's irreplaceable; my best friend, and my mother's powerful love."

This was Lila's confession, pouring out of her heart to me one day with obscured sadness in her eyes. I gently placed my hands around her shoulders and turned her to face me. "Lila! My dear girl, don't despair. Your mother's love has never left you; it will eternally be with you."

She smiled back at me pleased. "Thank you, I will always remember that."

She left me with a warm hug, convincing herself as well. While I hoped my belief touched her heart, restoring her peacefulness.

Novel No.9

ACROSS THE OCEAN

I was fifteen when my mother stripped me of my friends, my young cousins, and other family members dear to me, but worst of all, my sweetheart: my seventeen-year-old boyfriend, my first love. He had been forbidden to me by my mother. Therefore, no goodbyes had been allowed; I just vanished out of his sight with my broken heart and he was left searching for me in vain. She announced that she had made the decision for us to immigrate to North America, and that was final. I was happy in this part of the world, that was my comfort zone. This took place in the late 1950s, our status and existence in this small city in Italy was not the best, but we lived in a fair condition, which satisfied me. I thought we were happy, although we missed my dad. He was not with us at the time; a temporary arrangement that should have soon been over.

Apparently plans had been changed; my mom felt, it was necessary for us to join him. He had emigrated three years prior. My father had accepted a government assignment for work on the railroad. At that time, he had to leave us behind. The change in our lives that was going to take place was disturbing, especially for me, but I had no say and no choice. The three of us, my mom, my younger sister, and myself, boarded the famous Andrea Doria and crossed the Atlantic Ocean bound for New York City. From there, we would continue our journey by train to Canada. We had never traveled such distance before; a few questions regarding our safety quizzed in my mind. Once we boarded our ship, I felt reassured, admiring the luxurious décor and the size of it. During our voyage, I felt fine, but my mother and sister were incapacitated by the journey across the Atlantic Ocean. I attended to them dutifully, and in whatever spare time I had, I would scribble in my notebook and read up on deck. That was my escape from my thoughts of what I had left behind and the unknown ahead of us. One could feel the serenity of the universe being surrounded only by the ocean and the deep blue sky, with no land in sight for many days. Before I realized it, we arrived in New York. We were emigrants, the last ones to disembark, and it felt good once we were on land. A representative from the travel agency was there waiting for our arrival.

"Graziana Delgata!" Cheerfully, she introduced herself, extending a welcome hand in greetings and fluently speaking our language.

A pleasant lady, she was wearing a heavy tan coat with the soft fox fur turned up around her collar, protecting herself from the bitter cold. We, on the contrary, were not appropriately dressed for the New York climate. I noticed her raised eyebrows when she saw what we were wearing.

"You must feel cold," she stated. "We will get your baggage and dash to the limo, where you will be warmer."

We were at her mercy as my teeth were jittering. In no time, we were taken to a place and warm tea and coffee was served with marmalade and toast. During our drive, with much interest, I curiously checked our surroundings. It was seven-thirty in the morning and the city was bustling with life. I noticed the skyscrapers and I was impressed. As cold as it was, N.Y. looked promising. Soon after, Graziana directed us to board the train to Canada and we were on our own. I was to be in charge for the rest of our voyage, watching for our destination and looking after the well-being of my younger sister and my mother — both still nauseous from sea sickness. I tried to be brave, but anxiety, combined with fear, was building in me due to my inability to speak English and fear of facing the unknown. As I looked out the window while on the train, I was not impressed by what unfolded in front of my eyes. This new country seemed strange and so foreign. The structures of the homes looked small. This reminded me of the fairytale stories in my early childhood: like the three little pigs' house and that of Little Red Riding Hood. I noticed some were constructed in wood and were only one level. This was much different from our stone and mortar buildings on three levels and attached to each other in continuity. I remember being so concerned about the names of places. One was Thorold and one was Toronto. I could not pronounce it right. I worried we would be taken to the wrong place. But when the conductor announced our arrival to this little place called Merritton, he motioned for us to get off; I looked out, in dismay.

"Mom," I said, "where on Earth are we? This cannot be Thorold. I have never seen a train station this small."

Mom raised her eyebrows with a worried look and did not respond. She was just as puzzled as I was. The train stations we left behind were big and bustling. Then I spotted a man followed by another, making their way toward us. At first, I could hardly recognize him. Once I noticed his big eyes beaming with joy at seeing us, I knew it was my dad. My uncle, Tony, his brother, was with him following behind. I was so happy to see them. My worries vanished and I felt reassured. They were both dressed like seasoned Canadians, all bundled up. On getting out, the cold hit my body and I was caught by surprise once more. Oh! How I felt that cold. As much as I tried to cope, that miserable cold was so hard to bear. We had arrived in the heart of winter in January and Niagara was buried in snow. We had left the central part of Italy, which was cool in the winter, but never had I experienced such below zero temperatures. Once I saw the piles of snow, I soon realized our shoes were not right to even get off the train. We had no boots and no heavy coats. Watching my dad's face and body language told me he noticed our reluctance.

He said, "You stay right here inside the station. Your uncle will bring the car right by the front door on the opposite side. You will get into the warm car and we will be on our way."

I felt relieved already. Dad, with his over-protectiveness, was taking charge. "Thanks, Dad. That sounds great." I hugged him to show my appreciation.

We were taken to a brick two-story house that was to be our new home. My father informed us that we needed to share the premises with Uncle Tony's family of five.

Dad apologetically explained, "Jobs here are scarce, the pay is poor, we cannot assume a big debt. We need to live together to share the expense."

He had written to us to inform us how he had to abandon his government job in Alberta due to the unbearable condition of it. My uncle Tony, his brother, had helped him come to Niagara. My father felt Ontario was more promising with some family around. With his relocation, the move prompted him to send our emigration papers to join him. This small town at the time had a population of fifteen thousand. I noticed the streets were deserted.

"Where are all the people, Dad?" I asked him.

He responded, "Here, not too many people walk. Most of the folks mind their business. You stay indoors, you drive to places."

Being so cold, who would want to venture outdoors? I certainly would freeze to death. So would everyone else, I thought.

"Dad, these streets are different. Are there cobblestones under the pile of snow?" I was full of questions. "Dad, I don't know if I can get used to this quietness and the cold is too much for me."

My dad responded, "This is why I was reluctant. You know I went to the emigration three times to write up your papers because I knew you would have a hard time adjusting."

But I continued bitching. "I hate it here, Dad. I wish we could go back all of us together. I prefer to live in a city."

He looked worried and concerned. "You know that is not possible!"

My dad was a kind man. I knew I was being unfair, behaving like a spoiled brat with all my demands. I tried to be more compliant.

"Do not worry, in time you will be fine. You will make new friends and once spring comes, it will be nice," he tried to reassure me.

But still, I could not help compare what I had left behind. My new surrounding and discoveries did not appeal to me. Often, I found myself slipping into deep sadness.

Comparison, comparison. It would not leave me.

I kept wishing I was back in my bustling city near the Adriatic that we had left behind. Over there, we had lived in the center of the city close to an outdoor market where the merchants were loudly competing with one another. There were people everywhere and they walked everywhere. I usually struggled through the crowds, but after our move to Canada, I could not bear the feeling of deadness around us. Not being able to speak English was a major problem, and these uncertainties caused anxiety with every move. Although we did not have an abundance of food back home, it was organic and flavorful; the food back then was tasteless. Our taste buds could not get used to the different flavors, so we did not feel satisfied after a meal.

My dad had arranged to enroll me in school immediately.

"Good, Dad, I cannot wait," I said to him.

I thought with going to school I would be happier. Find new friends and be with people. I vowed to apply all my intelligence into learning English. Another disappointment awaited me. I left high school in Italy, but here I was placed in a lower grade with much younger students — actually, children — because of the language barrier. Every day, I mercifully waited for the teacher to spend a few minutes with me at the end of class.

"This is my nose, this is my ear..." I would repeat these phrases over and over.

I was miserably unhappy. I felt degraded and demoted. I could not defend myself, being speechless and obedient. My dad had to go to work every day. Therefore, he was unable to assist my needs. However, in those days, you did not complain. The teacher was not to blame. I felt her sympathy, but she was overloaded. Every day I felt the burning flame inside my soul. I wanted so much to go back to my native land. All I could do was dream and fantasize. We had no money and besides, where would I go? Who was going to receive me? I felt misplaced, alienated and trapped. I found myself in a strange environment with no choice but to cope. Adjusting was difficult.

My dad was an educated man back home. Here, he worked as a laborer in construction. The pay was poor, jobs were scarce, and one could not choose. We barely had enough to meet our needs. This was our beginning in Canada. The church was our refuge. Our entertainment consisted of our family, Sunday afternoon rides, sightseeing in the countryside in our old car on limited time and gasoline.

I spent a lot of time indoors reading my pile of books brought from abroad. I kept dreaming that someday I would return to my land in my own environment and find the love I left behind. Time is a great healer, and we started to adapt and make the best of our situation. It did not take me long to learn English, and slowly we made friends. I noticed the different behavior, the different mannerisms. I kept practicing what I had been taught: not to judge or discriminate. Acceptance was much harder back then. The government did not offer the opportunities that are available to us today. Computers were not in existence. We struggled for survival.

I know my mom missed our old life, too, in a way, but she kept saying, "We are here together as a complete family, and that is important."

I knew she was right. It took ten years to find ourselves in this country. We adopted its customs, we educated ourselves, we became Canadian citizens, and we grew with the country; we moved with the time. Our determination plus the good work ethic brought from the old country helped us achieve many goals. My dad, with his engineering mind, prospered and built a steel plant. He employed many people and contributed generously — a true asset for our new country. As for myself, once established with my husband, the opportunities of entrepreneurship presented themselves to us and were successfully met and carried forward. Job creations through business developments fruitfully rewarded this country and, in turn, us. Once we felt we belonged, our great ambitions materialized in realized dreams and the benefits were overwhelming. When I recollect our hard time and suffering, I know they were the pains of a learning process. We felt displaced in the beginning. It is rare for one to arrive in a new country and to find instant joy and fulfillment.

We have been in Canada sixty-two years. I consider myself, with my family, privileged to live here and be part of this great country. I now understand the people, because I am one of them. I sympathize with the newcomers. I know if they give themselves a chance, in time, with willingness they will succeed. I can honestly admit that once I reached a prosperous position, trips abroad were available to me. That desperate desire I once had has turned into the strangest revelation. When I went to my city and revisited the people I once knew, including my seventeen-year-old boy, the love of so many years gone by, I smiled. By now my heart belonged to another. I could not wait to return to Canada, which I consider my country and my home.

Although I like to walk the path of my past, to listen to the pleasant music of my mother tongue, my unforgettable language, and to indulge in the tasty food, my comfort and happiness will always lay on this side of the ocean.

My friends are many. The love I receive is the love I have spread out there. I was once resentful of my mother's decision. Now, with my wisdom, I know she made the right choice. Our relocation brought a lot of suffering in the beginning, but I will never forget my mother's words, and how many times she stated: "This is Paradise. We are so lucky to live in Canada."

Novel No.10

THE GLORIOUS GAME OF GOLF

This is dedicated mainly to the new players, who have decided to take up and adventure in this game.

Congratulations! You have chosen to play the most popular sport in today's existence. My first advice to anyone with the intention of taking up this game is to enroll in a golf lesson program and take some private lessons with a golf pro. The place to start would be calling one of the golf courses, or wherever they offer classes in golf recreation in your local area. A lesson with a golf professional will give you the basic fundamentals of golf and familiarization to your golf clubs. The rest is practice, and apply what you have learned.

Remind yourself it is only a game. Regardless of the results of the game, the rewards of participating in the game itself are immeasurable.

Take yourself on the golf course. A good habit to get into, before the game, is to direct yourself, with your clubs and a bucket of balls, to the driving range.

Here, you prepare yourself for the game.

After a short drill, you can proceed on to the first tee.

Stop and think for a minute, and look around yourself. Now, take inventory. Here you are, in golf attire, assuming the weather is warm and pleasant and you are outdoors. You can be alone or you might have chosen to play with a friend or a complete foursome. Your clubs are beside you. The expanse of the course in front of you; all in green grass, it is lush and inviting. The practice from hitting few balls has put your body in motion, which is to your advantage:

A-physically.

B-psychologically.

By applying these requirements. you are ready to enjoy the game:

The grip is the foundation of the swing.

The aim, for that perfect shot is for the center of the fairway.

The set up in a proper posture will help generate power.

By balancing your body, you will gain control.

Your club face should be positioned square to the target or the ball will curve.

Your confidence, reassuring yourself you can do it, helps perform with quality shots. After a short practice, you are ready to move on to your game.

Relax and enjoy and engage, knowing that you have prepared properly and ready to have fun. You are on the first tee, the fairway extends, leading you on to the course. Or the possibility of some water body in front of you. You are surrounded by nature. You drive your ball from the tee to the middle of the fairway, to the green. What a great accomplishment. Now, when your ball has reached the green, you are on the dance floor with your ball. Take a good look at the ball position, walk around the green. Study the hole, are you downhill? Uphill? Concentrate, take a mental note. A total different approach is needed here. This is the most important part to become a good golfer and crucial for your score. Putting is a skilled, slow approach. The green itself, is it slow for the ball to roll, is it fast. You need to recognize the condition. Your putter position needs to be held in a pendulum modem, gentle, the stroke should initiate from your shoulders movement only, execute with precision. One putt is great to complete your hole, two is acceptable. Three putts disappointing, four or five is not acceptable, but happens to all of us.

The very fortunate zero putt is a jolt of joy. I have witnessed a few, including the occasional rare one. Golf is a pleasurable game. Once you are hooked on the game, it is very rewarding for life until you are able to play.

The more you focus your attention on your action, the better the results.

Remember not to be hard on yourself. Golf is one of the most difficult games out there and you need to remind yourself and realize it's just a game. Try to play relaxed, you are there for fun. You like to see fairway drive long and straight; good chipping and putting will result in a good score. Yes, all of us care about a low score. We need to feed our ego. Forget about the score; take the game for whatever... rewards are beneficial to you being in other ways, eventually the score will come.

My warning to you is: one day you might have the ability to perform like a pro. Therefore, you will feel elated about yourself and the game. But the chances are you won't be, so be willing to accept being a total failure the next time you play. "This is golf! The game can also be frustrating."

When you perform well, you cannot wait to go back and play, because you think you have conquered it. Then you play badly, you are also eager to get back on the course, because you want to prove to yourself that you can do it.

Golf can be disappointing also, and you must not take it to heart. From my experience, it is wise to take it in a good stride.

I'd like to share with you my recollection as a beginner golfer. One of my golf pros, Travis Glass, who is a gentle and patient teacher, said to me, "To achieve a good drive: once you bring back your club and your arm reaches your chin, it is time to bring your club back forward and follow through."

I am thankful to him for this maneuver. When I am playing and I remember to send that message to my brain it works all the time, of course, when combined with my positioning and the rest of the requirements for a perfect shot.

I was foolish enough to believe back in my day that this game could be conquered in no time. How foolish I was and how little did I know.

Over passing time, the frustration accumulated. The more frustrated I got, the more frustrated I became, all for this game of golf.

I joined the Nine Whole Leagues at the local Golf and country Club.

I persisted to play with the league weekly. It never occurred to me that I must have been a burden for my fellow foursome since I was a beginner.

Nine holes were more than enough for me. My husband again kept insisting that a golfer is not a golfer unless you play eighteen holes. Since I was hooked on the game, I was going to play it to the fullest.

My next step came when the spring season rolled around. I proceeded to join the Eighteen Holes League. This presented a big challenge; I needed to play good, now for my sake, and for the respect of my foursome. These girls were not only serious, but competitive about the game. Of course, they needed to be, this was the weekly league. We had to abide by the rules. Good, I thought, this will really motivate me and turn me into a good golfer. Besides I liked to follow the rules to perfect the game. Whenever I had the chance, I would take myself to the driving range. There for hours, I would practice and practice, mainly the long drives. Finally, the travel of my ball was gaining distance. In observing that, it gave me some pleasure. The chipping was important, if the chipping was good, the putting would fallow. Most of us neglect practicing chipping and putting. We all seem to concentrate more on the drive: fairway shots, again, is to show. The saying goes, drive for show and putt for dough. The short game is so important, it makes up sixty-five percent of your shots.

I remember one morning in particular. I was playing badly with my eighteen whole companions. We had completed the first nine holes, ready to go on the tenth hole for the next nine. I turned to my partners and said, "I have had enough of this game for today, I am going home." They looked at me startled. But I ignored them, left, went home, childishly, got myself under the covers and wept my frustration out all for a bad golf game. In looking back, I think, How foolish of me.

I must also warn you that this game can be addictive. Before you know it, you will find yourself either on the golf course playing a game, or on the driving range practicing. I can honestly say it's not a bad place to find yourself. This practice is not only good for the game, but the brain, the waist line, and the fresh air for your lungs. You have all to gain and it is for you, and you only.

This is what I was doing every time I had a chance; the driving range became my place to escape. It got to be a joke that if anyone was looking for me, they knew I could be found on the driving range or on the golf course. It became a great therapy for me. Many times I shook my head, realizing how golf had become so pleasurable. But originally, I felt it was an imposition upon me by my husband.

The appreciation of this game will materialize itself only after the inventory of its benefits start to take place. Many times, regardless of where I find myself in any part of the world, alone or in company, I am so grateful to know this game, thanks to my husband. In company or by oneself, you can have the pleasure to explore the beautiful courses. You meet wonderful people and indulge in the beauty of nature.

This takes me to when I was given an assignment in one of my writing courses entitled: A special place.

This is what I wrote.

It is seven o'clock in the morning; I make my way and descend into the sloped valley of the driving range, toward the golf course. I take my clubs, a bucket of balls, and proceed. Then I stop for a minute, I notice the place is all set up and the spots are all empty. "Good!" I say to myself. "I can pick the best spot, and no one can see my bad shots." Besides, this tranquility is all for me to enjoy. I take a good look around and all I see is nature at its best. The air feels warm, and the peacefulness is soothing my soul.

As I start to position myself and am just about ready to address my first ball, two birds fly right by me at ground level, chirping and singing at each other. They land very close to me. So here I am, instead of continuing with my practice of golf, I stop to sit on the bench and I am totally immersed in admiring the two lovely birds. One is orange and black, and has some streaks of white feathers, the other has two shades of blue and black feathers, and they seem to be in harmony with one another.

"Yes, this place is lovely," I say to myself. As I look around me, the surroundings are breathtaking. What a great place to meditate on an early morning to start the day. Why not? I thought. And who is going to stop me? I close my eyes and tune into my senses. Connected to my hearing, I detect the rippling noise of water running close by me. I open my eyes and follow the sound. Very close to the right of me, there it is a small running creek covered by shrubberies and wild flowers cascading gently on a bed of white river stones. "How beautiful!" I say, talking to myself. What a way to start my day with this heavenly scenery to enjoy. I walked back to my post and started my golf drill energized. Yes, now I was ready to play.

Novel No.11

THE FOREST ADVENTURE OF MELBOURNE

With a strong desire in our hearts, the long voyage ahead of us was hardly considered a sacrifice. We are grandparents, willing to go to the end of the world for our children and especially our grandchildren. On November 18, 2002, we boarded United Airlines in Toronto and headed to the land of the kangaroos: down under Australia. Our visit entailed Christmas with my daughter and her husband and our three grandchildren in Melbourne.

At this time of the year in this part of the world, nature is at its best and the climate is warm and pleasant.

This was my second trip to Melbourne. The country itself and the people had left a good impression on me from my previous trip. Now, I had taken my husband with me. Our intention was to enjoy the wonders of Australia and our young family.

We were to stay with my daughter and her husband and their three children: Mat, nine, Dario, eight, and Danny, five. They lived in a two-story stucco yellow house, well fenced and gated. The front of the house was surrounded by a stucco wall that came half way up, and then topped with a black iron fence with an automatic locking gate. The back and sides of the house were also fenced with a stucco wall topped with a row of bamboo wood. A foliage of soft greenery, had been planted. This softened the appearance of the outer fence while making it high and difficult to scale.

All the high fencing around the entire home seemed strange,

especially the back part, but eventually it grew on me. We needed a few days to recuperate from the long flight. After being well settled and we caught up on our sleep, we could start our exploration especially of the outdoors and nature from this fenced and gated yellow house. There was a palm tree right outside our window from the family room. It was often full of birds chirping and singing. They sure made you feel that you were in a tropical land. The aura around us was motivating. One wanted to get out there and really see what this intriguing part of the world had to offer behind all the fenced homes and the running rivers. The people themselves seemed pleasant, but I was questioning why they were all fenced in and sheltered. My inquisitive curiosity on walking the streets and the paths was not satisfying enough. I was looking for more answers and motives. Not only I was inquisitive to satisfy my own self curiosity, but I had also worked up my grandchildren into a discovery mode. I certainly was going to motivate them on the adventure.

It was Saturday morning, and usually I start the morning by coming down the stairs from our bedroom with my broken made up notes singing "Oh, my a beautiful grandchildren are going to love this sunshine day, because we will take them on a discovery tour to see the koalas" My loudness is disturbing to the family. I know my singing bugs the boys, and I hear their protest.

Mat, Dario, and Danny complained once more for my out of tune singing. "Oh, no, not again. Mamma!" But I soon put myself at their child level and I work on their enthusiasm for something funny and happy for the day ahead. With this manner, I win them over and they cooperate, and I get their full attention.

I proposition them and promise them that today is going to be a real fun one. "You get ready and we will have the treat of our life." I stated we would start the day by going for a drive out of the city, and go find some koalas and some tropical birds. Everyone agreed. Afterwards, I promised them the follow-up was going to be treats of ice cream and cappuccino and all the goodies that we had seen in the markets the previous day. We all got ready and piled up in our burgundy Jackeroo; seven of us, my son-in-law Roger, my daughter Lia, my husband Roy, and my three grandchildren.

We were all cozy in our Jackeroo. I started to amuse the children with my story telling, which they love. After we agree to start singsongs as we leave the city, the children are in their glory, and so is my daughter because we are all together and loving to do what we really enjoy doing on a beautiful Saturday morning: venturing in nature. We enter the national park. I was not so sure about my son-in-law, if this is what he would have liked to do. Maybe he preferred working on some assignments or doing other things, but he went along and it all started on a happy note...

Before we knew it, we found ourselves looking at a tropical wonderland. Lush greenery, amazing trees in every shape and colour, and the ground was covered with all kinds of tropical shrubberies and plants, wild flowers in bloom with a tremendous smell, especially the eucalypts. it was just a paradise that you wanted to get lost in.

My son-in-law announced, "We are going into the forest. How far do you want me to drive?"

I answered him, "Oh, Roger , just keep on driving until we find some koalas to show the children." I think he was doing the driving, but not really engaged as the rest of us. We were mesmerized by the surroundings, and with the children singing and me cheering them on and joining them like a child. I was pointing at this here and that there. We were so captured with our visualization our heart and soul were immersed into it.

My son-in-law again asked, "How far do you want me to go?"

I just kept saying, "Roger, drive on."

He replied, "Mamma, let me know when to turn around."

I said, "Roger, from my experience, you never go back the same way you came from, you always take a different route. You learn more and you change the scenery."

My son in law obliging, replied, "Whatever you say, Mamma."

He kept on driving and driving. We were still looking for the Koalas.

Then we noticed some strange looking trees. The branches seemed dry, almost like plain straw piled in bunches in a silvery colour, and sure enough we saw the koalas sitting high on top, sleeping. The children were ecstatic, and we all got out of the car to take a better look and pictures. Now with our discoveries, we are really captured and totally in a magic state. What can we discover next? As we continued to drive along we would often stop for better observation of the wild animals. At one point, we got out of the car and my son-in-law, with the boys adventured down the embankment of the forest to admire some trees, and birds, and more wild life.

All of sudden, we heard this strange howling sound. It came from a big animal. We saw a big boar pig with a big thick horn running through the forest. Suddenly, he stopped he took a look at us, and he started to make a charging noise, turning toward us. Roger, with three of the boys dragging behind him, was running and climbing the slope back toward the car as fast as he could. The boar in pursuit. They were running breathless . That scared the heck out of them, including us closer to the car. With that experience, we hopped back in the car and decided to do our observations by staying close to our vehicle only, and not go too far off the road on foot.

As we continued on, we noticed that this was really a haven for all kinds of animals, not only the birds but the bats, and the undesirable snakes, green in colour, and so-called flying snakes. They jump from one tree to the next, and they are venomous, and hardly noticeable unless you are really aware to catch them during their leaps. With so much greenery and different colour twigs of the trees, it gets confusing for the naked eye. The snakes could be mistaken for branches of some sort until you see the movement, and they can easily jump on top of you, and with no mercy, you are gone. The snake part started to give me cold feet as I absolutely detest them. My spell from all this fascination was starting to wear off. We had been driving for a long time by now. The realization of being too far into the forest made me call out to Roger. I asked him, "Keep on driving and do not stop any more, try to find the way out as soon as possible and a place to have lunch."

He again replied, "Whatever you say, Mamma."

He drove and drove, and the road was getting narrow and narrower, and not another car in sight, or human life, only us seven and the wilderness of the forest with its wild life. It was getting overwhelming as we moved on. The branches were brushing against our windows, and the car was struggling to maneuver the narrow path. The singing had stopped and my mood had changed as fear started to creep in. It seemed that we were getting deeper and deeper and no opening to make a turn or signs of directions of any kind. I started to worry, but did not let on. It had been hours, but now we were all realizing that it must be late and starting to get dark. We should have long been out of there. Instead, we were getting deeper into it. We realized that to turn around to drive in the same direction we had come from would have taken us into the night. There was no space to turn around. Besides, I was afraid of the flying snakes and the bats. I just prayed that there would soon be an escape out of this situation. I kept looking in the direction of the sun to see some sunlight, but there was only thick brush and trees and darkness.

Then my son-in-law announced that he had something to tell us. All of us anxiously awaited. "What is it?"

All of a sudden, he brought the car to a dead reverse with a thundering noise. "Guess what?" he said. We thought he had come up with a solution. "We are out of gas."

In disbelief, we shouted, "Oh no!" Then we really panicked.

"What are we to do now?"

I started to pray quietly. By now, my daughter was crying, and all the kids started to cry. My husband never let on, but I am sure he was worried. In the meantime, so much was going through my mind. I felt responsible, as it was my idea. I had encouraged Roger not to stop, to go ahead, thinking that there was a road to turn or come out on the other side soon. I heard stories of people getting lost in forests and I thought how easy it had been. We had innocently been pulled in by a magnet until it was too late.

I am sitting there with my silent Holy Marys as darkness settled in. That increased my worry. The cell phones. "Yes, let's try the cell phones," I said. Nothing, they would not pick up anything. In a panic, I exclaimed, "My God, does this road lead anywhere?" Since no one had come across us, I realized that we had been around for hours and had not seen a sign of human life or vehicles. As I said that, we spotted a car coming from the opposite side toward us; a small car. Immediately, my spirit with the children lifted.

"Oh, maybe this is our salvation."

We all were telling Roger "Stop that car!"

"Please, let's stop that car!" we were shouting in unity. "They could get help for us."

He totally ignored our plea, plus, he was telling us not to do anything. In no time at all, the car disappeared. Our little light of hope was gone and here we were again. Lia was getting really mad at her husband and all of us started to badger him. We had missed the chance on his insistence. Our fears and quietness started to turn into anger and accusations and resentment. We were fighting now. Roger seemed dead serious about the gas. But when he saw we were getting out of hand, he announced. "It's a joke!" He smirked laughing away "Mamma. Since you are such a forest lover, I wanted to test your endurance that you really wanted to be in this forest at any cost." He decided to play on my feelings, at the expense of the others. That was such a bad joke, that we found it so hard to believe and forgive him for pulling such a stunt. As a result, we were all angry at him and ordered him to get us out of this place as soon as possible, at any cost, since he was the driver. We still had quite a way to go, and finally by early evening, we emerged out of the forest. But we came out on a dirt road into no man's land. A vast extension of farmland. Finally, we found our way on some normal road that took us to the main highway and much later, back safe in our fenced- in yellow house. By now it was nine p.m. The poor kids were starving and sleepy, and all the treats and other fun things that we were supposed to do were taken up by the journey in the forest that took all day. We were lucky to be out of there now that night had set in.

I gathered my grandchildren and promised them that mamma would sing that song tomorrow morning again, and since it is Sunday, we will make sure that everything is going our way. We will venture in the city and close to the main hub with the rest of the people of Melbourne. We will get all the goodies from the stores that are available only in the city. We will be going on foot, and no joker with us.

My innocent grandchildren nodded in agreement, ready for their bed without protest. I am sure they had enough of this day with all the excitement and no treats. They would be looking forward to the promise of tomorrow.

Novel No. 12
BRING OUT THE BEST IN PEOPLE

There are leaders and followers. The leaders are gifted people that bring the best out of their followers. They possess a certain charisma that attracts others to them. In order to bring the best out of others, you need to transmit, empower, and pass on enthusiasm to them.

It is not an easy task, but with dedication and persistent hard work, it can be accomplished.

First, and foremost, you need to believe that there is good in everyone. After having recognized what is the strong positive gift of this individual, focus on it, reinforce it, praise it, and before you know it, you will be rewarded with the rendition.

Now, it is up to you if you happen to be in a position of leadership to take this good accomplishment and bring it to a higher expectation.

Take a strong company for example. It can only be successful if it is formed with strong leaders that are the anchor for followers. These leaders need to dedicate themselves to enhance the performance of their employees.

How are they going to achieve that? Caring charisma, inspiration, and challenge will only set the stage. You need much more than a stage setting, you need the performers to act on the stage. These actors need to be trained with strong discipline. In order to achieve good results, you, the leader, need to set standards, rules, and goals to be reached.

Your job as a leader is to:

a) Lead.

b) Commit.

c) Assist and sustain.

d) Delegate, authorize, and bind by contract with escape clause.

e) Encourage, motivate, create new challenges, and develop new strategies.

f) Be a good listener and act upon.

g) Judge positively.

h) Recognize, reward its merits.

i) Set higher standards.

Most of all, be in control, keep the team on its path. It takes respect toward the leader, and also great respect toward the follower. Earned trust does produce good performance.

The good relationship you build in your circle will create harmony, where there is harmony, there is loyalty.

An Excerpt No.13

A PASSION FOR LEARNING

When we are fortunate enough to be self-motivated and possess in our inner being a passion for learning, we should consider ourselves lucky individuals. Regardless of our interest, the mere fact that we are open-minded to the willingness to acquire knowledge is a plus in our life. The great opportunities offered to us today are amazing. Therefore, for any human being to want to remain illiterate or not take advantage of these possibilities open to all of us, is such a great loss on his or her own part. We can choose to expand our knowledge and enrich our lives. Anyone can search for knowledge of a preferred interest. It is at our finger tips with the click of a mouse.

The revolution of our technology today is mind boggling; we can learn so much in the comfort of our homes or while in transit and the classrooms of our schools. The findings will lure us to dig for more and more. We have the choice to register the knowledge to expand our brain; which in itself can be rewarding and phenomenal. The accumulation of knowledgeable information we store in our memory bank can only render us brighter and empowered. Unfortunately, I grew up not in the time of computer era. This is why I have been struggling ever since... to place myself in today's modern world of everything being revolutionized by our technology. Humbly admitting that for people of my generation it isn't easy, but I feel it's a necessity for survival. The practice requires constant repetition, and a lot of focus. When you become proud of yourself, thinking you have conquered it — Yeah! Cheers! — only to find out updates have changed it all. With patience and determination, start over and temporarily reconquer the knowledge. At one time, I considered books and schools the best places and sources to acquire knowledge. Which they still are today, with the leading commodity of computers. Our sophisticated cell phone has become our constant companion. The click of a button and it responds to our needs.

As far back as I can remember, I always searched for what I could learn next. At an early age, I recognized that books were precious and full of information on any interest. Our schools were the places where learning was offered freely for the pupils willing to learn by the dedicated teachers they staffed. Our educators were highly regarded and respected. They also had more authority to implement.

Their discipline and severity were accepted. We lived and respected the rules. We were eager to do well, to please not only our teachers, but our parents.

Most of all, our own self benefit reaps its rewards.

Being a reader, libraries were also my favorite places, along with bookstores. From a young age, I considered these places sanctuaries. The longing in my heart for books was my strongest passion. The desire was to place myself in these premises that contained books. They were considered treasures for discovery, for any subject that got the best of my curiosity. Because of all the information available to me through books, I knew that whatever my subject of interest was at this particular time in my life, I could conquer it by simply browsing through books. I used to regard to them as my precious weapons, my books.

I started out in a small town in Italy, where in those days reading material was almost limited to your text books and not much else available. With the assistance of a teacher, and my good parents, I was lucky enough to be sent away to school in the big city. Here I was, able to indulge in enormous bookstores and libraries that had shelves and stacks from floor to ceiling to treat my soul and content my heart.

Then the move to Canada took place. I knew the first of my possessions to be packed were my books, which made it across the ocean. Once in Canada and North America, I was in my glory when it came to books. It got to be a joke in my family as they were my addiction. I could spend my whole pay check in a book store.

From my collection, I taught myself so much such as bookkeeping, which is not one of my passions but a necessity. Interior décor, which I love, brings me back to my young years playing house. An interesting book in any subject truly captures my heart and soul. During my life of learning, my interests expended more and more to fulfill my needs. Psychology was always at the back of my mind. People intrigued me, and I love people; I needed to understand them, relate, and communicate. With excellent teachers, taking courses, attending lectures, and my selected, wonderful books, I was able to dig into information, which brought results. Empowered with knowledge understanding followed. A better look at life occurred from a different prospective. My love for nature and flowers and the actual hard work of doing the gardens all came from my collection of written information from books, magazines, visual pictures, and from attending lectures and seminars.

As life moved on, my passion for learning stayed with me and the desire for more never left me. When I stumbled in the lectures of philosophy, its learning felt good, and the outlook on life made a big difference. It made me see only the good on this earth and appreciate people even more. My choice has been to stimulate only love and seek beauty in everything and everyone. Never judge and never fear. When I was fortunate enough to live and travel in various part of the world, I always searched for a library close by. Going on a cruise, my tranquility is better contained in the section of the library. Either to treat myself with a good novel, or spiritual, or philosophical reading to soothe my soul.

My conclusion is that good knowledge results from good information. When we empower ourselves with information, it's a great asset and the obstacles in our life are less of a challenge. Only then, this world becomes a better place to be. For oneself and for the benefit of others to share.

As I've gotten on in life, my love of learning has never ceased. I continue to pursue, an old desire that I can recall from my childhood — to write — and be able to do it well in every aspect of the English and Italian language. I know it will be a little harder for me, since it is my second language. I am a great believer that where there is a will there is a way. My books and my research with the aid of the internet are going to help me along the way. I have taken steps to make sure every night I listen to one and half hours of beautiful Italian grammar, so both languages are good music to my ears. My laptop computer has become a part of me. My books are still my number one toys. The wealth in my life is knowledge. All derived from the passion to learn, whether a hobby or interest, and always with love.

Novel No.14

THE WAR IN MEMORY

A recollection of the Second World War.

A recount of what actually occurred then, from the eyes of a ten-year old boy in that period and time.

Location: Castelliri, Italy; a suburb of Rome, twenty kilometers from Monte Cassino, where the war was profusely concentrated.

Time: Spring of 1944.

***

Anthony, breathless, was running in an open field. He needed to reach his shelter outside his home quickly. But his whole body was taken over by fright, his legs buckled, dragging him down. Two fighter planes roared above his head. His little white goat, scared and disoriented, was keeping pace with him. They were looking for refuge. The planes were flying at low altitude now in hundreds, shooting down at the people vigorously and at random. The bullets were churning the ground, and one hit the corner of the house, and their path became blocked. A shower of stones and dust created a pileup of blowing gristle sand. Anthony and the goat were gasping for breath, their vision was blurred, their lungs polluted. The instinct for survival gripped them in full force. Pulling the goat along, Anthony made a dive into a deep ditch. His body shuddering out of control, he slumped to the ground, exhausted. The bullets kept coming down like falling fireworks. As he lay there shriveled like a cocoon, he prayed for the bombardment to stop. "Please, God, spare us." He thought of his Mom, Dad, sisters and brothers. Would they survive this hell, he wondered? Only time would tell. He needed to wait this out. After what seemed an eternity of roaring machine guns, there was a short calm. Courageously, he peaked. As he moved, his little goat tried to get underneath him for protection.

The propeller fighter planes were quieter, but circling above beneath the cloudy sky. The American planes were fighting the Germans tenaciously. The zone was under constant attack. A German commando was set up close to their area. Anthony, then ten years old, lived in constant fear for his life. The sudden attacks came without warning. One day in disbelief, he observed a fighter plane shot down by the Germans. It twirled down in a ball of fire. On hitting the ground, ironically, it ended up on a reservoir of gasoline tanks. The inferno lit the sky and the smoke polluted the air. One by one, the tanks exploded. The daily surprises never ceased. Anthony, perplexed, observed the pilot parachuting down from the burning plane. He watched as the German army captured the pilot and took him prisoner. The first bunch of German soldiers that arrived in an ownership way forcefully occupied their home.

His dad, with sadness in his eyes, warned them, "They are armed, and will shoot to kill. We need to follow their orders." As much as they didn't like the invasion, they obliged.

But to Anthony's surprise, these first soldiers were civil. But once the SS joined, they became mean-spirited. They stole, raped the women, and used their weapons with no hesitation.

Anthony watched entire families being bombarded, including their animals. He witnessed his own relatives gunned down.

The days and nights that followed were unpredictable. One afternoon, an announcement came from the town crier, "The Germans are leaving. You are free to come out of hiding and move about." Anthony, his family, and the rest of the folks were relieved.

Little did they know, it wasn't over. The American troops were coming through. The citizens of the area were rejoicing. They believed the Americans would restore peace and security. When they arrived, Anthony with other folks watched them marching through. They did not fear them, as they thought they were kinder. But another surprise awaited them on this particular Sunday afternoon.

An urgent knock at the door came with a frantic messenger. "Quick, hide your women. A bunch of drunken American soldiers are coming. They are armed and they are seizing and raping our women."

Scouring around frantically, they immediately hid their mom and their two young sisters. A man hole not far from the house led into a tunnel for the rain water to flow, leading into the river. The girls were lowered in the murky narrow passage, at the mercy of the rodents and other creatures in there. Anthony sat breathless, jittering in his skin. The drunken soldiers arrived, looking for signorines. After the search proved fruitless, they left. A sigh of relief came out of Anthony's dad; the young boy was still in shock. They watched the soldiers hunt continue to the neighboring homes until they found their prey, young or old, to satisfy their need.

The war ended May 18, 1944.

As time passed, the terror slowly lifted from Anthony's heart and soul. But the scars lived on for a time. The observations were gruesome and the endurance was nearly too much for a young boy or anyone to take. This is what comes with distractions of war. Such experiences are bound to leave emotional marks.

Anthony had been one of the fortunate ones. The long-ago experience of war has taken refuge in a far corner of his memory. He grew up to become a fine young man. At nineteen, he immigrated to Canada, where he found freedom and success.

Novel No.15

LIVING IN MEMORIES

Gail Tucker, slammed the door as she exited her apartment . 'Oh how I wish I wasn't going to that dam place to-day.' She mumbled to herself. Here she was again alone, imploring with her eyes rolled up . 'Why am I so disturbed lately? But I have no choice! I have to go to work.' Reluctant she made her way to the car to drive to the office. It was another nebulous day in Ottawa , as usual. . . The temperature sub -zeros at now mid- March. The long cold and bitter winter, was still freezing one's face in full force. The sun had been totally out of site for days on going. This morning was no different, with the icy road and traffic to negotiate it added to her gloomy mood. The head office of the financial brokerage company she was working for had been making tremendous changes lately, shuffling CEOS, setting new rules. Continuous meetings. . . lecturing's. . . The demands were enormous the pressure was on. Not to mention the irate clients with their phone calls , pulling out and withdrawing their investments.

Gail had not anticipated that, this morning, a surprise would be waiting for her to brighten her days for a temporary future. She walked to the coffee station. There she helped herself to another cup of coffee to boost her caffeine fix.' I need this other cup to help me go through all those file of complains. Before that phone starts ringing.' Lately she was talking to herself. She was just sitting down when she heard some chatting outside her door with a strange new voice with an English cadence. Out of curiosity she walked to the door, compelled to go take a look.

"Oh. Gail, we were just coming in to see you." Said Mr. Johnson.

Gail, with some embarrassment tried to hide her nosiness, with a smile on her lips, she graciously answered.

"Oh really! By all means Mr. Johnson, come on in."

Mr. Johnson was the head of the department, commander and chief of the company. A distinguished man in his mid- fifties, with a receded hair line, intelligent, showing lines of stress on his forehead.

***

This morning, Mr. Johnson walked into her office with an air of confidence and pride. The gentlemen with him as well. Strange as it seemed the air in the office brightened in more luster, and the sun, peeking to come out behind the clouds.

" Good morning Gail. I want to introduce you to Mr. Alvin Jansen, our adviser and counsellor for our new department. He will be set up in our office to initiate the marketing campaign in our board room."

With a gracious smile Gail Tucker extended her hand for the introduction. "Nice to meet you Mr. Jansen, welcome to our office and Ottawa. I am Gail Tucker." The pleasantries were exchanged. Mr. Johnson continued.

"Gail I place Mr. Janson in your capable hands, you will look after his needs. He will remain with us until we have mastered his skills. He comes highly recommended, one of the best in this field."

"My Pleasure Mr. Johnson," she turned to Alvin Janson, flattered and pleasant.

There had been rumors in the office to hire a qualified

empoweree for the troubled occurrences among the CEOS. Now it finally materialized. The details were given, Mr. Jensen had been requested from London, England to lecture and guide the corporate managers due also to the lack of profits in the finance industry. He was a gentleman in his late forties, of medium stature , well dressed and refined in his European fine suit. He began his meetings and lectures in the most eloquent professional way, with written slides , visual example videos, plus his best manners. Gail, his assistant, admired his knowledge and felt hypnotized by his voice. . . Since Alvin Jansen had started his program, the managers were gregarious, encouraged , the Karma in the office favorable. As for Gail, to her surprise, she couldn't wait to get to work in the morning. Beyond her control, the devotion and obligation toward Mr. Jansen had exceeded her expectations . . . Gail Tucker was a modest young woman, in her early forties, shoulder length hair, a pear shaped face with big brown eyes. Her demeaner, portraying kindness and gentleness. She had no children. At a young age, she had married a restless fellow. He was crazy for water sports, therefore her marriage ended in divorce. She looked after her ailing parents that lived in Ottawa. She was dedicated to her work . Gail, had never been happier than at this present time. These months working with Alvin Jansen had brightened her days, her evenings, and life altogether.

***

Eight months later, alone in her family room, life returns to the previous existence.

***

My eyes quickly gazed at the empty seat positioned in front of me. Tears relentlessly found their way, freely rolling down my flashed cheeks. My soul is tormented, my heart feels empty - my dearest beloved is no longer with me.

The flickering fire continues to glow from the fireplace. It's sparkling hues of bluish and orangey flames dance as if nothing has changed. My shivering body is automatically drawn toward it's warmth. The feverish need of comfort - physically and spiritually - is rapidly flowing through my veins. Yes, it is manifesting in all its craving form. I proceed to rub my cold hands; which brings upon me a subtle soothing relief. I absorb the warm pleasurable heat released by the fire.

This was our favourite spot; the cozy corner of our cold winter evenings. Here, many times he took me in his arms. In ecstasy, our love was consumed. Oh how I looked forward to our evenings together. The relaxing timing was ours to recap the chit chat of day's events in laughter and joy . He was interested to listen to my daily report. Likewise, my beloved would share his plans and his dreams, good or bad. Our togetherness was precious until the late hours of the night . Now the two inviting low-seated chairs were still here, comfortably positioned ready to accommodate two occupants. But now only one would be occupied. The one chair would remain vacant, in disillusion causing me much pain.

Every night, my aching body slowly lowers on its soft cushiony seat, seeking relief. But no sooner do my eyes' gaze return at the empty seat. My body starts to shiver, with my brain flooding in memories. A deep sigh surges from my lungs; as my vision of him blurs. My eyes dart around in vein, searching for my companion's tender loving face, while my ears tense as his voice echoes. But only quietness reigns; occasionally intermitted by the slight crackling of the fire. My emotions are stirred and feelings slip lower to a sombre mood. The restless discomfort follows as I try to understand the reasoning. It seems greatly unfair. I fuss about adjusting my body seeking comfort while my soul searches to be appeased from despair. My instinct takes over with my lips mumbling in prayer. In denial, I forbid the dark clouds to reign over me and close my eyes. My being is begging for the stellar blue sky to dominate . I keep my eyes closed and continue to daydream that my lover will reappear. I ask myself 'Where is he now ? Is he with another? Why aren't you, my dearest, sitting beside me?'. With my thoughts still fogy and my vision still blurred I keep begging for serenity. A warm light feeling zips through my body and I ask myself. 'Does he know how miserable and empty my heart is? Can he feel how sad my soul is?'

***

Once late fall rolled around with its gloomy dark days, his body got restless - like nature in it's transformation – he had been slowly changing. I watched the transition take place. It signalled alarm bells. Mounting despair traced deep scars in my heart. I chose to ignore it. My worst fear in its revelation surfaced in its ugly form. One evening he calmly announced. "My dear beloved, it was nice knowing you, and your love will be treasured in my heart as my souvenir. I must move on and return where I belong." I fell gravely ill within a short week ; and my heart was slowly failing the ticking beat.

In great dismay my desire for life started to slip away. It took much courage to pull myself together, allowing my earthly journey to continue on.

I ask myself " Will my immeasurable love for Alvin, slowly dissipate; as the memories linger on. Will this last for ever in eternity?" They bring some pleasure of the happy times and a deep sorrow of the now sad times. I know his touch and the love we shared will reign for ever in my heart . I realize my true love had to be denied.

***

Time has passed. . . On most winter evenings, I slowly get up from my chair, walk away from my fireplace toward the large window. I stare at the outdoor; the snowflakes are coming down like soft fluffy cotton balls. The ground is covered in a white mantel; the trees are glittering with bent over branches from sparkling icicles. It's pretty and peaceful out there. I take a deep breath. I resign myself in gratefulness; thankfully rejoicing in my memories . When the subconscious plays tricks on me with sorrow . I pray the good Lord to help me accept the loss. As I know my beloved is also feeling the same pain. I think to myself "We were two lonely loving souls thirsty to fulfill our needs. When obligations and duty called upon us, our love was sacrificed remaining only in memories."

Novel No. 16

SOPHIA

WITH LOVE IN HER HEART

Sophia was fretting around her bedroom like a disoriented butterfly. She had gotten up earlier than usual because a big day lay ahead of her. It was her first day of school; first grade. Her mom had insisted the night before to rise early in order to inspect her appearance, especially the serious dress code implemented by the school. A lustrous brand-new black uniform with a crisp white collar and a red bow tie laid out on a chair beside her bed — the combination of the uniform signified she was a first grader and mandatory.

Luisa Galante slowly opened her bedroom door and walked into the room and cheerfully greeted her, "Good morning, my darling. What an exciting day ahead of you today, dear." Sophia didn't answer, pouting miserably. The mother had anticipated the uncertainty of her daughter from her erratic behavior the past week. She was a patient, caring mom with a keen observance and intuition. These last few days she had been extremely cautious around her youngest daughter. In a gloomy mood, this morning she was reluctantly dressing against her will.

Once Sophia was dressed, Luisa complimented her, "There you are, Sophia, now you look like you belong to the Academy of St. Mary's School. You will love it there, dear. You will see," she encouraged, smiling.

But Sophia remained silent. She frowned, and proceeded toward the mirror to take a good look at herself.

"No," she said, stomping her feet on the floor and screaming in defiance. "I am not going anywhere!"

She burst into tears and ran back to sit on her bed, grabbing and hugging a cushion for comfort. She did not like her image. Her mom was forcing her to go to this Catholic school. She was miserable.

Luisa patiently followed her, trying hard to pacify her daughter with kindness.

"Sophia, you are going to meet so many children your age. You should be all excited," she exclaimed, standing beside her, patting her shoulders. It was hard these days trying to cheer her difficult daughter. Luisa's husband, Ronaldo, Sophia's dad, was away a lot these days due to business. Therefore, the responsibility was in Luisa's hands. But Sophia was getting difficult. This morning was worse than ever. With no provocation, she started crying again. In no time, the fresh appearance had lost its luster. Her eyes now were red and swollen.

"Honey, please stop, you are making yourself sick over nonsense. We need to get going," Luisa pleaded.

But Sophia had no desire to go to school, or anywhere else out of her home for that matter. Her despair was all due to her hair that had been shaven off and she was now totally bald. This really bothered her; this was the reason, why her home had become her sanctuary and refuge. But today, she was being forced to go to school of all places.

"No! Mom, no! I don't want to go! Please, please, Mom, don't make me," she protested, pleading.

Everyone in her household had made remarks about her sparse hair. Mom and Dad honestly believed shaving her head would make her hair grow fuller and stronger. They always commented how important it was for a girl to have a full head of hair, which, unfortunately, Sophia lacked.

To make matters worse, Luisa had bought her a red wool toque with a bow hanging behind. And Sophia was being forced to wear it going out. Today was no different. The ordeal mortified her.

It was getting late, and Luisa was getting nowhere with Sophia. She thought it better to get her husband. As much as she hated to wake him it was necessary. "Ronaldo, I need you here with our difficult daughter."

Ronaldo had heard the commotion, jumped out of bed, and made his way to the daughter's bedroom with a stern look on his face and ordered, "Sophia, change your tune. You know you have to go to school."

She took one look at her dad and knew it was an order. She couldn't disobey her father. Against her will, she grabbed the toque and shoved it on her head.

"There, Sophia, you look pretty. The toque completes your outfit," Luisa said. But somber Sophia felt sad and far from pretty. She was the only one who really knew the horrible feeling in her heart of being bald.

"Mom, I look like a freak. No one is going to wear a hat to school. Please, Mom, don't make me go," she begged.

"Sophia, stop giving us a hard time," scolded her dad seriously. "Besides, once you are there, you will love it."

Sophia was the youngest of seven children from an affluent family. She had developed such a poor self-esteem and was extremely critical of herself. She often pestered her older siblings, especially sister Rosalba. "Rosy, why are my eyes sunk in, my face long, and my lips narrow?" she questioned. "And look at this protruding chin." She repeatedly beat herself down by comparing herself to her older sisters.

"Sophia, you are still a child, give yourself a chance to grow," her sister, Rosa, would patiently respond.

Although still a child, Sophia wanted to be like them. But Luisa would scold her, "Sophia, stop all that negativity about yourself. You are kind, obedient, and loving. That's what's important. You are my beautiful baby."

Today, she was being dragged to school by her mom. The fear was overwhelming, and she was literally shaking from head to toe.

As they arrived at the classroom, Sister Debna was at the door to greet them.

"Oh, look, Sophia, it's sister Debna," Luisa said enthusiastically. "You are a lucky girl, Sophia!"

Sister Debna had been her Catechism teacher, was familiar to the family. There, she was decked out in her religious attire, wearing a black tunic with her head and part of her face covered in black and white. The gentle smile on her lips gave the aura of kindness. After her charming greeting, Sister Debna took Sophia by the hand and led her to her seat.

"Welcome to St. Mary's school, Sophia. You can sit right here on the first row," she said, in a calm and reassuring voice before she walked away to greet other parents and children.

Sophia gave a faint smile in agreement while trying hard to control her shattering nerves. She wanted to hide in a corner where she could observe but not be seen.

Looking at the classroom, the first thing she noticed were four rows of single benches, meaning eight children would sit in each row. Thirty-two altogether.

Oh, my! I have to meet thirty-two new children, she thought.

The room was large and bright. An enormous blackboard covered the entire wall behind Sister Debna's desk.

No sooner had Sophia taken her seat than a young boy approximately her age was assigned to sit behind her. She didn't want to look at anybody. Sophia was shy, but at the same time, curious. She twisted her eyes sideways to get a glimpse of the pupils being led to their seats beside and behind her.

Her attention turned back to her mom when she noticed her speaking seriously to the teacher. Subconsciously, she wondered, Is she talking about me? Indeed, she was. Luisa felt compelled to warn the teacher about her daughter.

"We have a little problem with Sophia; we have shaved her head to reinforce her hair growth. She needs to keep her hat on. I must warn you: Sophia doesn't like meeting new people at first, but once she gets acquainted she is fine."

"Not to worry, Mrs. Galante, Sophia and all our students will find comfort in our classroom."

In those days there was no preschool. Therefore, the children were placed directly into the first grade at age seven. The classes were taught at their age level.

Once all the children had arrived, the teacher called their names and asked them to stand up, signaling their presence. When Sophia stood up, all the children started laughing. It was her red toque with her dwindling bow. This was exactly what Sophia had feared.

Sophia burst out crying and put her head down on the desk, wishing she could die and never have to look at these kids ever again.

Infuriated, the teacher slammed her ruler on the desk and in a loud imperative voice, ordered, "From the first row in line, I suggest you make your way to Sophia's desk and apologize sincerely and shake her hand in friendship. I want to tell you that we are one big family here. This is a Catholic school, where we teach and live in God's grace."

Continuing, she said, "It is a mortal sin to ridicule and laugh at someone else's expense. This is my classroom. I expect respect from everyone, and for all of you to pass on genuine love to your fellow classmates. Are we clear here, and understood?"

"Yes, yes, Miss Debna," the children responded in unison.

"Then we continue with the presentation of the class," she added.

After the children had made their humble apologies, Sophia was ordered by her teacher to sit erect. Now, with her ears perked, she tried to catch everyone's name. The name of the boy behind her was Massimo.

"What a beautiful name," she muttered. "It resonates." Quickly, the name registered in her memory.

Soon after, the teacher started teaching and turned to the blackboard to write the alphabet.

Suddenly, she felt a strong pull on her hanging bow. A sharp pain pierced her heart. Oh, my God! The pull would risk her toque coming off and leave her bald head exposed. Her sudden instinct was to turn and strike. But as she turned, two big brown eyes beamed at her, humbly and docile. She refrained from striking and stared at him. His meekness softened her little heart and her fury turned to pity and kindness.

"I want to be your friend, I like your hat," the boy whispered. He seemed sincere and shy, like her. She believed him, so instead of striking without thinking, she extended her hand in friendship.

This was the beginning of the relationship. First grade at this Riverside town in 1927. From that day forward, Massimo became Sophia's best friend, her favorite classmate, and her idle. A good-natured boy, Massimo was caring and polite. He greeted his young friend daily, respectfully and protectively.

Sophia lived in a palace, erected high on the hilltop overlooking the town. She had four sisters and two brothers, loving parents, and a staff of servants at their service. She was privileged with the commodities of life. Since Sophia was the youngest, her sister and brothers fussed over her immensely. She was spoiled and overprotected. In the meantime, their good intention of overprotectiveness was turning to abuse that they never realized. She was intelligent and smart, but in a strange way, lacked confidence. Her shyness crippled her in many ways.

At the other end of the spectrum was Massimo, who came from a family of seven. His mom, Giova, his dad, Alfiero, two sisters and two brothers. His family earned a living working the field, good, hard-working folks who ended their days tired from hard labor. After school, Massimo was needed to pitch in with his share of assigned work: feeding the chickens, taking his little goat to the pasture, and gathering dried fallen branches for firewood. The chores were endless. He was accustomed to fend for himself. Their possessions were meek, and their food came mostly from the fields.

Sophia's dad was a tycoon; he built bridges and roads and accrued immense assets from east to west. He employed most of the town's young men, plus some skilled folks from surrounding towns. A clever fellow, Ronaldo was also loving and kind. He fed the poor and helped the needy without discrimination. He often arrived home loaded with goodies that he would buy from the local merchants to help them out.

"Luisa, give this to Mariana. It's the fresh catch of the day," he would say. Mariane was the family cook. He would buy from the local hunters or fisherman, bags of fresh fruit, and muscatel green and yellow ripe grapes, even when the harvest was over.

"Luisa, dear," he would call his wife. "I got plenty here for all of us. Call whoever you think needs some of this food, and share our wealth, in gratefulness of our good Lord."

Luisa was also a generous woman herself. "Yes, of course, my love," she would answer. "I will ask Vincenza to pass some on to our neighbors. I am surprised you did not bring anyone home with you tonight to share our dinner."

"I feel guilty. My horses were loaded. I could not afford to pick up anyone, although there were a couple of people we could have fed," he responded.

"Ronaldo, we will make up for it," she added. "Today is Friday. Sunday morning, we will ask Tommaso to do a cookout outside our open atrium — sausage on a bun — and Vincenza will serve tea and coffee with warm taralli (biscuits), right after the nine o' clock mass when people come out of church. That will be our good deed for the week, dear."

"He will need help, Luisa. Who knows how many will show up," he answered.

"Ronaldo, you forget we have seven children. Gian and Arduin can help. Tommaso, Vincenza, and the girls can help. They need to feel part of our mission. Isn't this what charity is all about? You give of yourself. How else are they going to learn?"

"You are right, dear." He walked over to her and kissed her on the cheek. "What would I do without you, Luisa? You have given me seven beautiful children. You are such a good mother and wife; sometimes, I underestimate you. Sorry, dear."

That's how the Galante's family lived and operated. The environment in Sophia's home was wholesome, with plenty of love and abundance of life's goodness.

Her friend, Massimo, was lucky to attend the same school as Sophia due to the Catholic faith. St. Mary's was the only one in town. They were both devoted Catholic and went to the same church.

Their amicable friendship continued as the years passed. The two had now grown into their teens. They had gone through grade school and high school together. Sophia felt comfortable with him, because of his kindness. Massimo was now seventeen, and so was Sophia.

The young boy had grown into a handsome young man. His black and wavy hair, slicked back, revealed his perfect facial feature. His lean body had grown to six feet in stature. Sophia admired him in his Sunday clothes when he attended church service. He was well groomed with a suit and white shirt and tie — the only outfit he owned for church. Most of the girls in town had their eyes on him. Massimo continued to be polite and courteous, with much loyalty toward Sophia. She was his special friend, although their time together was only while frequenting school.

School was out, and Massimo had not seen Sophia for a while. He missed his shy, strange friend. He would not dare enter the palace where she lived without an invitation. The high stone wall structure surrounding the palace was held shut by four huge double doors on the east and west. The structure gave the impression that they wanted to keep the outside world out and that's the way Massimo, in his young mind, interpreted the situation. Or so he thought. As kind as Sophia was to him, unfortunately, the parents were often away on business. The brothers were in charge of the household. Especially, her brother Renato, the first born. He loved to be in command. Any young suitors for their sisters had to go through his scrutiny. Sophia was last on the list.

***

At Massimos's residence, changes were taking place. Returning home one evening after a hard day's work from the fields, Massimo's mom greeted him at the door holding an envelope close to her chest. Giova had a surprise for him.

"Massimo, dear," she called out, with teary eyes

"Mom! You seem mysterious. What is it?"

"This came for you today," she said, handing it to him with sadness on her face.

He took a quick look and automatically knew. "Mom, I am being called to the army," he said, proudly.

"Massimo!" she cried out. "You cannot go to the army. Can you get out of it? You are my third son, we need you here in the fields."

"Mom, what are you saying? You know I must go. It will be good for me. Papa always said the army makes a man out of young guys. Besides, we have no money. I know in the army I can further my education."

Pensive, he dismissed his mom. But one thing bothered him. He needed to see his dear young friend, Sophia, which he had not seen for a long time. She had reigned in his heart. I cannot disappear without telling her, he thought. He wondered how he was going to get to her in that big walled place she lived in. Whenever around the piazza, her Miss, Vincenza, escorted her everywhere. He wasn't allowed to approach her being chaperoned. Now, he was pensive and taciturn to work out a plan. The next evening, although in doubt, he gathered his courage and made his way to the palace to seek her.

"I seem to have an obligation toward this girl, although, I have never revealed any of my feelings to her," he muttered.

After he entered the courtyard of the palace, the immensity was intimidating, but he knew once Sophia appeared with her sparkling eyes he would feel encouraged. He tried to reassure himself. He rang the doorbell and took a deep breath. In no time, a gentleman, who he presumed to be the butler, wearing a black and white uniform, opened the big brown door.

"Yes, sir," he said while scrutinizing him from head to toe, "what can I do for you?"

"I would like to see Miss Sophia, if I may," replied Massimo, stuttering.

"Is she expecting you, young man? Who may I say wishes to see her?"

"I am a classmate of hers, Massimo Romano, Sir." He strangely obscured his eyes with a strange look on his face, said. "Wait here please." and walked away.

Massimo's body was nervously shaking like a tree branch in the wind. He didn't know if it was this immense place or the anticipation of seeing Sophia again. He wished his crazy body to calm down. The butler soon reappeared and startled him out of his miserable thoughts.. He had sensed Massimo uncertainty and gently gestured for him to come in.

Once Massimo stepped in the foyer, he felt a strong urge to turn around and run. He thought, A big mistake to come here.

"Please, step in the waiting room and I will be glad to announce you to Miss Sophia," said Tommaso.

Massimo had never been in this house before. How lucky my friend is to live in such luxury, he thought. He was admiring the décor of the room when Sophia's voice jolted him.

"Massimo! What a surprise! What brings you here?" she asked, with a puzzled look on her face and half a smile, more inquisitive than pleased.

Massimo immediately sensed discomfort. He had expected her to run toward him, greeting him, with a big smile on her face, much pleased. Instead his young friend's approach was somewhat cold and removed.

The surge of adrenaline his body had felt on his way walking there, now flushed up and down his spine like an icicle dropped from a tree branch hitting the ground. He forced himself to gulp a big breath to respond.

"You, of course," he said in a low tone. "Should I have not come? I know after all these years, you have never invited me. But tonight, I had to come. I have something seriously important to tell you."

He raised his eyebrows, frowning his forehead. What a big mistake to come here. What was I thinking? Why would my going to the army would matter to her? Her coldness, at this point was evident. His urge to turn around and run and never step in this place ever again grew.

Sophia sensed his discomfort. "Is something terribly wrong?" She tried to get a hold of herself, from her surprise. She had not expected him.

Then in the doorway, an older fellow peeked out, calling with a deep voice, "Sophia! Oh!" He took one look at Massimo "I was wondering what has been keeping you since you didn't come back in."

He spoke with a strange accent Massimo immediately knew was an out of town fellow. His spiky hair cut accentuated his square face, heavy set, wide shoulders, and over six-foot tall stance. A giant compared to him.

"Claudio, come and meet Massimo, a classmate of mine, I have not seen him for quite some time and he decided to drop in."

Sophia's friend came forward with an extended arm, ready to meet the new fellow. But a disturbed look and a creased forehead, his light handshake transmitted displeasure at this intruder disturbing his time with Sophia. At the same time, Massimo's stomach was churning in acidity as he asked himself, Who was this joker taking my space with the girl of my dreams. He chose to ignore him and with much courage, turned to Sophia standing between them.

"Look, Sophia," he burst out. "I have been summoned to go to the army. I will be leaving in a couple of days. I came to say goodbye."

"Oh! Massimo, I am sorry. Do you have to go?" She seemed sincere.

But who was this new friend? He bothered Massimo. He wanted to believe that she cared for him. Of course, only in his mind. How could she when she belonged to one class and him to another. While he was reasoning in his own mentality, to his surprise, the fellow grabbed her hand and placed his arm around her shoulder to claim possession.

Massimo gave him a disturbed look while his heart ached, wanting to smack him. He was overcome by jealousy. Sophia just stood there. He knew it had been a big mistake to come here in the first place. Humiliated, he excused himself to leave, forcing himself to shake hands with both of them, and left devastated.

The couple returned to their cozy niche to resume the evening. Claudio was her new boyfriend. He had been introduced to Sophia by her older brother. A fellow from the northern surrounding town, a son of an industrialist that had conducted many business dealings with Sophia's father. The parents knew each other and taken occasional holiday trips together. Claudio's parents had suggested Sophia was a good match for their son, and both parents had match made their union.

Sophia had gone along with their wishes, as that what they did in those days. In her heart, she seriously believed that Massimo was only a school friend, that he couldn't not be considered any more than that. Claudio was attentive and showed her affection, but her body didn't respond with excitement. She had accepted in her soul that this suitor picked by her older brother and parents was her duty, her feelings were not important. Sophia deep down in her heart, cared for her friend Massimo. All he was for her just a childhood school friend. He would never be considered marriage material.

Seeing him again tonight had left a disturbing effect on her being. She wondered if she felt sorry for him. Was it pity? Was it his big brown eyes that lingered with his gaze? But seeing him again the adrenalin had stirred a warm feeling in her being. It was questionable. Massimo had definitely revived the attraction she had tried to bury in her heart. Now, he was leaving.

Once back visiting with Claudio, he kept nibbling at her ear and cuddling her affectionately. Her mind was floating away in her own thoughts. She wished he would stop touching her and go away. Her restless body, since seeing Massimo, had been taken over by anxiety. She turned to Claudio, trying to gently get rid of him "Claudio, the ride from the fresh air in your sport car this afternoon has been too much for me. I feel a migraine coming on. If you don't mind, I would like to retire to my room and call it an early night. May I be excused?"

Claudio didn't like it, but he felt he needed to oblige, for now.

"Oh! I am sorry. Yes, of course, my precious, I certainly don't want you to be in pain. A good rest should help." He embraced her with a lingering kiss, and slowly walked to his sports car and left, not so pleased.

Sophia let out a big sigh of relief. Now she could indulge in her solitude and plan; since she couldn't stop thinking about her classmate. I must see him before he goes away. I must. But how was she going to manage to get to him. The escape out of the palace without being escorted? The watchful eyes of her two brothers, adamantly protecting her, her sister Rosa, her other siblings were everywhere. They would never approve of her going to visit someone from the low land. How am I going to escape? It was unheard of. She only had few days and Massimo would be gone. She didn't sleep well all night. The next morning, Alba the Governess was coming over to teach her embroidery. She would ask her to go with her to purchase the fine silk thread imported from Spain, which was sold by an outlet down by the lower level of the town, and maybe she could slip away to see her Massimo.

She was consumed by her thought, How can I let Massimo go without an embrace, or a proper goodbye. With her plan in place, there she was with Alba on her way to find her beloved friend. She turned to Alba, trying to sound sincere and innocent, she said, "Alba, while you choose the yarns, I will skip down to the Chickigno residence for few minutes. There are special angora wool yarns that the old grandmother produces herself by hand, I would like to get some to make some scarves for my family for Christmas."

"Of course, my dear, why not?"

Overcome with emotion, Sophia ran as fast as she could, skipping the cobblestones, hoping to throw her arms around her friend, and apologize for the cold treatment.

She found herself in front of a two-story stucco building, kind of run down and in bad need of plastering. She knocked on the peeled grey door that needed fresh paint. There was no response. Anxious, she knocked harder. A squeaky window opened up and an elderly lady leaned over. "They are not home, they are out on the fields. They will not be home until after sunset, usually late."

"OH!" Her heart sank. She was so disappointed.

"I can give them a message if you like, but not until tonight when they return."

Sophia looked around and thought, *how am I going to get back down here again? I may as well leave a message.*

"Yes, please, can you tell young Massimo that his friend Sophia would like to see him?"

The vigilant old lady curious, couldn't wait to deliver the message to Massimo.

It was kind of late when Massimo made his way home from the fields. After the news with his throbbing heart, there he was again, at her door. Sophia found her way to a secluded area in a far corner of the open atrium. There she let go of her emotions. She locked her arms around his neck and their lips locked, breathless in the depth of their passion. She had no fear of anybody from the palace seeing her or reprimanding her. She realized now that she had harbored a love for her dear friend all along. Now that Massimo had reappeared, it was evident how he had re-awakened her buried feelings to resurface uncontrollably deep in her soul and class distinction wasn't going to rule her heart.

Sharing and lost in the same euphoria, the two of them gave in to their longing. Massimo whispered in her ear, "Sophia, Sophia, my darling, I have loved you since that first day your bow dwindled in my face."

She smiled in happiness and sealed his lips with a warm kiss "You silly fellow, why didn't you come for me sooner?"

"You broke my heart the other night when I saw you with that individual, someone you had traded me for."

"Massimo, when I saw you the other night, my restlessness was off the chart. After you left, I couldn't wait for Claudio to leave. Just so I could in my peacefulness focus my thoughts on you, and only you, Massimo." She looked at him with languid eyes, continuing, "You see, my family arranged my union with Claudio. It wasn't my wish or what I wanted. I just went along like a good girl."

"Don't you believe in following your heart, Sophia?"

"All I know is that our bodies feel good together. If that is love, then I am in love."

Both could not believe their revelations. As they were overcome by their own feelings. Sophia's eyes filled with tears and the warm flow continued down her cheeks. They were tears of happiness, joy, and sadness at the same time.

"Massimo, you mustn't go. I cannot bear to be without you. You are my dearest friend."

"Sophia, you know I must go. Don't make it more difficult for me."

"I tried to put a lid on my heart, denying my love for you because I could not allow myself to believe that we could be together, or you would love a dork like me. Oh, please, Massimo. You mustn't go."

"Sophia it is mandatory. I must go."

"I will lock you up in one of these rooms in our palace, no one will find you."

"You silly girl. I think you are so beautiful, and a universal gift — all for me."

He locked her in his arms again and again until he felt her heart beat. He did not wish to let her go. They were both so young, heading for their eighteenth birthdays.

He sorrowfully relented his embrace, looked her straight in the eyes like a mature man, and said, "Tonight, Sophia, we must say goodbye. I promise you I will come back for you."

He had a fine gold chain on his neck with a gold medal. It had been given to him from his sponsor, the day he received the sacrament of confirmation.

"Sophia, this is the only thing I possess. I want you to wear it; a small token of our friendship. St. Christopher is the protector of safe keeping, he will protect both of us until I return."

He placed his necklace around her neck and hugged her gently one more time, hating to let go.

"I will always love you, Sophia. Don't forget me, and keep me close to your heart, because I sure will return."

After he left her, that evening he returned home with much sadness in his heart. Oh! He would miss his extraordinary friend immensely. The following day, he packed his mere possessions and left for the army.

In September 1939, World War II was well in progress. Massimo was a brilliant soldier, he had been trained well and had become an expert at firing the cannon with its artilleries. In May 1939 he was shipped to Africa, assigned to the frontline to fight the war.

Sophia longed for her dear soldier, and her heart would not give in to any other suitors, waiting and hoping for her dear beloved Massimo to return. Much later he did return; sick and wounded. Struggling on foot on his journey, fighting malaria and finding refuge in churches, and abandoned places to make his way home.

He was hospitalized for months. After a long and near-death experiences in and out of consciousness Massimo finally pulled through. Sophia's love and prayers kept him fighting for his life. He returned to his duty to complete his mission.

***

After a devoted long wait, the war was finally over and in 1944, Massimo finally returned. He marched to find his beloved Sophia faithfully waiting for him. As no one could stop or deny their love.

A life they shared united in marriage for 65 years. They believed the power of love from our universe brought them together from that first school day to mature old age until death took them apart.

No. 17

A POEM

SHADOWS OF THE NIGHT

My heart is throbbing, my legs are buckling, my riddled body is wobbling.

In a ghostly transparent motion, I snake around the sparse doubtful crowd of the late night.

My eyes scornful, dart from side to side — there are mostly males here.

A few short skirts show bare legs, enhanced by uncomfortable high heels.

The ladies of the night are desperately still at work.

My ruffled bills are rubbing safely in my bra.

I have reached my own quota; my tricks are over for tonight.

A hiding thief in colored skin with luminous flashing eyes and vibrant white teeth appears.

He jumps out and grabs my arm and reaches for his loot in ownership.

Two bills are savagely shuffled back between my breasts.

While he dictates an order in command. "Tomorrow night; same place, same time. Increase your favors."

My fragile shadow now moves faster in quicker steps.

My throbbing heart slowly calms down, resuming its placid beats.

I make my way to my refuge. My own bed is inviting.

My body slumps down in defeat.

Thank-God! No more sex tricks for tonight.

A Poem, No.18
AUGUST
MY WEEPING SOUL

The month of my dreams you had always been.

As you approach, pain and tears feel my heart,

a reminder of that dark and gloomy day when I lost you.

The replay is fresh and the wound reinforced,

I can never forget you.

Struggling in-vane,

fighting hard to catch your breath,

that was being stripped away.

My pain echoed deep as my longing wish to spare you was ignored.

I watched you slip away,

on that dark August Day.
Your love and wisdom with me remains.
The happy memories flow back, slowly,

like the crystal water on a calm river bed.

They bring me back a smile,

but it soon fades.

A part of me went with you.

August was family love and shared celebrations.

That far away day of August brought many changes.

We all know our life must go on.

But, Dad, it is hard.

Your love remains solely as my souvenir.

I was told: time heals and the pain would subside.

Then why is the sorrow in my heart not relenting?

As each day passes by,

I miss you more.

Novel No.19

AN INTERESTING JOB

September 5, 2005

An official-looking package arrived in the mail. Once I scrutinized the papers, my attention was quickly aroused. "What? A house in Italy? Plus, some monies? The estate of my late cousin has been left to us and is to be shared with two other families here!" I exclaimed to my husband as he curiously stretched his neck to peek at the papers over my shoulder.

"Let me read it," he said, so I passed the sheets to him.

"Yes. It instructs you to carry out the necessary formalities for the transactions of the monies and property."

"Oh, my Lord! As if I don't have enough to contend with," I responded gloomily. "Canada is a long way from Italy, and it looks like a nasty project," I continued. Since no will had been drawn up, the lawyers had reached us in Canada as the assigned heirs.

***

I started corresponding with a young lawyer in Italy, located near the property involved. The work began, from letters, to faxes, and phone calls. The file expanded immensely. My progress needed to be related to the other two families who were entitled to this inheritance. They pressed me for progress reports relentlessly.

The inquiries on my part had begun, but the results of the work was slow, stressful, and time-consuming.

In the meantime, I was toying with my own vague memory.

"I need to see for myself if that house is worth all this fuss," I said to my husband.

Before long, we booked a trip to the small town on the other side of the ocean. In front of my vision there it was the spread-out town situated on a hilltop with the church peaks standing erect as the large bronze bells delivered the time. The population had diminished incredibly due to lack of industry. Therefore, a lot of older people were seen walking vaguely on the narrow avenues, not many young people had remained. One good bit of news was that a main highway now connected the town to the city in a short drive. This quiet, peaceful town had become a popular holiday and summer retreat.

***

We walked up steps, trying hard to steady our footing on the uneven cable stones. It was hard to keep focused on the surrounding structures, as lot of them were in bad need of fresh paint and repairs. Before I knew it, there we were at the address we were looking for. We were standing in front of the house. My husband and two other friends that had accompanied us from another area of the outskirts of Rome.

"This is the place that has become our inheritance?" I said, eyeing the three-story structure. In their company, I felt more animated.

The property had belonged to my great aunt's family, which included several cousins. The double doors were shut, cobwebs dancing from the corners of the wooden doors and stones. By knocking, no one would appear to open the door, or lean out on the above side terrace or second floor balcony. The place looked desolated and abandoned. Forgotten memories of long ago started to surface in my mind and flood my vision, some not too pleasant.

It was hard for me to enter this home, now that nobody was left. There had been times in the past when we were welcomed with joy. Celebrations had taken place here with my family — my aunt and uncle and cousins. Their hospitality was that of genuine love and affection. It was difficult for me now, but I was chosen to execute this matter with respect, for the sake of my parents and the other two families.

The house was in a fine, desirable location around the corner by the piazza in the center of the town. I had no choice than to enter and execute what I had come here to do. As we went through the rooms, we were somewhat shocked to see that it was fully furnished, left intact with all the personal belongings. I observed pictures on the walls of relatives who were familiar to me, part of my childhood.

Continuing my tour, I discovered that the rear of the house was set on a slope four stories high with several balconies and an unobstructed view. The mountain peaks were far away toward the horizon. Il Matese, were covered with snow, they had always been.

The place was overwhelming. So much was there with four bedrooms, a linen closet, an armoire full of clothes barely worn, coats neatly hung on wall hooks, purses, and uncovered floor tiles with bank books thrown on the floor. Previous visitors have been in here, I thought.

We continued our tour, going through more wings of the house. We came into a room of preserved food, a wine cellar stocked with lined-up bottles, each labeled and dated. A huge cistern echoed our voices. As I looked down into it, it felt creepy, cold, and dark. Goose bumps covered my skin. There was no end to this place.

The property itself needed extensive renovation, but I could see how it might be turned into a real mansion of hospitality, for whoever had the desire or the energy to own and manage it. Despite the opportunities it offered, I had no desire to have anything to do with it. There was no room in my heart or willingness in my soul to make this place re-flourish.

I turned to my company and said, "Let's look for a somewhere to sleep tonight. It's getting late."

My husband and friends looked at me startled. "There are four bedrooms here! With beds made up! Why not stay here?"

"No," I replied, "I couldn't possibly do that! I prefer to stay at a hotel on the way to the city, to put some distance between us and this house."

We found a pleasant inn by the river, where thus removed, we could discuss the situation with more level heads.

"I have to tell you, visiting that house was most unpleasant for me and I have no desire to own any of the contents," I said firmly.

They looked at me in disbelief while I tranced myself back to our inspection tour. My thoughts went back to one of the bedrooms, where a dresser drawer was partially opened and an exposed a torn book got my attention. It was entitled something about love. Was it a diary, or someone's journal, or even a historical record of the family?

I wanted to take that book with me, but my anxiety to leave took over and I left without it. I think about it to this day. I never did go back to retrieve it.

The next morning, I made a trip to the cemetery to visit the deceased family whom I knew had worked hard and accumulated those possessions. With a heavy heart, I was convinced all the more that everything they had left behind did not interest me. I called my young lawyer and instructed her to list the place for sale.

That was some years ago. The place was sold for less than its value; the communications with the lawyer continued for a short while, then stopped. The relatives all got their share of inheritance from the sale of the house, as for the bank books on the floors with monetary savings, who knows... swindled away. We could have continued to argue about other values and goods involved, but in the end, it was proven there would have been little to gain.

This experience has only reinforced my belief that material possessions on this Earth are meaningless. Greed serves no purpose. A peaceful soul is one's only contentment and salvation.

Novel No.20

TOGETHER BY TRAGEDY

Marco and Liana's story

It was two in the morning when Marco Garland staggering on his feet, got into his car with the intentions to drive home; on the front seat his drunken body passed out. Hours later he was awakened by a knock on the window. Totally confused he managed to roll the glass window down. His eye sight blurred, his head throbbed, his stomach nauseated. He greeted the officer vomiting.

The officer immediately knew what he was dealing with. He called for back-up, Marco Garland was taken away in his drunken state as his breath reeked from alcohol.

It wasn't unusual for him to ignore his sober friends pleads, but, most of them were as drunk as him. His first intention had been to slip outside for fresh air. The party had really gotten out of hand after midnight. The loud music, the mixed drinks, sex interludes had started to take place; it all added to his chaotic stupor. On this foggy night in mid-April once more Marco's Father Dr. Garland senior was called to bail out his son from his addiction to the fast life and alcohol.

While in Rome Marco and his family were desperately dealing with his episodes; on this same night in mid-April 2009, a short distance away the earth decided to act in its calamities. The uncontrollable distraction that took place, many lives were lost.

Abruzzi's devastation 2009. One particular young girl was touched to the core. A deep-rooted sorrow darkened her existence.

***

Liana Romana's catastrophic revelation took place on this mountainous top town in Abruzzi Italy. The region is majestically laid out extending in land continuing along the Adriatic coast. Looking down the rugged valleys with its running creeks is breath taking. Nature itself without physical efforts glorifies in offering wild flowers and greenery in different shapes and colours. The pristine air fills the lungs reinvigorating energy. There on top of rocky crests sprawled in different heights laid a small town. The sky above remains cloudless and serene most of the time. The climate is cooler in the winter months changing into early spring with placid temperatures. The older people used to tell stories of how a large population lived in this town many years ago but heavy rain, landslides and earth quakes, divided the terrain into boundaries and separated the area into small towns. This particular one had remained with a population of three thousand five hundred people who lived here at this time. It contained one elementary school, three churches, a scattered zig-zag row of multilevel homes. The structured stone homes were attached on mounds of solid rocks and tuff hills of earthly creation. At the base of the valley the river Tronto runs through in a multitude of angles swaying through its bed in different depths and shapes. Here, is where most of the creeks end up in the rainy days of spring and fall. They usually run low and dry up in summer. The majestic large body of the river ends its journey at the Adriatic Sea.

Liana with her family lived in the lower level of the town. Most of the habitants were of modest nature and tried to earn a living from agriculture, working the fields and some from their artisan trades. The industries were next to none and the education limited. But back in the old days, the education was compiled and serious. The studies took one well into further knowledge of life skills.

In the center of the town there was a two-story stone structure with several classrooms; this was the main school where Liana started her primary grades.

The students were compelled to wear a black tunic uniform with a white collar. Liana vividly recollects wearing a pristine collar ; the color changed as she progressed to the higher grades.

She started school at seven years of age. At that age, one went right into the real learning process of reading and writing, learning to add and subtract and multiply the simple operations of math. The school was six days a week, no recess. Classes started at nine in the morning until one o'clock in the afternoon.

Liana remembers starting her primary grades in this two-story building on the second floor in a class of thirty-some students. They all looked alike with their uniforms that were mandatory. The uniform gave them a feeling of equality. The girls would be in one class and the boys would be in a separate class. From this early age it was known that for some reason the two genders had to be separated. A male teacher was at the head of the classroom. He was always well dressed and groomed. Good hygiene and proper dress code were implemented. As for the teacher, he or she was to be a role model to follow. Every morning the pupil's hands were extended on the desk and an inspection followed. The teacher checked their clean nails and ears and their hair needed to be well combed and free of lice in order to be in the classroom.

The rules were laid out and they were strict to be respected and obeyed. The students were disciplined. Liana among them followed without objections learning was her main interest. If one chose otherwise, the teacher did not hesitate to implement punishment. You knew this was a place to learn and do what you were told. One would not run and complain to the parents for any misgivings; because they would take the teacher's side and you would get a double barrel of punishment for any wrong doing.

Liana always chose to sit right at the front desk, across from the teacher's desk. She loved school and she had a passion for learning. The girl figured by sitting so close she would not miss anything plus she could see the teacher's writing on the board clearer and listen better. No one knew she was nearsighted, in bad need of glasses. No intervention had ever taken place to measure her vision, no money, no doctor in that field existed in this small town. This is why sitting at the front helped her troubled vision. Regardless of her efforts; it was still a chore sometimes to read the blackboard. Poor Liana resigned herself to her problem, quietly without complaints as she knew her parents couldn't take her to the major cities without money.

***

Every morning the class began with the Lord's prayer, since it was a catholic school. The teacher would sit after checking everyone row after row. He would place a ruler on his desk and the ceremony of the posture came every day. "Students, sit well and erect. The posture is important. If you hunch over or slouch in any way, your attention span will suffer and you will not perform as well as you should."

"Yes Mr. Rizziero." They all responded.

He would pick up his wooden ruler to show them and seriously he would say. "You see this ruler? It will automatically reach you without warning." The ruler kept the students alert. Mr. Rizziero didn't hesitate to use it. It reached the studious Liana few times but as the time progressed by the end of the school year, the teacher's threats worked; he picked up his ruler less and less to correct them. Later in life when Liana was complimented her response was "I try to walk with an erect posture automatically since it was imbedded in my brain at a such an early age it has become a part of me."

The teacher was from one of the surrounding towns. Short in stature, dark black hair, well-groomed with a docile kindness that governed his face. Since he was a truly devoted teacher, the students respected him. He didn't fail to recognize the eagerness of some of them including Liana. She was intelligent and eager to learn. By that, he was encouraged to give much more of himself in helpfulness. Liana excelled in every subject. She was one of the lucky ones. Mr. Rizziero had noticed and recognized her love of learning. After talking to the principal, and showing him her well-deserved marks. A recommendation was agreed upon. It was almost the end of the year. These folks were poor, money was scarce. The teacher and the principal hated to have some of their brilliant students miss out in life. All due to the lack of funding for further studies in this abandoned town. They took it upon themselves to write letters to the main province. Nothing could be done unless the students in question could attend the higher grades in the cities. The teacher relentless continued to investigate without success.

Finally, a miserly grant was offered to the school for one student. Mr. Rizziero felt sympathy for his number one student Liana. He decided it was time to pay a visit to Liana's parents at their home. One Sunday afternoon on the Lord's day he was at their door step. Mr. Antonio Romano opened the door to find Mr. Rizziero standing there. He was honored and surprised at the same time. "Please come in, Signor Rizziero, I will get my wife and Liana, they just stepped out back. Si accomodi make yourself comfortable." Mr. Romano was fretting and nervous. The teacher remained standing waiting to greet Mrs. Romana and her daughter. In no time they cheerfully appeared walking in to welcome the unexpected guest.

"Mr. Rizziero ! Ben venuto! 'welcome' what a surprise what brings you here?"

The teacher blushed he was shy by nature; besides he wasn't accustomed to going to student's homes. "Mrs. Romana, I came to talk to you and Mr. Romano regarding your Liana. We are almost at the end of the year. You must have seen her marks, I know she cannot further her studies here. The principal and myself especially are concerned.

As you know she is a brilliant student. It would be a sin for her not to continue on with her schooling."

In a caring interesting manner expressed his concern to her parents. While Liana listened attentively, holding her breath. As her teacher continued on. "Signor Romano, I was wondering if you and your wife have any plans for your daughter to continue. We, at school would like to prepare her for the exam of admission to attend the higher grades in the city."

Mr. Romano shook his head pacing the floor responded. "Yes, we are aware of the situation we are in for our Liana and it makes me sad. It is all due to our system, not being able to study further in town. We would like to do what it takes to send her to the city but it takes money."

"I am happy to hear that. I would recommend you should do everything you could. We would like to help in any way we can. The principal and I received a small bursary from the province to reward our students, it's hardly enough to buy the books. We will present it to Liana as she well deserves it."

"Signor Rizziero. Thank you I appreciate your concern and your kindness toward our daughter. My wife and I would do anything to help her achieve her dreams. She is a good daughter, and studious."

"This makes me feel better Mr. Romano, I am glad for Liana, we will do our part to help"

They thanked each other and Mr. Rizziero left after of course Mrs. Romana, insisted he accept an espresso, and some biscotti.

***

The parents were magnificent, proud and good family people; they wanted so bad for Liana to have all the schooling she deserved. In the meantime, Mr. Romano was pensive rubbing his temples, how can I earn money in this abandoned town so limited; in order for my Liana to go to school in the city without money, which is hard to come by.

Mr. Romano loved his family and was a hard worker beside being ambitious. The opportunities didn't exist. His heart ached and his soul was tormented. In desperation, he started to knock on doors of the artisans offering to do any hard work they may have just so he could gather enough money for the first semester. He decided to extend his travel on foot to the surrounding towns to look for any odd jobs he could find. He was prepared to do anything in his power to earn some cash. He started on his journey early morning searching for jobs. Many nights he returned home desolated and discouraged. One day he stumbled into one of the farms where Mr. Brandini, and few others were working on this machinery that had given up on them. They couldn't continue sifting their wheat. He stood there watching, studying the situation for a while. The men were sweating covered by the dust and grime. It was the end of June. The sun was beaming the heat unbearable. He had an idea and moved forward "Mr. Brandini, can I give you a hand here, let me try,"

"Oh! This darn machine has had it. I think we have to call the guys across the river to get here with theirs if we want to finish this pile of grain before it gets drenched and ruined by the rain. You see how hot it is? Those clouds in the sky are going to break. We will be getting a down pour; my grain will be gone."

"Mr. Brandini, let me try something." He had watched their maneuvers, which didn't seem right to him. He rolled his sleeves, searched the farmer's tool box, grabbed a rusty screw driver, and went to work. He seemed confident and knew what he was doing. In no time the machine kicked in and was ready to go in full force. Mr. Brandini all smiles patted him on the shoulders, he let out a big sigh relieved. "My friend where did you come from, thank heaven, you might have saved my grain. Can you stay and work with us just in case this old clunker gives up on us again?"

"Yes, I love to stay and help you guys, why not"

The farmer was delighted and the wheat was all done by early evening. Mr. Romano, went home glad to have been able to help the farmer. Mr. Brandini couldn't wait to relate his event to the neighbours, bragging about the fellow that came to his rescue. He owned lots of land and machineries; he needed a mechanical brain around. He said to his wife "I have got to go to the piazza and find that Mr. Romano, I can sure use a fellow like him around here." It didn't take long to find him as most of the guys unemployed gathered at the piazza by the only bar, lingering on their cup of brewed orzo since they couldn't afford anything else. Mr. Brandini accosted him, smiling, slapping him on the shoulder. "Eh! Good morning my friend. Tutto bene? All is well? That was the norm to say like a greeting. Let's us have an espresso? What do you say?"

"Oh! Good morning Mr. Brandini, si tutto bene, all is well. Things would be better if I could find some work."

"This is why I am here. I was thinking..." He hesitated, scratched his head " I could use a fellow like you around my farm, with all the tractors and other machineries, my acreage of grapes to be pruned , sprayed; if you are willing you can start tomorrow."

Mr. Romano's eyes glared wide open and his mouth widened speechless in a big smile. "Are you serious?"

"Eh! Antonio, I wouldn't be here If I wasn't serious." Extending his hand.

"Thank you, I will be there, first thing in the morning, or I could come even today?" Never bothered to negotiate or ask for what he would be paid. Any money was better than none. Some people just worked to be fed.

"See you tomorrow." He shook his hand and left.

Mr. Romano couldn't wait to go home to his family to announce the big news. He had been in the army, there he had learned to do some electrical work and repairing machineries.

From then on, he would rise early morning and return home late at night. The voice soon spread. All the farmers from the surrounding towns working the fields needed his expertise with their machinery repairs. He became in demand mostly from his self-learned trade developed by his own intelligence. He felt the universe had blessed and rewarded him. Now thankfully, he could provide for his adored wife and family especially his daughter. He arrived home one Saturday night, with an envelope, in his hand full of liras, his hard-earned money.

He Called over Liana put an arm around her shoulders and said. "Liana, choose your school for your studies, set your goals, learn as much as your heart desires. Daddy can manage to pay for your education as long as God gives me the strength to work." Never procrastinating the unexpected in life beyond his control.

Liana was moved "Dad you are the best dad I know. I promise I will make you proud." she hugged him and tears of love and joy ran down her cheeks.

***

Time passed life was good. Liana moved and enrolled in the best school in the province. Her dad with his hard-earned money was able to send her to the best school. He was also able to hire a tutor for her. A high priest, since it was known in those days that the priests had the highest education.

Liana took her studies seriously and applied herself totally. At the end of her semesters, she was well prepared to write her exams. Later was ready to attend University.

Every now and then her dad would come to visit her. She rejoiced in adoration, and hated when it was time to part. She knew in her heart how lucky she was to have such a loving family. When the visits were distant she worried and missed them miserably. . . time passed, it was time to move on into her higher studies and prepare to attend University.

Spring was slowly turning its magic this particular year. It was April, the weather was gloomy, cold, following with relentless rainy days. Especially this particular afternoon, the sky was dark and the air misty. While she was being tutored, a knock on the door interrupted her lesson. The priest's assistant with a gloomy look on her face excused herself and asked to speak to Liana. "Sorry to interrupt, there is a gentleman at the door asking to speak to you Miss Liana."

She immediately got up, alarmed, who could be asking for her here at this time? Other than her daddy that usually came. In quick steps she made her way to the waiting room. There immediately saw her dad's brother that lived in northern Italy. Totally surprised shouted "Uncle Lio! What brings you here?" He sorrowfully smiled. After giving her a light hug, in a low voice said "Liana, we need you to come home. Your mom is not well,"

"Oh! What do you mean? What is wrong with her? Where is my dad?"

"Liana, I came to pick you up, we have no time to waste, your dad is taking care of things at home, they are waiting for you."

She was confused, didn't know what to think or make of it. "Get your things and we need to be on our way." She looked around and like a zombie gathered her books, excused herself and left.

The priest had been informed by his assistant "A tragedy has occurred at her family's home. Liana needs to go home immediately." Liana hadn't noticed or heard their low colloquial conversation.

Her uncle had hired a chauffeur and he was waiting for them outside. As she got in, she noticed the somber look on the driver's face, she felt something was amiss. In no time they were on the road speeding away. She kept quizzing her uncle but he was evasive. She resigned not to ask any more questions. The uncle didn't want to be the one to reveal the bad news. He was mortified, wishing the shock wouldn't be too much for his niece. Once she arrived near the town, the eeriness hit her ... Once closer to some sections of the town, rubbles and debris were blocking their passage way. The driver had left them not far from their home as he couldn't go any further they needed to go on foot.

"Uncle Lio can you tell me what has taken place. Things are not good here I see. I slightly heard of an earth quake ... you know I don't listen to the radio. Has something terrible happened to my family?"

He didn't respond verbally, he shook his head, and then "there is hope, will see..."

They kept walking toward her home. When Liana's legs buckled, "Oh! No! Don't tell me."

The closer they got to her place the more the realization verified itself. There was no more home. The rude awakening in front of her eyes was some people working removing the pile of rubble of stones and mortar and debris, a total disaster. The neighbourhood was destroyed including her home. She shook uncontrollably sobbing outload screaming "My Mom! My dad! My little brother, my sister, where are they?"

"We are trying to find them, hopefully they are still alive under this mess"

"Under this mess! Oh! No! My beautiful family."

The uncle hugged her, "Liana it happened during the night. This part of town received the strongest tremor, 6.9 magnitude followed by many aftershocks we were told. We cannot give up, miracles happen."

"Miracles! Oh! My God! How! Look at this mess. I cannot believe it. My family! Where are they? I cannot be without my family. I should have been here with them." Liana went totally insane banging on the workers and digging removing stones with her bare hands, in a lost stupor.

The grief took over and Liana collapsed in shock totally succumbing in terror. One body after another, after hard digging from man and women and children, the dead surfaced mutilated. A bad scene for any human being to endure. After a week of digging, the bodies of her beloved family were retrieved from the rubble. Liana's heart sank deep into sorrow and her being died with them. Uncle Lio took care of the funeral arrangements as Liana couldn't function at all. Once the funerals were all over, uncle tried hard to lift her spirits, her depression had set up deep in her core with no life left in her.

Her uncle and aunt Mary, against her will took her to a doctor. After a few months of no cooperation or response on her part, the doctor suggested they would be wise to consult a psychiatrist. Liana motionless moved along with them in a zombie state as she had lost all interest in life. She was admitted at the psychiatric ward for evaluation and hopefully a cure. Since her dearest people were gone. her existence had no more meaning or value.

Uncle Lio with his wife were kind to her and visited her daily at the city hospital. But she remained wrapped in her own loss without response. When they tried to talk to her about her previous goals and go back to school, she just ignored them silently.

As time passed without progress from the city hospital, she was later transferred, to be hospitalized in Rome which was renowned to have the best psychiatric care for trauma patients. After much counselling and antidepressants that she often discarded, Liana started to show some animation.

She had finally started to leave her room and go to the lunch-room with the other patience. The nurses were encouraged by her new effort. She was now eighteen, wasting her youth in depression.

Young Marco Garland in his twenties had of lately been hospitalized. From a distance, he had watched the girl just starring at her lunch. He slowly made his way to her table and stood there. Liana didn't lift her eyes. He mumbled something to her. No response. She didn't want to hear nor care to engage in conversation with him or anyone. He proceeded "HI! Are you not hungry?"

Nothing, he may have been speaking to the wall. He started to volunteer information about himself. "I am in for some addiction of sort here also. What are you in for?"

She snapped back irritated. "I don't want to talk about it!"

"Why not! It will do you good."

She got up and left, finding the invader disturbing her privacy, preferring to be in her misery.

He felt sorry for her, and thought She is in bad shape. I will try again. Marco was super intelligent. His main studies were psychology, interrupted by his own problems. He watched her walk away pitifully.

A waitress from the kitchen walked over to him to retrieve her tray. "All done with your lunch?"

"Yes, it was good."

"I see this one here wasn't touched. Oh well, maybe one of these days." Left it at that and walked away with the trays.

Her comment motivated Marco even more. That mysterious creature that snubbed me. He creased his forehead muttering to himself. Hoping she would come out again tomorrow, or he would check the garden. . . in case, she would decide to be outdoor.

Marco was from the suburb of Rome. A fairly good-natured fellow, tall and slim with big brown eyes and a dimple on his chin, that made him attractive. Thick black hair cut military style accentuated his features. He was popular with the girls and his friends, until drunkenness would take over. Then he was only a pitiful wasted fellow. Since he had not been able to cope on his own with alcohol addiction; he had been hospitalized on the insistence of his parents to fight the battle with alcohol that was ruining his health, his life, and interfering with his studies. He was a gentle soul when sober. Unfortunately, his drinking episodes had gotten out of hand. It needed to be stopped before it destroyed him and the people around him.

He had not been able to stay in a relationship due to his drinking. His problem created a lot of friction with his siblings, parents, much pain for especially his mom. He had finally agreed to sober himself for good this time. Now discovering this mysterious girl, she intricated him.

The next day he continued searching for the gloomy looking girl. No sign of her anywhere. Liana had not left her room all day. She had resorted to reading and sleeping. She hated daylight, the darkness promoted sleep and she preferred to be lost in her dreams to re-envision her siblings and her dear parents. She would do anything just to be with them once more.

Dr. Mauro and the nurse walked in "Good morning Miss Liana, how are we doing today?"

She hesitated then responded "What difference does it make. Do you want to know how I feel? I feel my world is totally empty. I have no reason to live."

"Nonsense! You have your whole life ahead of you." Encouraged the doctor. "At such a young age? The world needs you out there if you give yourself permission to do so. Are you taking your medication?"

Liana didn't respond and avoided looking at him. He turned to the nurse, asked to look at the chart again. Everything seemed to be recorded accordingly. "Miss Liana, some fresh air will do you good. I encourage you to leave your room and engage in activities its therapeutic." He looked her straight in the eyes condescending. Shaking his head with his nurse walked out. Dr. Mauro badly wanted to help Liana but needed her cooperation. He turned to the nurse saying "I will reassess her case, including her medication. I suggest to encourage her to participate in activities as much as possible."

"All we can do is try, doctor." She responded

Liana had not left her room in over a week. Her appearance wasn't at its best. The nurse had an idea if it would work. If only Liana would cooperate.

The next day nurse Matilda walked in cheerfully smiling with a lady in tow "Miss Liana come on, get out of bed. It's a splendid day out there. Get washed up and dressed" She turned to introduce her friend. "I have invited Diana here, my hair dresser, to do your hair. She will apply some make up on your face as well. Later today your aunt and uncle are coming to visit; they will not recognize you. We want to surprise them. Come on! Let's get going."

Liana, didn't seem to anxious, but when she heard the mentioning of her aunt and uncle coming, she thought she better wash up and get herself decent. In slow motion she started to cooperate. Diana was a chatty middle-aged lady, she kept Liana distracted and fully absorbed in her operation. In no time she had her appearance turned admirable.

"There you are Signorina Liana, look at yourself in the mirror! You look so beautiful, ready for the run-way in Milan. Now here once you follow up with the pink dress your aunt sent you, you will be ready to tour Rome."

Liana like a robot did as she was told. After all if uncle Lio and her aunt Mary came she felt duty bound to please them a little.

When aunt Mary and uncle Leo arrived, they hugged and praised. "Liana, you look absolutely stunning. It is lovely out, let's get out of this room. A little sun will do you a world of good." coached her aunt.

"I will say so. I am told you are not leaving your room much.

Liana, honey, you need to try for your sake sweetheart. Your mom and dad up there want you to live a full life. If not for yourself do it for them. I am sure they know what you are going through." her uncle continued.

She gave him a sorrowful smile and broke into a good cry. "Now, now. Liana, you are spoiling your beautiful face. You looked so pretty with the make-up and the work the lady had done, don't ruin it." Aunt Mary, kept caressing her back to alleviate her crying spell.

After some encouragement, they signed her out for the afternoon, she went along with them. They strolled along piazza di Spagna. They adventured toward the amazing Trevi fountains.

"Here Liana some coins to throw in the fountain for good wishes." Uncle Lio said and handed them to her. Slowly Liana was captured by the beauty surrounding her. The flowing fountains, the statues, the architecture, the history told by uncle Lio. She was enjoying herself and participating. Sentimental music could be heard fusing the air. People were bustling and mingling by the coffee shops indulging in their gelatos. When uncle asked "Eh! Girls are you interested in treating ourselves with one of those marvelous gelatos?" Liana was the first to respond "Yes! Let's get one."

Uncle Leo was delighted, "Great let's, pick your flavour"

From that day on Liana seemed to regain some life. She had returned tired, she slept well, without the aid of sleeping pills. The next day she felt motivated to stroll around the garden to adventure in the sunshine and fresh air. The warm breeze felt invigorating, gently blowing her long hair lifting away her sad thoughts. The flash back of the rubble covering her loved ones seemed to dissipate somewhat as days passed. The pain in her heart kept flickering. Oh; how she missed her mom and dad and her sister and brother. "Please God! Help me cope." She would often implore.

She was sitting on a steel bench absorbed in her thoughts when a voice, startled her, and broke her spell. "Hello! There! Here you are. Finally! I have not seen you since that day at the cafeteria. I thought you were discharged!" said a familiar voice

She just mildly looked up. Oh! that annoying character again. She turned her back at him. Without responding. He walked around to face her, extended a hand "I am Marco, how are you?"

She didn't respond, remained seated. "What is the matter? I am offering you my hand." Then, as if someone else was directing her body, she extended her arm to meet his hand shake.

"I am Liana Romano. As if you care to know." defiant she smirked.

"Nice to see you again" With his head bent in a gallant behaviour. *At least she is not running away today* he thought.

"Would you like to take a walk with me? I usually walk alone every day. Its better with company."

"No. I was just about to go back in. I have been here for a while."

"Come! it is pleasant. Look at that serene blue sky. Isn't it hypnotizing?" He proceeded to extend his arms to help her up.

She lifted her head avoiding looking at him. Marco smiled at her in kindness. He was usually a charmer, clever in approaching girls; why was this girl being so difficult? He thought to himself.

"Let's enjoy a stroll together, if I am not invading your solitude that is."

She didn't respond, but she nodded, motioning to move forward. Marco didn't know how to take her. They started to walk side by side. 'Encouraging' he muttered.

As they moved on, this creature seemed to spread an aura of comfort for him. He was overwhelmed to have this young strange girl beside him. For some strange reason the universe out there had placed this strange girl on his path once more. He felt pulled toward her. Since that day he had first noticed her, her image had re-played in his vision and dominated his mind. Then she had vanished. Now that she had resurfaced, there he was pulled toward her again. He questioned himself Is it pity? Attraction? Or a need for both of us.

***

Marco's teen years to present time had been a challenge. He had gone through some unbearable moments himself from his with-drawls. The shaking that would take over his body had been hard to cope with; sometimes the attacks seemed to last an eternity. His craving of alcohol menacing. To be hospitalized had been absolutely a necessity. The drunken episodes were happening more and often lately to hinder his life plus that of others. He came from a family of six, two sisters and a brother. He was the first born. His dad was a cardiologist and his mom a language professoress. His parents were highly respected and regarded. When phone calls would arrive to his family from various places, especially from the police department, advising them to pick up their son; it was painful and embarrassing. They usually would find him passed out, consumed by alcohol, plus fines to pay for driving under the influence. He had been jailed a few times driving while intoxicated. Marco's problem had become serious. The addiction was hereditary, his parents had been told. As time passed and got involved into more social life; his episodes occurred often, and totally out of control. At first, he had been taken for counselling. The sessions didn't work. The counsellor advised he be hospitalized. "If he didn't receive medical help his future was dangerously questionable for himself and others."

After many pleadings from his mom and dad and siblings...Marco had agreed to be hospitalized he was now addressing his serious malady.

Two souls come together.

When Marco was sober, he was personable, loving and kind with a gift of gab to attract everyone's attention around him ; but once he started drinking, he couldn't stop. The alcohol would take over flowing in his blood and his brain. His being would turn into a totally different person. The relationships with young girls would not last. Now he had found this beset Liana, his attraction to her was different than any other young woman he had ever met. Pensive he thought She is definitely mysterious and troubled, I need to find out ... I like her. A magnet pulls me toward her.

Their walks continued as days passed. For Liana an awaken feeling of well-being would zip through her body after returning to her room She didn't know why or cared to question it. Maybe the universe itself willed it to her. The good aura around her continued. From that day forward she started to be more cooperative. Her willingness to comply with the nurses and the doctor continued to bring good results. Her progress was soon recognized by the counsellor and hospital staff. Her aunt and uncle were much encouraged by her awaken spirit in life. The friendship with Marco grew as time passed. They spent much time together bonding, talking about their problems. Marco understood when she revealed to him her inner turmoil. "I was away at school. My dad did everything in his power to provide for my education. My mom, my sister, my brother we were such a close family. To find my home crumbled in a pile of debris, my family under the rubble buried alive. It has been a scene that I cannot take out of my mind. I cannot live without them. The people so dear to me have been destroyed, taken away from me. I want to die too and just be with them. Ever since that horrible day I have had no more desire to live." She broke out sobbing out loud. Her body shaking uncontrollable just like Marco's body shook from his withdrawals. He hugged her soothingly caressing her back. He held her in his arms until the shaking subsided. "Liana, listen to me. I am so sorry about your loss. I understand how you feel. I cannot replace your family. If you will have me; I will be with you as long I will live."

Marco was truly passionately, overcome by love and caring for this human being. "Listen to me Liana, for our unfortunate reasons, we ended up in this place. Both of us needing to resolve our serious problems; for you to overcome your depression and no willingness to live, and for me if I don't solve this addiction to alcohol; I cannot continue to live! We are two unfortunate souls brought together by our grief in destiny. I am sure that by supporting one another, we will survive."

How right Marco was. He had been studying Psychology at the University of Rome when his studies had been interrupted by his drunkenness. Many times, he missed classes and often carried his booze in his back pack to indulge. He had been expelled more than once. The matter had been getting from bad to worse. They poured their hearts out confiding in one another.

Six months later, Liana and Marco had become inseparable and their love for each other truly intoxicating. They both felt the need to be together, from the core of their humanely existence. Marco, had survived his temptations and had abstained totally from alcohol. With the medical help he had received, the love and adoration from Liana; his future looked promising. The doctor had encouraging news. On his recent visit Dr. Roberto Scoglia with a big smile on his face had announced to him "Marco! I must give you credit. You have done extremely well and made me proud. In a couple of weeks, I would like you to be an outpatient and be discharged from the hospital" He patted his shoulder "You will be fine, my young man."

Marco took a deep breath, with a big grin on his face he responded "I have to be! I have every reason too, I am in love doctor"

"Good! She is a lucky girl. You are a fine young man, with a stellar reason to live."

He was a local fellow. His family would come, he could live on campus resume his studies or live at home. Liana what would be Liana's fate? She had been doing well lately.

Her education had also been interrupted from that traumatic day. She had no parents to take care of her, the aunt and uncle had their own children and grandchildren to worry about. When Marco took her in his arms to announce the big news; Liana suddenly pulled back bursting into tears. "Amore mio! My love, what's wrong? I thought you would be happy for me." It took a lot to pacify and calm her down. Finally, between wiping her tears, she responded.

"You are going to leave me. I have no one else left in my life. No family, no money, no home to return too. Now that I had found you. You will be gone too; my world will be totally empty once more."

"Liana, what are you talking about? I will never leave you. You are going with me where- ever I go you will too. We are going to get married. We will become one body, one soul."

Liana's body shivered in fear. At this point she felt plain scared, all over again. Marco tried hard to reassure her.

She had met Marco's family, they were Romans. His mom and dad seemed polite and courteous toward her. Her own insecurities combined with a low self-esteem sometimes surfaced out of control to cause her discomfort. Marco's siblings intimidated her especially Maria Rosaria, always gave her the cold shoulder. Liana invaded by these thoughts...was not coping well. Her mentality was still fragile, therefore playing tricks on her. Acidity churning her stomach causing much pain with anxiety.

Marco was discharged. Once Liana remained alone her state of mind played havoc. Once Marco left the hospital she felt abandoned... she plunged into depression with a relapse. Although Marco came to visit every day to reassure her; she still felt alone and destitute.

Marco and his loving family didn't abandon Liana; they were good loving people and it took their devotion to alleviate her sorrow.

***

Marco resumed his studies with set goals. His love and devotion for Liana grew even deeper. His relentless visits every day kept her alive. After a long struggle from the gloomy days to the more up-beat ones thanks to Marcos insistence an assistance. The gentleness of his parents helped a lot. They offered their sincere kindness.

Time passed and after few months Liana was reunited with her beloved Marco by moving in with him... They were inseparable. She had every intention to resume her studies. She took Marco in her arms and with tears of joy. She said "You are the most precious human being in my life. If it wasn't for you. I would have had no reason to live. You and your family have helped me and revived my heart and my soul."

"Oh! mio amore, you have no idea; how happy that makes me to hear you say that. Don't forget we were meant to be together. My body was being wasted with alcohol. You replaced my inebriation in me with your potion of love."

"Marco, I have one more announcement to make. I need to return to school. I want to go to medical school. I want to dedicate myself to help other people out there. Just like you and your family have helped me."

He sealed her lips with a long breathless kiss, after he released her, he held her at arms-length to admire her. "I want to tell you how beautiful you are. Darling, with your intelligence. You will be the best care giver I know beside my Dad."

Liana was accepted in medical school in Rome with Dr. Garland's help. Once immersed in her studies, every day was a new day. The relationship with Marco's family grew affectionately. Her experiences in watching the pain and suffering and death of the patients in the hospital, doing her residency helped alleviate her loss, her pain, and suffering. It all belonged to a far dark night of long ago. She cherished the memory of her parents and the pain was placed in a corner of her heart. Her duty at work was demanding. Liana loved to be lost into it.

She graduated with honors. When the medical degree in cardiology was handed to her. Marco with his Mom and Dad and the rest of the family, were there to cheer her on.

She walked over to them. Marco hugged her "Congratulations, Dr. Garland!" The rest of the family followed. Doctor Garland senior was the last to congratulate her. "Welcome to our team, I know you will make an excellent doctor. You chose the heart, I am sure you will save many lives. With your diligence no one can beat your success."

"Thank-you Dr. Garland; with your help and my gratefulness."

Marco had also graduated. The two saved souls with great minds were united in matrimony soon after their degrees; both of them totally devoted to their profession. Since their encounter had begun to helping one another they would both now dedicate themselves to helping others. "Yes! Darling" said Liana to Marco. "We want to make a difference for our people in need."

"I agree. Thanks to that strange girl, that has turned out to be my wife, whom I will devote the rest my life, since she gave me mine back."

"Oh, Marco! Where would I be if you hadn't pulled me out of my misery?"

They locked themselves in a long embrace for strength and support.

Dr. Garland Senior had prepared an office for their practice right in a magnificent building in the centre of Rome, walking distance to the hospital. Their knowledge was widely spread and in no time the two new doctors; were highly recommended.

Liana's life and family had been destroyed by the Earth Quake. Strange as it seemed, fate, had rescued her. Marco and the Garlands had been a gift from above. Every heart she saved, she rejoiced. Only then by surpassing these crucial times she would say to herself. "The good Lord must have spared me for a purpose."

Novel No.21

THE MARRIAGE VOWS

Wherever I go these days, I run into friends or acquaintances that are quick to relate to me their mental state of displeasure with occurrences in their life. Often when the phone rings in my home, the same ordeal takes place. The conversation is usually with distracted parents that need to talk. Most of them have one thing to relate: the marriage break up of their children. Or their own! Some of my friends are eager to vent how their quiet household has turned into chaotic disarray by being reoccupied by their adult children and grandchildren. The stories continue, all related to the same family matter.

By traveling abroad, I found out that it is a global problem. Especially, if it's their first, or a recent happening. They expect sympathy and advice, because they feel their pain is bigger than others'.

The majority of the older parents find themselves in a shaking situation that threatens their existence. Once I related this to a friend of mine, of the new individuals with the fresh experience; her reply was, "They need to sweat it out, just like the rest of us." Eventually, when one gets used to it, things will smooth out. Or at best, learn to live with it and make adjustments to the new developments.

By being a good listener, I felt their anguish and pain. I could sympathize with them from the experiences in my own family and observing developments around my circle. The happenings strongly motivated me to write and focus more with some research on this special subject. The marriage vows. What are the marriage vows? What do they mean? How are we interpreting these vows? What do we intend to do with these vows?

What does matrimony mean to us? A lot of question marks are divulging toward the sacrament of marriage these days. A lot of couples supposedly in the bliss of love are still putting themselves through all the work, the emotional ordeal that comes in the preparation of a wedding celebration by putting themselves through a big financial expense!

When the wedding ceremony long dreamed of and planned for takes place, it's the biggest day in their life with all the glory. The marriage vows are recited and a promises are made between the groom and the bride to love and cherish in sickness and in health, for better, for worse, to be true to one another until death do them part.

This can take place either in the Catholic church with the ceremony conducted by a priest, an Anglican church, or in whatever other faith they belief in, or by the justice of the peace. Some couples choose to seal their commitment among the two of them in a set scenario of their preference. The locations and set ups of marriage ceremonies are getting more and more creative, to stimulate the enthusism of the couple themselves and their guests.

Regardless, their intentions at this time and place is believed to be a true commitment to love and to cherish each other until death due them part. The big or small wedding party will proceed, and the honeymoon is supposed to be a continuation of the heavenly happiness for these two human beings. They consider themselves so fortunate to have found each other and united in matrimony. As a rule, their love is to blossom in the creation of a family and receive the gift of life. This was preached in our Bible, "To grow and multiply." The intentions are to live through their married lives in harmony and sacrifice to cherish one another. More importantly, to nurture and guide the offspring that we, with the phenomena of our creation, God the omnipotent, have placed on this earth. Some couples choose not to have children, which is fine also. Most couples, regardless of their gender, like to enhance their union with children to feel complete as a family. These children are the innocent, trusting souls at our mercy. They are our donated gift as result of the performance of our love. These innocent children contain a bounty of affection to give us in return. Especially when they, in their infant state, melt our hearts; continuing with their unconditional love until tender age. We should be grateful and feel so blessed to have them. Should some couples be denied this blessing, there are many children out there in desperate need of love and a home. The rewards can be immeasurable, providing all your efforts are geared in the right channels. Some couples prefer pets; they cherish their pet. Whatever one prefers, it's a matter of choice, as long as it brings harmony in their household.

Unfortunately, we see more and more marriages fall apart. Some in a short time, or some later on in life. The divorce is hitting our society in a very bad way. The rate is alarming, and it has become a way of life, bringing distraction to our young people, mostly. Although, surprisingly, some older couples choose that rout, also. But the younger generation, most of all our children, are the ones that pay the biggest price.

Here, we find ourselves in a state of turmoil, not only for the couple themselves, but even more disruptive, when children have been brought into this world as the result of their professed love. All they will observe is hatred and resentment between the two parents they love equally. Here is where their confusion starts and their world begins to crumble. One has to look deep into this matter of occurrence and ask why? Are our young people giving up too easily? What is going on with our older generation, also? Have they caught this virus from the environment, to break their union with their partner?

The divorce rate is rampant, bringing with it a lot of agony and pain in many homes to the couple themselves, the children, and the grandparents. Everyone involved pays the price.

Who is to blame? Is it our society? Is it a revolution of our own doing?

Often, all of these questions are unanswered. We can only analyze with logical reasoning, but we really need to take a good look at this situation.

We need to see how we can rectify and restore some foundation and security in our homes and family unions. We need to reassure our children. Many older people at their retirement age find themselves with their married sons or daughters with grandchildren moving back into their homes.

In some cases, the children become the responsibility of the grandparents. The problem is that some of them have a hard time dealing with their own physical body getting on in age and poor health creeping in. The extra demands placed on the poor grandparents are hardly fair. Their lack of good health will not be able to give the children the quality of care they deserve, although they have good intentions.

I ask myself, what can society do to turn this catastrophic phenomenon of divorce around? We should be able to do something to rectify these marriages of temporary arrangement. How do we change the mentality and thinking of human beings?

This is a revolution that we are caught in. What are we thinking? Have we become selfish? Are we looking for self-gratification? We need to come to some sort of solution first between the partners. We need to restore love and harmony in our homes. How can it be that these two individuals that once loved each other have come to resent and hate one another so much? These feelings of discontent will send wrong messages. In return, the results will create adverse behavior toward each partner, and yes, especially our children. This chaos just keeps expanding, making our world much more difficult. Where do we start the rectification? Are our beliefs disappointing us? Our Clergies are losing control. Are we disappointed in them? Our science has made such advances that morality is taken for granted, and has created such a revolution for our young people and the rest of society to be so liberated. We have no respect for our bodies and everything is acceptable. Even if we have been geared toward our faith, we pay little regard because we think that our immoral behavior is condoned. And we are not scorned by society because this is the norm.

The ratio of marriage breakup in my research has reached at an alarming rate of fifty-seven percent. The U. S. being the leading country, overriding Sweden, Italy, and Spain, where family unity and respect are still dominant. These countries have the least, but they still have many cases. This figure has also had an effect in my motivation to write this article (The marriage vows).

It is definitely necessary for us to revaluate its meaning, reanalyze the statement in our vows. Once matrimony has taken place, it is absolutely a must that either party needs to give of themselves one hundred percent. A relationship to make it work takes compromising with more giving than taking. It is not easy, it takes hard work. If all of us could realize that no human being is perfect, we would not think that the grass is greener on the other side of the fence and search for a better pasture. Eventually if the better pasture turns out to be more complicated, making our life much more difficult. We need to accept the good with the bad. One should work on bringing out the best in a person, concentrate on the good qualities, because I strongly believe there is good in everyone. You need to recognize it. Once you concentrate on the positive, it will flow with rewards. Where there is a will and determination to make a marriage work, there is a way and you shall succeed. The benefits are gratifying for the well-being of the whole family. I really think that the primary reason of marriage failure is brought on by too much stress. Too many demands are placed on our young families in this era. Our young couples are stressed out from every direction. The high demanding jobs they hold, resulting in both partners being always in demand with little rest. The woman is no longer just the homemaker, the nurturer of her family. Many are in high power stressful jobs, along with the household choirs and family rearing. At one time, the woman served a different role in life. She was married to have children, be a homemaker and the subordinate of the husband. She was to be obedient, submissive to her male companion, willing to sacrifice herself for the well-being of the family. The female gender of long ago complied because this was expected of them and besides, there was no way out of a committed unhappy relationship.

A lot of the women were suppressed in unfavorable situations but kept the family unity regardless. They were forced to remain there because life did not offer any better; divorce was scornful. If one found herself in an abusive relationship, she lived with it. Jobs for women were scarce. She was totally under the partner's jurisdiction, for a roof over her head, and the necessities of survival. The liberated woman today has made great progress, has gained much respect in our society, she can hold a high rank position, which is great, but is this part of the price we are paying for our family break ups?

Some children go home to find empty homes, the parents are both out of the house, occupied with their jobs or whatever.

The children I find are also placed in every sport available, or what is offered out there. This is the trend, this is the new way of life in this era. Everything is costly; two salaries are needed in order to supply the demands for the family. Bigger homes, more than one car, and yes, everyone in the household needs to have his own computer, his own cell phone, iPod, and all the new technology has become a necessity to live in the millennium. All these gadgets have become a necessary evil. It is a vicious cycle for the whole family. Everyone is pressured by the demands of life and what society imposes on us. The parents are tired, the kids are tired, the chores are endless, and time to rest is minimal. They cannot keep up with the demands, and before you know it, the explosion occurs: the inevitable family breakups and disintegration.

Once the household has become an unpleasant place, the parents start their fighting match, or even worse, they start the avoidance of one another. Often, they seek the consolation or sympathy from their fellow workers or elsewhere outside the home. The distance starts to take place between the two mates. The children are confused at this point. They also will seek advice and try to fill their needs by turning to their friends. Their mental state is not quite stable at this period of time. Their emotions can be easily shattered. Some are lucky enough to survive the rough ride on their own. Fortunate if a sincere caring person happens to be in their life. It is very hard for them to keep up with their school work and their peers, while most often their grades fail together with their self-esteem. Unfortunately, there have been many cases where predators take advantage of the situation.

And our poor vulnerable children or young adults pay the price. The results can be devastating for the rest of their lives. We, as parents, get so caught up in our own wants and needs that we do not realize at the time the consequences our break up brings. We desperately need to restore the permanent commitment of two people in marriage for life, with no reservation or question or doubt it is going to work. The marriage has to work by both parties, they should feel holy committed one belongs to the other for the duration of a lifetime on this earth. Nothing comes easy, it is hard work to struggle with the demands of life and live in harmony as a family. It is not only necessary to be in complete accord in the immediate household. A wife or a husband should eliminate any outside interference that might mar the well-being of their immediate family.

Why does the feeling and the euphoria that once was such profound love between these two individuals transforms itself as such to reach the point of dissipation and resentment toward one another; instead of lovers they become enemies? I am told the amygdala that causes the full-blown infatuation knows no fear. Most lovers when originally attracted to one another become marinated with endorphins. This, combined with other chemical reactions in the body packs a powerful punch. How can we renew this effect of feelings in two people that has worn off in time? The couples drawn together by these feelings committing themselves without marriage run the risk of a greater separation than married couples with the actual documentation of marriage. Those that go into a union uncertain tend to separate. There is a big difference between commitment in a marriage and cohabitation. A marriage is a unit, cohabitation is a roommate with sex, with an easy escape should one become dissatisfied. All I can tell you is that people that understand their values are less stressed. Their offspring find themselves in less challenging situations. Although there is always pain in a breakup for everyone involved, one more than the other, but most of all, guess who? ...

I was told by the children themselves, plus from a relative of mine in marital and family therapy in New York when I asked, "What was the worst part of the separation followed by divorce?" that it's, "The shuffling back and forth." From literary research, the new step-mother or step-father figure brought into their life. The laments, the crying spells I have personally witnessed from our young people is heartbreaking. This happens while the parents will move on to other unions, trying to experience the same jolt in their search for love and romance. The children are forced from one relationship to the other. One needs to consider their feelings and expectations

Was it better in the older days when the families remained together and suffered in silence? In this era, the beautiful nest that is supposed to be a heaven of love and creation of family sanctuary, becomes a place to run away from. This is what I am told by many broken marriages. The first sign is to avoid confrontation with the partner by staying away from the home that they so wanted and desired at one time. On this subject matter, my conclusions come from being a keen observer of real cases in the process and results. I dedicated myself with my heart and soul to do as much research as possible. Being a writer, every word, every action sends a message, and you cannot help being tuned in.

Yes, I believe that in some cases to make a marriage work, can be very challenging. In extreme cases, there is no avoidance of separation or divorce. Therefore, I am not saying that every union is severable. While the marriage between two partners is supposed to be sacred, unfortunately, there are cases where we need to sympathize with some unions that are struggling in their existence. We must feel and condone some break ups that bring nothing else but pain to the whole family. I was attending a wedding reception few months ago. I happened to be seated beside a widow and her son. We engaged in plain conversation about marriage, and some comments on the happy couple. The widow simply stated to me, "I was married fifty-five years, a marriage from hell."

The son soon replied, "My dad was not nice with me or my mother. He was bad and mean." I was told he was an alcoholic, abusive in every regard. My heart goes out to certain cases that bring so much pain and suffering, neither I would condone physical or verbal abuse, infidelity. In some cases of having tried and failed, the separation or divorce is the crucial route to take. Does one ever divorce herself or himself of this original union, especially if children are involved? Did the parties realize that once they take the initiative of divorce?

Our Catholic church at one time did not recognize divorce. But with times changing, they have accepted it, offering an Annulment. Calling it a declaration of Nullity. It means that the marriage was invalid, because at the time the two people took the vows, the necessary elements to make a marriage work were not there. It is only in the tribunal of the church that a marriage is dissolved for the parties to move on to other unions. It is my belief that often we see certain couples who do not match or are not right for each other, but they proceed in their union. Who are we to dictate, judge, or advise, especially when it comes to our own children? Some partners develop totally different behavior once married, or refuse to assume responsibilities for the chores and care of the children and financial troubles that puts a lot of stress in a marriage. I have also been told by a few of our young people that they have fallen out of love, they no longer love their partner, or I have been told one never loved the other! I am asking myself why they went through all the charade of marriage, children, the works if they did not love their partner.

Again, comparing to long ago when a woman remained in a commitment of marriage because they had no alternatives, were dependent on the man to go to work and provide, a lady married with five children related to me one day. "I was so unhappy with my husband, I wanted to leave him, but had no place to go."

We have made great progress and come a long way in our independence; we are no longer suppressed and forced to stay in relationships that do not bring us fulfillment. Is it good in certain respects, but devastating and confusing in others. An original family in harmony is easier to live with than an extended family. There is always someone suffering in secret pain in the extended family. Without misgivings by anyone, there is that emotional turmoil that will go on in the heart and soul of the participants. Regardless of the reasoning, this subject is so vast we are still facing an alarming statistic. For the majority, there has to be something we should be able to turn around what is going wrong in our society to a positive long-lasting relationships with love, trust, and sincerity.

Most of all, from our unity, we start by setting a good example in our homes. Yes, I believe that is a good place to begin. Our education system can also help by teaching our young people respect, honesty, love thy neighbor, and treat others the way they want to be treated. Then, of course, I honestly believe our faith has a lot to do with our guidance; one needs to believe in order to stay true and on course.

These statements are the result of research and findings and personal wisdom on how couples can restore and rekindle their love of the first attraction toward one another. I wanted to find out how we can bring peace in our marriage. How can we restore our original professed love? The attraction that once led us to this particular person that became our soul mate. Why has the affection gone to the wind? Many questions boggle my mind; it all brings me back to let's try to search our soul and see how we can re-establish a lasting relationship.

It sure is comfortable to have your original partner to love and grow old together. I am told that true love requires chemistry, compatibility, and commitment between two individuals.

A couple handling their problems and disagreements with good communication is number one.

Kindness toward one another. Once they start to criticize, naturally either one will turn on his or her defense mechanism.

Contempt, regard your partner with disdain. Shutting your partner out, refusing to listen, and turning into a stone wall is unacceptable and will lead to more trouble.

A good idea is to start solving your differences with a soft gentle voice, without lashing out at your partner with insults. Automatically, the other party will respond accordingly. In turn, you will have a good listener that you have captured with your own knowhow.

In disagreements, the main approach here is not to be the aggressor in a mad rage. Use your diplomacy tactic by being at full attention, absorb and explain, facing your partner and making eye contact.

An apology and hug usually eases the tension, reinforces your marriage, and automatically turns your resentment into renewed love.

Stubbornness will hinder your marriage. A husband willing to lean toward the influence of a wife will turn his marriage in a strong and happy one.

It has been a proven fact that a marriage will not be strengthened by trying to change one another. From my own experience, people adapt, but do not change.

By compromising, acceptance, and appreciating what is good in a marriage will bring harmony from eternal issues.

Avoid negative emotions. Negativity is detrimental to a relationship.

Express what you are feeling inside: Request your needs, your wants, request it.

Listen attentively to one another; it is so important! After all, isn't a marriage a union regardless of the kind of commitment? Two people are supposed to become one.

Be aware when you are stressed out. Recognize it, follow up by excusing yourself, and take time out for relaxation. Stress itself brings explosion.

A good idea is to have less expectation from your marriage, not extra fulfillment.

Never assume, your partner is not a mind reader; reveal your needs, your desire at that moment.

Be spontaneous with caress, touch, affection. These gestures will heal and improve a relationship.

Engage in conversation and listen to each other talk: a wife should be focused on her husband's needs also, likewise in one another's involvement and understanding.

Some individuals develop a secret inner life, a desire or wish that they keep to themselves. There should be no secrets in a marriage and between the two partners. This can lead to trouble. If one happens to meet someone outside of their marriage that they feel they can reveal or share this side of themselves with, they risk the extramarital affair.

Be open and honest with your mate.

Avoid at all costs the need to relate intimately to anyone outside of your marriage.

This in itself will make you vulnerable, before you realize it, you are in conflict with your loved one.

Yes, keep in touch with a simple hello, a phone call, and three syllables daily as a reassurance and reminder, "I love you."

Most of us neglect to be considerate, or even have the notion that by expressing our love belittles us. Or especially, more the male gender thinks they lose their macho or masculinity.

We have the ability to read people's hearts if we are tuned in, and act upon it with love lust. Especially, toward our mate.

Always speak the truth, and give joy to the people around you, especially, your family.

You need to be empathetic, to possess the ability to feel the pain of those around you. This could be your spouse, your children — any member of your household.

You need to promote good behavior and be a great encourager, not only your partner, but your children especially.

You should accept people unconditionally. Should you have the fortune of wealth and mainly good health, be a generous giver do share your wellbeing and bounty with others.

Always recognize the need to be able to balance logic and compassion.

Control words that come out of your sweet lips: speak only with kindness; the power of our vocal cords can heal or condemn people around us, especially our loved ones. Once spoken, we cannot ever retrieve them.

Does how much encouragement and praise we give our mate mean we are working on bringing out his or her gift of possession? Let's examine our own souls and actions.

Are we exuberant with hospitality? Are we doing our utmost with our gift of hospitality? Do we make the people close to us feel special, wanted, warm, welcome, and, most of all, celebrated?

How much are you giving of yourself? If someone, especially in your home, is sad or hurting from daily crisis, are you supportive in lifting their spirit?

Every one of us is looking for happiness. Once happiness reigns in our being, it spreads around us. If you can love your family, especially the ones you are with, the way you want to be loved, the rewards are to your advantage and to that of your family.

Will our good deeds make a difference? I think if we seed goodness, we will be rewarded with such.

Our marriage will proceed like a ship on the vast ocean. With a good captain and a supportive assistant, and surrounded by a well-trained crew, will reach its destination in perfect balance and harmony.

If our marriage is contained in a full circle, it can bring us to our mature old age where we can enjoy the golden days of our lives. We can look back at our trivial past. Sit back together, contemplate and rejoice in taking inventory of our branches that have sprung out as the result of the production of the union from our trunk. If we loved, if we created, if we multiplied, abided by the rules of the marriage vows, life can only bring the two partners the sorrow of someday this union beyond their control will come to an end. The promise they made when they recited their vows will have actually come in completion of their journey.

To love and to cherish until death do we part? With a good life to be had. The branches and the leaves of your love seeds a great legacy to leave behind.

Novel No.22

NATURE ON PLANET EARTH

This planet in which we live and call home has been created for us in a round ball formation. The soils contains substances in nature, in form and colour.

It also comes with great water bodies, starting from small veins that form our creeks, to the flowing calm and running rivers, the placid lakes, the seas, to our grand extensions — our oceans.

Our mountains erected in different heights with indestructible beauty. Others come in volcanic formations, brewing deep down in their cavities; occasionally, erupting their lava, causing destruction, but also in beneficial contribution by adding a new look to our Earth. The dark charcoal formation turns into stone and is used for a strong foundation.

Then we have our lands covered in vegetation, with an array of trees in every shape colour and form.

Our submerged rocks also come in so many shapes and forms and colours. They create unbelievable sculptures for admiration.

These are the earthly contents that form our planet. We are the living creatures along with other animal species to occupy it. Our globe long ago must have been a heaven, lush and unspoiled by any living creatures.

Our modern way of life and technology has put a big dent on our mother earth. We have managed to pollute our waters, contaminate our soil and the air we breathe.

Yes, our planet Earth is a masterpiece of creation by some almighty power.

We are fortunate to live in certain parts of the world where, we can enjoy the seasons. This is another gift of nature that comes with the weather effect on our planet Earth. Climate change creates different sceneries with our seasons, which we call: winter, spring, summer, and fall.

They contribute to the beauty of our planet in its own special way. Let's take spring; it is my favorite season. Spring is time to renew. It manifests itself automatically by force. The sun illuminates our planet with more direct sunlight; it is like a wake-up call. Nature starts to slowly transform from the dull and droopy life to a new, warmer one. The blooms and greenery eventually move on to create a magical place. If we tune in to our being, we can feel the same effect taking place in our bodies at this time of spring. We want the time to stand still and the gentle breeze to caress our bodies in renew, like the rest of nature blooming on our heavenly Earth.

Then comes summer. It brings us serenity, longer daylight, warm evenings to admire the celestial sky in star-bursting clarity, cool drinks, time to work, time to rejoice with family and friends, outdoor gatherings; warm and beautiful in peacefulness.

We have fall! Fall comes to us with lots of good deliveries. Our trees start to turn their magic from green to cheerful yellow, burgundy, mauve, brown. The changes occur gradually, never stopping to amaze us. We enjoy it all with admiration. The harvest, our gifts from our seeding, this is the contribution back from our Mother Earth. We cannot forget our vineyards, the bounty of grapes in color. The wine, its tasting, its many flavors, and spirits transformations, luring us to our dinner table.

Winter! Some of us love winter, some don't. Winter can also be enjoyable — the beauty of the snow fall, our cozy homes with fire places and burning logs emitting warmth with a crackling fire. The outdoor air, crisp and pristine, clear of germs for our lungs to freely breath. The Earth in its white mantel, the snow. The fluffy white powder rests on our grounds, trees, and rooftops. It creates light with an angelic feeling of calmness. The icicles are an added décor to our surroundings, hanging like crystal chandeliers. Our warm clothes keep our bodies snuggled in comfort. Great winter sports can enhance the spirit of the winter months.

There is an abundance of good things for us to enjoy and glorify.

Yes, indeed, our great creator is omnipotent. It is up to us to look and recognize the beauty in gratefulness and indulge in its pleasures. All of this is for us to enjoy on our Mother Earth.

Novel No.23

RISE ABOVE THE TIDE

We lived in Melbourne, Australia on a work visa for a period of time. We loved the country and its people, with their unforgettable hospitality. To our surprise... No one had warned us about the annoying miniscule black flies that were adamantly persisting in getting in our noses, lips, and every part of the body they could invade. I had invested on different chemical spray to defend ourselves, but it was useless; nothing deterred them. The continuous days of scorching hot weather and clammy heat with no relief in sight was getting to me. Although summer is my favorite season. The relentless hours of hard work had dragged my tired body to a merciful state. The gnawing for a break from it all had reached its peak. I wanted to return to Canada even in its cold freezing state which I had detested... Therefore, the necessity to escape was harboring in my heart and my soul, desperately seeking my return.. In March, three years later, finally! My return home in the north occured. After glorifying myself in the lovely summer and reacquainting to my life in Canada, fall soon approached.

With the colder temperatures setting in, the desire to travel again kept churning in me. This time, I knew my destination of choice would be our historical Europe. I had been amiss for few years. This had been an annual summer ritual to look forward to before being devotedly committed to going down and under. But at this particular time in 2005, my husband and I were still without plans, due to some surprising bothersome occurrences taking place in my life.

Needless to say, my spirit was low. I had become resentful and depressed by disappointment news I had been told by my doctor. My husband, trying to cheer me up, had arrived home one evening with a sheet of paper in his hands.

He handed the paper to me and said, "It contains information for a week getaway to the Amalfi coast. Would you like to go?" he asked.

My ears immediately perked up along with my curiosity, as travel has always been my passion. Without reading the itinerary, immediately, I responded, "Yes, of course, providing my health issues don't stop me."

A couple of weeks earlier, an unplanned, innocent visit to the doctor had resulted in a precipitation of alarm and fear. The shock of the news had ceased my tomorrows. "Where did this come from, Doctor?" I asked him.

"I don't know. Your lungs have three spots, one of your kidneys has a cyst. We need to do further tests."

"What do you think, Doctor? You know, my dad just died of lung cancer! He lasted only three weeks after his diagnosis!" I reminded him, shaking.

"It could be cancer, or maybe not. I cannot tell you until we do an MRI and investigate further."

My serene and happy world had suddenly collapsed. My days now consisted of going from one doctor to another, causing confusion and delays. Many appointments with specialists were months away, prolonging the unknown in agony. I was getting discouraged.

I detested our medical system because of the slowness, and I felt helpless in moving forward. At one point, I said to my doctor, "We are supposed to be lucky to live in Canada, free medical assistance and everything that comes with it. In reality, it stinks.

Medical assistance to put your mind at easy ; it's definitely not available when you need it. One can die waiting." I soon realized I needed to speed up the procedure as my patience, in anger, had run out. I relentlessly started my own research, and I was willing to pay for my care. I went over to the U.S. where, with no hesitation, my tests were promptly done and my answers quickly available.

But guess what? Back in Canada, the doctors were still dragging with their answers after I had done the provision for them. Talking about health crisis, I came to the conclusion their sympathy was nonexistent.

While I was struggling with my anxieties caused by my maladies, my husband had proceeded with his inquiries for the trip. Although, up until the very last moment, there were serious question marks surrounding our voyage. But in resolution, I made a strong decision. The hell with everything! I'm going, and I will deal with whatever… on my return, as I feel fine with my silent killer.

We got on a bus to begin our tour, commencing from our city. There, on the bus, surrounded by familiar faces, I was handed my tickets and the fun began. The bus was filled with laughter, music, and jokes. All negativity in my mind was erased. We flew to Rome, where upon arrival, we were picked up by a deluxe tour coach that whisked us off to Positano on the Amalfi Coast.

The sun was glorious and the sky a mantle of serene blue; the scenery all around was magnetizing, incredibly mesmerizing. There, in my vision to enjoy, Positano set sprawled on terraced hills above the Mediterranean Sea. As we toured, the sun rays continued beaming without a cloud in the sky, and the blowing fresh breeze in the air soothed my warm cheeks. I took long walks on the beach, welcoming the waves flapping on the shore to gently cares my tired feet. The homes and our hotel were erected on rocks like magical structures. We walked and drove up and down cliffs, through roads so narrow our fellow travelers had to move the parked cars to make way for our bus to squeeze through.

We were there in autumn, and the coast was lustrous and sweet. Even in the winter, I'm told, the climate is ideal. The setting above the Mediterranean Sea with its fresh caressing breeze gives you an aura of wellbeing. As we strolled through the piazzas, the sound of Neapolitan music treated our hearing. It sounded intoxicating special, and it came from everywhere. The karma was harmonious. We were serenaded on our bus, in the streets, and the shops, but most of all, those lyrics touched and reached deep into your hearts.

The body itself felt rejuvenated. The pleasurable feeling was wonderful— the food, the gorgeous giant white grapes in Muscat flavor, the white and purple figs teasing your taste buds, and yes, always that music. The company was gregarious, with contagious laughter; everything around made you feel harmonized and alive in a real setting. My cloud of worry became a nonexistent nightmare. As for my health issues, they were finally resolved in a good way, but mainly, from my strong will and a positive attitude. Since travel is part of my life, I often find myself with these setbacks.

I often ignore my health providers and take matters into my own hands. With my stubbornness, I have not missed out on my good time and new discoveries. With luck, it has worked out to my advantage many times. I try earnestly to educate myself and acquire as much knowledge as possible. Most of all, what works for the mind brings great results to one's physical body. Therefore, my motto in life is maintaining a beautiful positive outlook. I am grateful for my own existence, and I love to share the well-being with the less fortunate. My good deeds bring satisfaction, and my rewards are immeasurable. Should my life reach the end of the travel, I'm satisfied I know I have done it all.

When life gets you down, take yourself to the beauty of nature. Give a smile in kindness to a sorrowful face. Strange, but truthfully, joy will enrich your soul.

Novel No 24

FINDING SERENITY

Gloria, a young wife and mother, with a gleam in her eyes and a big smile on her face glided through her new home. "Come on, Susan, let's check your bedroom, darling. No more sleeping in your old crib, you are a big girl now. You actually have a bed of your own sweetie; look at your new bed!" The room was done all in a small floral pattern in soft multi-colors, the white iron headboard in a classic design with an organza ruffled bed spread. The dazzling pillows complimented the wall paper and the spread. She was blabbing away while her two-year-old daughter happily skipped along in delight while being led by the hand.

Every room they entered was a pleasure to admire. Finally, our dream has come true, thought Gloria, letting out a sigh of relief in gratefulness. The young couple together, especially Eduard, her husband, had worked earnestly to make this happen. He had been putting in hours of hard work until late at night in constructing it himself. Two-days ago, their new furniture had arrived and everything had been placed in its place. They were both gifted with artistic creation, therefore, they marveled on what they had finally been able to put together for their enjoyment. The aroma of fresh salsa permeated from the stove in the kitchen, the karma around landed itself for celebration.

Gloria's eyes glanced at the clock set on the wall. It was later than she had realized. Hurrying along, she said, "Susan, my darling, Daddy will be home soon. Let's set the table and get ready for supper."

"Mommy, I want to play with my rocking horse," she insisted in her spoiled mood.

The grandparents had bought her a good-sized rocking horse and she loved to ride it, burning her energy.

Gloria would do anything to appease her little one and make her happy, so she said, "I will tell you what, we will carry the horse to the kitchen; you can ride it there while Mommy attends to our dinner."

Now that her tour was complete with great satisfaction, she figured they better retreat to the eating area and concentrate on the completion of the meal for her hard-working husband's return. The kitchen, of course, was equipped with the latest appliances. A fantastic stove, with large expandable burners, the oven with all the fancy features, not to mention the lucid cupboards, were her shadow reflected in luster. Young Susan, although a toddler, felt the anticipation of the new household to be joyful. She was trotting away on her horse, bouncing as high as she could. Gloria talked to her daughter a lot as if she was an adult. "Susan, why don't you get down from your horse and come and help Mommy set the table?" But her pleas were ignored, the horse was priority.

This is our first evening in our new home. Let's make it special. I will cook some veal chops for us as our second course, after our pasta. Eduard will like that. How blessed I am? This is all I wished for in life: a new home, a loving husband, and a beautiful baby. These were the thoughts going through her mind. Eduard was coming home from work and she was going to prepare a special supper for them to feast on and celebrate. The young couple had lived in a dark and gloomy one-bedroom apartment in a basement quarter for four years, since they had been married. Gloria couldn't wait to be able to afford a decent place of their own and, most of all, with daylight and sunshine. The living discomfort consciously motivated her to saving every penny she could toward a down payment of a decent quarter to call home. After much research and serious study, their dream of owning their own place had finally come to realization. Poor Eduard was holding two jobs to supply his income. He was a commercial accountant and besides working on his home choirs, he did some carpentry for people to supplement his income. The long hours had been doing him in lately.

Nevertheless, he was proud when he arrived home to admire their new labour of love. It consisted of a recessed bungalow with a circular driveway with plenty of green space for their family to grow and enjoy. The backyard was set on a ravine lot, the backdoor led to a large stone patio, built by Eduard's hard manual labour. The landscape continued sloping down to rock gardens and a rumbling crystal-clear running creek under a crossing man-made bridge. All hand laboured by Eduard. The unobstructed view from the neighbors filled the surrounding area with pristine air. The interior, although not large in square footage, felt airy, sun light poured in delightfully with bursting energy from room to room through their large windows. Fresh paint and new furniture created an overall complete feeling of wellness with pleasure.

Gloria was so grateful. Their wish had finally been granted She thought, Now, we can live happily ever after, never anticipating the series of mishaps that were in store for them. The next morning before leaving for work, Eduard had hugged Gloria and kissed her tenderly, holding her longer than usual, not hurrying as usual to leave for the office.

He whispered in her ear, "Darling, I don't feel like working late tonight. I will try to come home early." He seemed reluctant to leave. Twice he went over to Susan's room to admire his beautiful still-sleeping daughter.

Gloria was anticipating preparing dinner. Oh! The evening before had been terrific, tonight she was going to try to outdo it with a delicious meal. Her new pan was placed on the stove. She was going to fry garlic and scallops, with that green extra virgin oil. Her mom had been preaching about it being so healthy and had dropped a bottle off for them that morning. Now, here she was, ready to create another terrific meal for the family when the doorbell rang. It was the front door. Hesitant, she left the stove and disturbed, went to go check who was at her door. The lady across the street was standing there.

"Hello, I am Doreen Flanagan from across the street. I wanted to drop off this fresh pie to welcome you to the neighbourhood and introduce myself."

"Oh! How kind of you, thank you. Won't you come in?"

"No thanks, I can't. Another time. My baby is just about to wake up, I must get back."

"Thanks again, I am sure will enjoy it; I will serve it tonight for our dessert."

After waving good bye to the new neighbor, distracted, she turned around to get back to the kitchen, carrying and admiring the crusty cherry pie. Although the lady had declined to come in, the chit chatting had taken Gloria longer than it should have. Immediately, a strange smell disturbed her. As she stepped into the kitchen entrance, a shocking vision awaited her: the stove was engulfed in flames reaching the ceiling. The smoke was intense, and in no time, the flames were spreading wild and their lovely home was burning out of control with Gloria and young Susan right in the middle of it.

Gloria, in a state of shock, at first heroically tried to put the fire out herself with water, making things worse as the flames rampaged wildly higher. She was totally confused, ignoring what was around her. Her hands were burning, her little girl was screaming. Like a desperate, insane woman not thinking of herself or to spare their lives, she kept fighting the flames and breathing the smoke. All she was thinking was to save her home.

Finally, with her lacerated hands and arms, some senses kicked in to grab Susan, and rolled herself out of the inferno. The fire had taken over; fate and the cruel destiny was stronger than her heroic attempt. She collapsed by the back door, rolling down the stairs. Little Susan managed to twist the door knob and run out screaming as loud as she could. The back neighbours were far away. She ran to the front of the house still screaming, "My mommy, my mommy!" Luckily, the lady across the street turned around to see the smoke and the little girl in distress. She ran over, distraught, the front of the house was clouded with smoke. Susan, as young as she was, kept running to the back of the house where she had left her mommy with Doreen, the lady, running behind her. Gloria's motionless body lay sprawled on the floor. The little girl was crying hysterically in total confusion. The neighbour managed to drag her out of the back entrance. Soon after, the blaring sirens were heard getting closer. In no time, the place was invaded by fire trucks, ambulances, and the rest of the neighbours looking on in shock. The ambulance arrived, called by the neighbours. The paramedics immediately took over. Susan and her mom were rushed to the emergency burn unit while the fire fighters tried hard to battle the raging inferno.

The ravaging flames had taken over, destroying and reducing their dream home to rubble and ashes. Some oil from the frying pan had spilled on Susan's head in the chaotic confusion of her mom's attempt to fight the fire; her head was in pain with patches of burns. The doctor on call shook his head in dismay and commented to his assistant nurse "She is lucky to be alive. As for the mom, it's questionable. Her hands and arms are burned and good part of her body; she is comatose."

Eduard was just about to leave the office. He had bought a treat for Susan, her favorite smarties. A red rose for Gloria, with three green stem leaves tied with a red ribbon that was to profess his love for his two dear girls. He had been fretting all afternoon to complete his work and couldn't wait to get home. When his secretary knocked on his door with a sorrowful look on her face, telling him to pick up line one, his hand shook and a strange notion told him something was terribly wrong.

The officer in charge said, in low tones, "Mr. Durante, it's Officer Gibling here. There has been an accident at your home. I suggest you get to the hospital first; your wife and daughter have been taken to the emergency."

A dark cloud stirred through his head and his eyes blurred. He couldn't think straight. "Officer, officer, what accident? What are you saying? My daughter? My wife? How are they?"

"Sorry, Mr. Durante, I think they will be fine. But I suggest you get to the emergency first. There has been a fire, we will check with you later." He hung up.

Eduard was stunned and remained perplexed. Clare had stood there in front of his desk. His secretary was a mature, caring lady, the motherly type. She grabbed him by the arm and said, "Come on, Eduard, I will go with you." She spared the details of the house, Right now, the two lives were of more concern. and insisted on driving him.

Once they arrived, a sympathetic nurse took them to see Susan first. When seeing his daughter's patched head, his heart sank into the deepest sorrow. "My God, what has happened to her? My wife, how is my wife?"

His legs were barely holding him up, the shock was debilitating. He made his way to Gloria's room. He couldn't believe his strong radiant girl he had taken in his arms and professed his love, saying good bye in the morning was there lifeless and unrecognizable. He broke down, sobbing incessantly. His world had totally collapsed.

Good old Clare tried hard to pull him together. "Eduard, come on now. We need to talk to the doctor. I am sure Gloria will recuperate. Susan will be fine; she is a child, they are resilient."

Dr. Rebrandin walked in. "Mr. Durante, I am the doctor on call. I have attended to your daughter and Mrs. Durante."

"Yes, Doctor, please, tell me they will be fine," Eduard said, trying to regain his composure between tears.

"Your daughter will be fine," said the doctor, animated and putting a hand on his shoulder in his attempt to comfort the young father. "She is a lucky girl and a heroic one, I am told. I can assure you, other than the trauma she went through, her burns are not severe. A couple of patches of burns not close to each other can be covered by her hair growth. We will keep her overnight for observation. You can take her home tomorrow, if you like. Other than that, she is fine. The stamina she possesses is radiant. I wouldn't worry about her."

"My wife, what about my wife?"

"She has severe burns on her extremities and upper torso, which we can take care of. Our main concern is she has slipped into a coma. We are confident she will snap out of it. I am told she was desperately trying to put the fire out herself instead of running out. She is lucky to be here and have a chance to survive."

Eduard listened in total disbelief, but managed to thank the doctor and returned to his wife's room. Desolated, he couldn't believe the turn of events that had taken place. He was gently caressing her forehead, hoping for a sign or movement of her body, to give him hope and strength to go on. But watching her just lying there was breaking his heart.

Later, he figured he better call their old landlady, Mrs. Evalyn Smith, and ask her if he could return to the basement address where they lived before. Trying to relate and explain to Mrs. Smith was going to be another chore, as lately she was going senile. He had no money left, since they had spent every penny to furnish their home and the most needed necessities. A hotel stay was out of the question, and his family was out of reach to help. His widowed mother lived on her pension, and his sister, Nanda, had recently been divorced and left penniless by her alcoholic husband with two children, was bunking in with her mother. How sad, he thought, I planned to help my sister out, and my mom. Now I am on the street myself, with my lifeless Gloria and my Susan. He couldn't help but feel sorry for himself. They had been living from paycheck to paycheck. Gloria had done a terrific job in controlling their spending. Their finances had accumulated after four years of marriage, all for their dream to live happily ever after with their new home. Gloria's parents lived in Scotland. They were set in their ways and didn't want to emigrate to Canada. They were continuously asking her to return home. Since she was the only daughter, they were resentful of her leaving. Gloria had every intention to return for a visit someday not too late in the future with her husband and daughter. The planned vacation was her next project after they were settled in their new home. Susan with her vivacious personality would bring them joy. She figured by bringing the grandchild to meet the grandparents would be beneficial for all of them. Maybe, just maybe, that would appease them.

Eduard had spent a restless night on the sofa in Mrs. Smith's basement, fighting his nightmares. He couldn't wait to get back to the hospital to be beside Gloria, hoping for the miracle to happen and pick up Susan the next afternoon. After dragging himself, in a somber mood to Gloria's bed side, the same scenario awaited him. When the nurse walked in, his futile inquiries of her well-being, he knew without saying, were answered with no changes. After shedding few uncontrollable tears, he made his way to Susan's room. As soon as she saw him, her face lightened up. "Daddy, Daddy, pick me up." There she was with her arms outstretched, reaching out to him.

"Can we go home, Daddy? Mommy, I want Mommy."

"Darling, we have to wait for the nurse, love, you need to be discharged. I will take you to see Mommy." Hoping that from some universal force, Gloria would be drawn by their love to wake when they entered the room. The plan didn't work. "Daddy, why isn't Mommy waking up? I want her to talk to me."

"Come, my love, let Mommy rest for now, we will be back

later."

"No, Daddy, I want her to talk to me now."

After bribing and convincing her, he was able to pull her away. The two of them returned to Mrs. Smith. The gloomy dark basement was theirs again, sleeping on an old couch, and Susan on a borrowed mattress on the floor. It took few days to find a day care for Susan. Which was another rude awakening for Eduard. Now, his daughter didn't want to leave his side. When he'd drop her off at day care, she screamed and cried, not wanting to be left there or have any part of the place, or the lady Liana, or the children around her. No words of consolation would calm her down. She wanted her mommy, and with her arms wrapped around his neck, she wouldn't let go of her daddy.

"No! Daddy, don't leave me here." Susan, left alone in this strange environment, felt abandoned. She had been so used to her mommy, the sadness settling in her being was like a black veil wrapping around her body, rendering her taciturn. The disconnection from her mom effectuated her as such: by not wanting to participate in anything that was going on around her. She would sit, moping in a corner. Liana's attempts, and the children around, to reach out to her were totally ignored.

After a week of the same behaviour, the supervisor at the day centre decided she better talk to Eduard. "Mr. Durante, I think Susan's is going through a much deeper sorrow which we are not qualified to help her. She needs professional counselling to get over the trauma that has affected her more than we realize."

"I understand." He took in a deep breath and turned his head. From the door ajar of the small office he could see his Susan crouched on the floor in the far corner. "I will take care of my daughter. Thank you, Miss Liana." He got up and proceeded toward his daughter.

"Darling, come on, let's get your things, you are going with Daddy."

She couldn't get up fast enough, and elated, wrapped her arms around his legs, fearing to relent her grip. "Daddy, I want to be with you and Mommy." She was terrified of losing him and being left behind.

"You will darling, don't worry." He picked her up in his arms to reassure her.

Eduard had been holding a position with a professional accountant firm. His specialty was in tax saving for his clients. He figured at this crucial time in his life, if Donald Dunken, the senior partner of the firm and his boss, wanted to keep him on, he had no choice but to accept his work from home since he needed to be the caregiver for Susan. After picking up Susan, he marched to his office and made his way to his supervisor. "Mr. Dunken, you are aware of my situation. I need to work from home. My daughter needs me now and she comes first. Otherwise, I have to take a leave of absence until my life turns around. But I badly need the money."

"Eduard, yes, of course, your family's well-being first. You can do as much as you can from home. I will inform the head office: keep your spirits up, eventually everything will work itself out."

Time passed, and Gloria's state remained the same. Day after day, after working from his basement quarter, Eduard with his little Susan would go to the hospital with no improvement in sight. The doctor had consulted with his colleagues, and kept encouraging Eduard to have faith. The miracle wasn't happening, and he was turning bitter. Susan, relentless in her questioning, was bouncing around him continually during the day like a stranded butterfly, asking for her mommy and demanding his attention. Although she was distracting him from his work, his daughter was the only thing that kept him going day after day. But at night time after putting her to sleep, having assumed double role of mommy and daddy, his mental state was shattering in pieces from the emptiness.

He had awakened in despair this one morning. The office had called and he needed to go in and meet this prosperous client with complicated income tax problems with his companies. It was necessary for him to meet him at the office and handle the matter professionally. He had no choice but to take Susan with him, so he would have to have their receptionist amuse her while his meeting was taking place. Oh, God, he implored, please, let my wife come to.

Days passed, and weeks had turned into months. Eduard was getting impatient with the doctors and nurses. "I want something done about my wife, maybe she should be transferred somewhere else where they can help her!" He was being irrational from his shattered nerves.

The doctor sympathized with him. "Mr. Durante, your wife has received the best care we are able to give her. At this time, there is only so much we can do. We just hope she will come to soon."

"How can it be that there is no sign of improvement?"

"Be patient. The situation is difficult, but it can change."

As the days passed and Eduard would walk into the hospital room and Gloria would be laying there unresponsive and unrecognizable with her bandaged wounds. His heart and soul was sinking in despair. He left the hospital once more with his head down, in a slow stride, thinking, how can my life with my beautiful young family have turned into such an irreparable nightmare?

He had been, and was, madly in love with his Gloria and his precious Susan. He questioned why God had abandoned them so, since life had taken such a cruel turn, shaking their existence. That night, after reading a prayer to Susan and putting her to bed, he kneeled down, took the rosary that Mrs. Smith had hanging on the wall, and decided to pray as hard as he could. He felt some peace come over him. He stretched his tired body on the couch, with a woolly blanket, and in no time, drifted into deep sleep.

He awoke the next morning with Susan pulling at him smiling, "Daddy, Daddy, come on, I want to go see Mommy, she is waiting for us."

He had slept well all night, and in his grogginess, tried to wake up and appease her, forcing himself up. "Sweetie, what are you saying? We will go see Mommy at lunch time, Daddy has to go to the office and you are going with me."

"No, Daddy we have to go to see Mommy now." She was stumping her feet, insisting. "She told me, she wants to see us." She was serious and adamant in her demands, pulling the covers out of his bed. Eduard was used to giving in to her demands, but this morning she was more insistent. He was to be at his office with the important client assigned to him. The phone startled him, and with Susan pulling at his legs, he picked up the receiver. "Hello."

"Mr. Durante, it's the hospital. Dr. Rebrandin wants to talk to you."

Eduard held his breath. Bringing a hand to brush his forehead, he looked up. God, help us, he muttered while holding the phone and waiting for the doctor.

"Hello, Mr. Durante, Dr. Rebrandin here. I have good news; your wife is asking for you and your daughter. You can come and see her as soon as you can."

A warm shiver filtered right through his body. "Oh, my God! Thank you, thank you, Doctor, we will be right there." In a euphoric state, he picked up Susan and lifted her up, twirling her around. "Yes, darling, we will go see Mommy; you are right, she is waiting for us."

"I told you, Daddy, I told you. She was calling me in my sleep, she woke me up."

Eduard, remembering his commitment at the office, placed a quick call to Clare to change his schedule, and in no time, the two of them enthusiastically were on their way to the hospital.

The clear blue sky, with the sun shining brighter than ever, was invigorating. Eduard let out a big sigh of relief and holding his daughter's hand, made his way down the corridor to his wife's room. There, his beloved Gloria was weaving her bandaged hand relentlessly. The doctor and two nurses were there, all smiles. Miraculously, Gloria seemed well-aware of her surroundings.

"She is well tuned to her senses, especially her hearing. Although we have tubes inserted down her esophagus to help her breathing and alleviate the strain to her heart. She is fine," said the doctor, placing a hand on Eduard's shoulder.

"A big step, indeed," continued Dr. Rebrandin.

When Eduard questioned him, he cautioned . "The battle for recovery is far from over. Many plastic surgeries are necessary to repair the burnet part of her body. Her upper shoulders and arms, and especially her hands, require a lot of skin grafting. But she will gradually survive it all."

A year had passed. Gloria was in and out of the hospital. She submitted herself to the many medical interventions required to repair her body. Lots of pain to endure, and poor Gloria, deep down at times, thought she would have been better off if she had ended up in ashes with the rubble of her home. When she looked at Eduard's sorrowful soul, felt her agony was shared with his feelings, it gave her courage. In false pretense, she kept smiling. Together with Susan and their strong support and love they would conquer all.

***

A year and a half later, after a lengthy surgery to Gloria's hands, the doctor called with more good news. "Mr. Eduard, I am happy to tell you that your wife will be discharged. We will keep a close watch on her, monitoring her as an outpatient. I think it will do her good and she will recover better being at home."

Again, in what had become a routine, he made his way to the hospital, holding Susan's hand as she skipped beside him.

"Darling, Mommy is coming home, we are going to be together again in our own new place."

"Oh! Daddy, which one? The house that burnt?"

"No, honey, we are going to have another, at the other side of town, for now. It will be just perfect for us, not far from your school."

Edward had instructed a realtor to negotiate a lease with the contractor of the new subdivision close to the school. He had been preparing himself, praying for Gloria to get better and be discharged to put the nightmare behind and resume their interrupted family living. Yes, of course, he had no doubt the dream of their happiness would eventually resurface once Gloria returned.

He stopped at the nurse's desk at the third floor of the hospital when he spotted the doctor. He was anxious to thank him. He extended his hand in a hand shake with his eyes shining in gratefulness. "Doctor, thank you for the care you and your staff have given my wife. It's been much appreciated by myself, my wife, and Susan here. Due to your care, we can finally have her back home again in our new home."

The young family settled into another new home. Two years later, they were blessed with a spunky baby boy to add to their joy. Gloria and Eduard with their two children realized that only death is irreparable. Given the chance to live, material things on this earth can all be replaced, and they are irrelevant, when love and faith reigns, happiness and rejoicing will follow.

Novel No. 25.

MY HEAVENLY GIFT

Agada's broken dream had fallen into ashes the evening of June 19, 2014, at the Toronto airport. Since then, her somber mood had been growing in leaps and bounds. The days that followed were dark and heavy. The cloud that reigned in her heart was ready to release its heavy down pour as the tears kept coming freely down her cheeks. The airport was chaotic that evening. The elevators and the escalators were blocked with yellow ribbons. Some strange occurrence had taken place. The daughter and son-in-law that were to fly with them and twelve other passengers were okay to go. They had been standing into the unmoving line for two hours. Once they presented their passport at the check in, the attendant of their airline wicket said, "Mr. and Mrs. Lorini, you will not be able to fly." Agada wasn't sure she heard right "What do you mean? We are not able to fly? Your passport needs to be validated three months after your return. You are due back July 1, /14. Your passport expires September 14, two thousand and fourteen."

Mr. and Mrs. Lorini looked at each other in disbelief. "No one told us or warned us about the passport." Indignant, they turned to the attendant.

"Do you have a birth certificate with you?" She asked.

"No! Not here, but we do have one at home."

"The plane will be leaving shortly. How can we get it here?"

"We can't! There is no one home."

"Well,' the attendant replied "you need to renew your passport and rearrange your flight. You definitely cannot leave on this flight."

She called a supervisor and Mr. and Mrs. Lorini were turned away.

But the Lorinis would have to return back home to Niagara. They struggled with their suitcases to get to the lower level down the escalator since the elevators were blocked. They were lucky to find a shuttle to take them back home, paying another fee.

The next morning, another hefty fee of four hundred and fifty dollars was paid to renew the passports. Mr. and Mrs. Lorini, with their suitcases still intact, were ready to return to the airport to catch to next flight. Before venturing back to the Toronto airport, they wanted to make sure by phone that there was space for them on the plane. They contacted the flight network and air-line. The cooperation from both was nil. After waiting all day, disheartened, they decided to abandon the whole ordeal and leave it at that. Their beautiful trip to Tuscany with their children had vanished.

It was now August 4th. Agada moped around the house annoyed and disturbed. To this date, no plans for their yearly trip to Italy or Europe had been renewed. The melancholy had been set in her heart since the ordeal… When the phone rang, she picked up the phone with a disheartened tone of voice.

"Agada, how are you?" the person asked at the other end of the receiver. She sounded cheerful in a high peak voice.

"Oh! Antonella, hi, how are you?" she answered, recognizing her cousin's voice.

"Good thing I found you home. What are you doing?"

"I am coloring my hair."

"Oh! Good, so you are getting ready?"

"Ready? Ready for myself. You heard what happened to us."

"Listen, Agada, this is why I am calling you. I am booked to fly to Rome tomorrow, why don't you go with me? You need to make up your mind fast. My travel agent has only two spaces left. You have fifteen minutes to call me back. Let's get out of here. Come with me, we will have a good time. We will be at our home town, you will have a chance to see the palazzo again. Please, come," she begged.

Agada's ears perked up. A flow of energy ran right down her spine, floating to her brain. "Antonella, are you serious?" she responded.

"I wouldn't be calling you if I wasn't. Please, come away with me. I need to get away from all this daily mess here."

It didn't take much convincing for Agada. She ran to her husband and asked, "Do you want to go with me? You know you are included."

"No, I don't feel like going anywhere anymore, now." He responded annoyed.

"Well, I am going. This is a great opportunity for me," she responded in a loud voice. "Just imagine, this is what I always wanted—to visit my hometown, plus the palazzo! The new novel I am writing is from the area. I will be able to take pictures, revisit the sights, relive my childhood. Sorry, my dear, with you or without you, I am going."

The next evening, there she was again, at the airport, booked for Rome with her widowed cousin, Antonella, a business woman, hard worker, mature in age, but vibrant in spirit and physically and mentally fit. A petit girl, full of love, for life and people; happy as a lark.

***

After a smooth flight at landing, a limo was ready to pick them up in Rome, and now Agada, sitting relaxed at the back seat of the

Alfa Romeo, was enjoying the scenery around her as the driver professionally zipped by, negotiating the narrow hilly road. They were getting close to her zone. The lush of greenery gleaming with the sunrays the hills and valleys were a treat to admire. Oh! Yes. How she loved nature, she thought with a pleasant smile on her face. "This is mesmerizing," she said to the chauffeur and Antonella.

Dante, the driver, noticing her feverish interest, pulled to the side of the road and stopped the car. He motioned for them to step out. "Look up there, girls," he said. "There it is, our town. We are in the valley by the river bank."

Agada was in awe, admiring the town spread out up above on the hill side. There it was, sitting on the same hill after all those years. The Spiro high crest mount stood out, reaching into the sky like a landmark. The row of houses was still scattered in a triangle at its base. Her old remote town, as she remembered it. The vision of the place stirred deep emotions in Agada's heart. A jolt of nostalgia made her go back in years. "Oh, my God!" she exclaimed, crossing her arms over her chest. "It's really still there! Still standing in the same shape," she said, excited. "The earthquake has not destroyed its form."

Then she stood still for a moment. Her voice trembled, and her eyes were misty, fighting back tears. Embarrassed, she wiped the streaks running down her cheeks. "Sorry, guys, I can't help it. My emotions are overpowering."

Agada had not revisited her place of birth for fifty-eight years. Today, her big, long dream was actually shaping into a realization.

The driver called out, "Enjoy, you are entitled to your feelings. It's okay… I have chauffeured many people from abroad, believe me, you are not alone. That old relic town of ours up there has its effect on the people that return."

She was in ecstasy, and didn't know where to look first. They crossed the old bridge over the river, its side banks were in an array of bloom, in wild colorful flowers and greenery. The placid running waters glittered to the reflection of the sun rays. The entire river bed was wide and full, flowing down in a calm, easy stream.

A flashback quickly came to her vision — the many years of her tender age. She had been here with her mom, her cousins, aunts, and grandma. They had gathered here to do il bucato, the laundry. They knelt down on rocks with a towel folded under their knees. It was here where they came to do the washing. The summer heat was unbearable, but the fresh breeze from upstream gently caressed their warm faces. It was hard work, but one of joy due to the gathering of family members in harmony to do their choir.

While Agada was reminiscing, the driver had negotiated the hills skillfully and she had survived the rough bumps without any effect. They had now reached the piazza.

"Sorry, girls, this is as far as I can drive. The rest of your destination remains on foot."

He courteously unloaded the luggage while motioning to a couple standing close by. Agada didn't know them. They promptly proceeded with the suitcases, leading the way. They were locals. Agada realized these two strangers knew everyone, where they lived, and were informed of who arrived.

They paid their fare and thanked the super obliging Dante. They were eager to continue on foot to get to their destination. Besides, they needed to follow the two locals, dragging their suitcases ahead of them. The chauffeur, before he departed, gestured with his arm and gently said, "Eh! Girls." He pointed out to his home. "I live right there, my wife, Sara, always bakes and the coffee pot is ready on the stove. Stop by, will you? You are coming to the piazza tonight, aren't you? You know there is music and the feast of fair August. We'll see you later, eh?"

"You are so kind. Thank you," said Agada, thinking how hospitable and warm the fellow was.

"Yes of course we will" responded her cousin. They waved goodbyes

Agada knew from years back that, August is the month when everyone goes on vacation. The people return from the main cities. At this time, is when they are celebrating the church events in the evening with music, dancing, plays, and food. All gathered at the piazza outdoors. The climate is warm and pleasant; the lighting décor enhanced by in art work glittering under the stars. The town folks and visitors mingle in friendship. A good time to get reacquainted and join the fun to be had by everyone.

But for now, Agada, with her cousin leading, needed to concentrate on her footsteps as she climbed the uneven road with its cobblestones. She was out of breath but continued, hoping to reach her destination soon. Antonella seemed to have no trouble. "You must be more fit, or used to climbing these hilly roads, my friend," she said. At the same time, Agada's curiosity was escalating to ignore her fatigue and huffing and puffing kept climbing away.

"We are soon to reach the palace," encouraged Antonella.

Il Palazzo. This is what their place was called. This was the place where her grandparents had lived. Where her mom was born and been raised. This was the place where she had spent her childhood playing with her cousins and had many family reunions.

The structure stood up high in the center of the town, overlooking the panoramic view with the circular horizon in sight of the area. One could see the other towns surrounding the zone. It was the landmark of the place called Molise.

Antonella's reminded her, "Our grandfather has played a big role in this town. He has constructed these roads, had employed many people, and built our bridges. He had fed the hungry, helped the poor, and shared his wealth. He was a legend in his time, a tycoon, well known for his good deeds."

"Yes, I remember some of the stories. Of course, my mother always talked about her parents."

So many years had gone by. The grandfather had long passed on. Times had changed; the remaining family had emigrated. The palace was sold. But the memory remained in the hearts and souls of the emigrated granddaughters.

A doctor from out of town had bought the place. He knew of the family that had emigrated to Canada and lived in Toronto. In his will, he left them the right of first refusal on his demise, should the place be for sale. Sure enough, Antonella was contacted. Since the nostalgia had never ceased, she and her sister bought the place back. This is how the palace returned into the original family ownership.

Here was Agada, now making her way to that never forgotten place of her childhood. As she entered the atrium of the residence, she noticed the big wooden doors to the east and west were still there. Some of the surroundings was dilapidated in its antiquity, but the part where they lived was well kept and the balconies remained. The memory was fresh, and she couldn't wait to get in. They were greeted by the other cousin, Tina, Antonella's sister, smiling and cheerful. She had arrived on vacation two weeks prior. Therefore, she had a head start in preparation of the place and food supply. As they entered the first floor, the aroma of a delicious Italian meal hit their nostrils. Agada had not been hungry, but the smell of that food stimulated her taste buds.

Tina quickly announced, "I have dinner almost ready, and I have invited five more guests to join us for your arrival."

A beautiful table was set up and this was to be their welcoming home.

Antonella pointed out, "Look, Agada, the stairs are its originals."

"Oh, my! Maybe I was six years old, but I remember. Then

when I was nine, I was sent away to school. But you know everything is vivid in my memory."

Once she reached the second floor, the first place she wanted to visit was a room outside the balcony at the far end. There, she remembered playing with her young cousins, away from the adults, so they would not be disturbed. Once she got there she stopped, puzzled. The door was barred closed with a railing.

"Antonella," she called out, "why is this railing blocking the entrance to that room?"

"Oh! Agada. Someone took that room away from my mother."

"What! Are you serious? That was my favorite. Who could have done such thing?"

"Don't you worry, I will take it back," responded Antonella, determined.

Agada nodded in agreement. "Of course, you have to. That is a missing link to the palazzo," She said, not realizing all the other missing links at the time.

Her cousin went on to explain how this lady now living in Rome had bamboozled her mother into giving her this room. But she was going to do everything in her power to reclaim it back. Agada thought, If I know my cousin well, she is certainly capable of doing so.

But now, she backed away, disappointed, and squinted her eyes in disbelief. "I will continue my tour. Three floors, wow!"

Antonella still leading the way, turned to her and said, "Look, my dear cousin. You will take the best bedroom in this house."

Selfishly, Agada did not protest as she was following her cousin in a daze.

"This cannot be true. After so many years, am I really in my grandparents' room?" she asked.

"Open the balcony, see what's out there," her cousin encouraged.

Once Agada looked out, the view was beyond any imagination, totally breathtaking, and the height made her feel close to heaven. The air was crisp and pristine, a real treat for the lungs.

The bells of the church broke her spell. They were almost at its height outside the perimeter of the palazzo. The bells rang every fifteen minutes, loud and poignant. It's striking was to keep the locals informed of the time.

"Oh! Thank you, Jesus," she exclaimed, making the sign of the cross after she heard the church bells.

The delicious dinner was served by Tina; the several courses were enjoyed by the rest of the guests.

Antonella seemed reenergized by the fabulous meal. She didn't want miss out on the celebration going on down to the piazza. She got up and motioned to everyone. "We must go to the piazza," She said, almost as it was a duty.

The flight had been long. The drive from Rome airport, daunting. But they were not allowed to miss out on anything.

Antonella, with her never-ending energy, commanded, "Come on, we will change our attire and get to the piazza to live it up. Of course, no down time, we cannot afford to be lazy, especially on our first night."

Where was Antonella getting her strength was beyond Agada comprehension. She realized they needed to descend the hill again. The elegant shoes were totally impossible to wear. No! She would not be able to negotiate those steps and uneven cable stones.

"The wedge flat shoes would have to do, I guess," she told her cousin.

"Agada, whatever feels comfortable for you."

"It's not only a matter of comfort, it's more a matter of not breaking my legs or dislocate my ankles or feet. I am not used to these ramps covered with cobblestones."

"The girls here wear heels; I don't know how they can walk with them. You get used to it after a while, I guess," stated Antonella.

The piazza was crowded with people. The festive decorating lighting were strung, in clear and blue, adorning the main church, the avenues, everywhere. It looked like Christmas in Canada. The warm breeze pleasant to enjoy outdoors. Agada looked up at the place where they lived; it was the focal point of the town, lit up with big lampions. The glitter of the lights and the music diffused everywhere with the loud amplifying speakers; it stirred energy and put one in a festive mood. The people were over friendly and kind. They showed much interest on identifying the placement of who belonged to whom with the connections of the past. They were caring, interested, and giving. Agada met and shook hands with so many people. The ones that were alive and could reconnect with the many years past. It was interesting. She ran into two classmates. Of course, she would have never recognized them if she had not been informed by the relatives. Then, long term memory kicked in and she could relive memories of her infancy. Her tongue rolled nicely in her first language. She felt grateful and proud, her few years of studies from way back then were paying back well now. She realized no one spoke the dialect. The proper grammar was heard among everyone.

"How beautiful," said Agada to her newfound friends and acquaintances. "I see how everyone joins in. The circles of people gets bigger and everyone is joyfully participating in friendship."

The next morning, Agada was awakened by the bright sunshine filtering through the balcony. Once more, she assessed her pleasant surroundings with pleasure. With invigorated energy, she stretched her body in delight, jumped out of bed and was ready for more venturing of her old town. Of course, the aroma of coffee brewing from the kitchen was enticing and inviting. The spread of fresh fruit, the warm baked biscuits… "What a royal treat," she exclaimed to her cousins.

"I will go for a long walk, through the town. I want to check the avenues, then visit the cemetery."

"Yes, we'll go together," they agreed.

On their tour, they found some of the streets heartbreaking. The earthquake of April 2009 had devastated a lot of the buildings; wooden posts were still holding some of the structures up for safety. Wild grass and weeds had grown on accumulated debris, blocking passageways on some streets. Her favorite church was abandoned. This part was disheartening. Then came the visit to the cemetery. There, she revisited the chapel of her grandparents. She was grateful to find their picture still there, covered with dust and cobwebs.

Agada searched her pockets for a tissue and cleaned the faded images and the marble stones, lit a candle, and recited a prayer.

The days flew by and the journey was soon over. Agada returned to her home in Canada with her heart full of joy and satisfaction for having relived her dream. The memories treasured in her heart will reign like a seal until all the days of her life.

Novel No.26

A POEM
LADY CHEEK PERFORMANCE

Her soft white feathers are sprinkled in romantic vibrant colours. Like a peacock, she twirls around.

Oh! Yes! The mood is set and the stimulation ready for the festivities. The wide eyes vibrate with love and attraction, resistance hard to combat.

Cheeky is all decked out, the show ready to begin. The stage is set, the costume enchanting, the room is full, and the audience breathless waiting. The curtains open, Cheeky appears slowly, methodically swaying. She turns on her magnetism by batting her eyes; everyone gravitates.

Silence follows. There in the mist of complimentary lights flashing, the lyrics erupt, soft, louder and clear to a pitch finale. The soothing melody is totally absorbed, the audience is mesmerized. The words have reached their hearing. Their souls are in peace and their heart filled with love.

Cheeky bows with pleasure and exits. The crowd claps feverishly in standing ovation.

Encore. Encore.

Cheeky smiles. Her act is successfully complete. She makes a return on the stage highly acclaimed. Shining, waving, bowing in glory, she slowly backs away.

Novel No.27

A PEBBLE ON THE BEACH

Pebble continued to cry outload, "Mommy! Mommy, where are you? Uh… uh… I want my mommy." His eyes burned as he wiped away his tears with the back of his hand. No one cared; his despair was ignored by the passersby. The child had found himself abandoned in the slums of Buenos Aires. Before leaving that early afternoon, his young mother, Romina, had embraced him affectionately, kissed his forehead, and sternly said, "Pebble, listen to me. You sit here, like a good little boy by this door step and wait for my return. Mommy must go now. I will find a way to get some money for both of us. On my return, we can go buy your favorite goodies to treat ourselves."

Pebble, doleful, had lowered his eyes. "Mommy, I don't like it when you leave me!"

"Now, now, my pumpkin, I don't like it either. I promise I won't be gone long. Please, don't make it more difficult for me." She knelt down and caressed his face gently with her hands to console him.

Through a forced whisper that came from his heart, Pebble managed to respond, "Okay, Mommy." As she moved along in a hurry, he watched her while his hand motioned in a wave. "Goodbye, Mommy."

The sun was up high in the sky when she'd left. The sun had since gone down as night came. It had gotten dark and frightening.

It seemed he'd had been waiting forever. No sign of Mommy. His body felt weak and defeated, tired, thirsty, and hungry. He stretched himself on the ledge of the doorstep of this abandoned building by the entranceway in total surrender and anguish. Days turned into nights, nights into days until Pebble lost count. The boy, desolated, wandered around the streets, returning often to check his designated awaiting spot. No sign of Mommy.

Time passed. Weeks turned into months, months into a year. Young Pebble at this tender age had no choice other than to resign to being homeless on the streets of Buenos Aires.

During the day, he managed to check garbage bins for something to eat. He often walked along the river, where he begged from tourists along the way. He rejoiced when someone dropped some money his way. The nights were the worst as he'd return to the place where his mother had left him. Hoping beyond hope for a miracle.

Most late evenings, he would doze off anywhere. Often, later during the night, some strange characters roaming around, homeless like him, would startle him and interrupt his sleep. Pebble, clearing his grogginess, he would look up to see what was over him. One night, two other homeless were poking at him, slurring words he couldn't make out. They were dirty, unshaven, smelling of manure, urine, body odor. At first, he was alarmed. Then he realized they could hardly stand from drunkenness. Pebble was about to retrieve his weapon of defence, but once he pushed them away, in their weak state, they wobbled on.

One particular Friday night, he was still awake when some younger hoodlums surfaced from nowhere. They were more challenging and dangerous. Pebble's survival skills kicked in. He grabbed his weapon in full force, swaying it right and left at their bodies. They were caught by surprise, after a few blows fending themselves, hurting, left him alone, swearing at him "We will be back, you scam bag, just wait." Said one of them. Pebble remained on guard awake all night fearing their return. He tried to change spot, so they wouldn't find him. The struggle had rendered him totally exhausted. One morning searching the garbage he had found an old knife. Great! This I need. He thought. Walking along the avenue He had collected a tree branch. He took the branch and carved it into a pointy stick. He guarded it and kept it with him. It had become his favorite weapon of defense lately. When the wonderers of the night, were weak — stoned on drugs, or drunk from alcohol — it wasn't hard to chase them away in such a state. But when the younger desperados came Pebble's body shook in fear.

***

His soul continued to feel tormented. Every day, Pebble asked himself, where is Mommy? Why she doesn't return? He watched continuously, eyes searching right and left, wishing for her to appear. It didn't happen. Pebble didn't know it couldn't happen. Romina could never return or see her Pebble ever again. She had gotten shot by a security guard trying to rob a bank. She was dead.

He still kept returning to that abandoned building where his mother had placed him. It was dusty, dirty, and full of dead bugs. But sleep there would take him to a dreamland of no existence. There he was this one morning as the sun came up for a new day. Pebble had awakened with his morale at its lowest point. Once more, his emotions had overpowered him. He had given into his feelings and broke into a good, hearty cry. Passersby were used to the squalor and misery of abandoned children around there, so no one cared or paid attention to him.

That particular morning, he felt reluctant to leave his spot. What if he did? She wouldn't find him. He still hoped. . . Then, he spotted a couple walking up the street. They were holding hands, smiling at each other. As they got closer, Pebble understood they were not locals. He noticed the woman staring at him, pulling her companion toward him. She stopped. At first, she stood there, quietly admiring him. "A young boy alone, dear," she exclaimed. "Darling, isn't he cute? Look at him! I wish I could take him home."

Pebble's ears perked up. He sat up straight. Wiping his eyes with his soiled hands, he smiled at the visitors. They were polished, kindness radiated on the lady's face. His melancholy subsided.

He looked like a dirt bag with his face smeared with dust and grime; the trace of the tears had left streaks down his cheeks. He looked at the lady inquisitively, forcing his eyes to clear and open wide. How he wished it was Mommy, but this lovely lady with luminous fair skin and blonde hair didn't look at all like Mommy.

"Hello, young man!" she said with a big smile as she kneeled down.

Pebble just gave her a faint smile. The stranger was not what he had wanted to wake up to. His mommy had black hair, dark olive skin, medium build, and brown eyes.

The stranger was Darlene Brooks, an English lady, with her husband, Morris. A tall woman, freckled face, softly spoken, she turned to her husband. "By his appearance, this little boy must have spent the night here." The lady was puzzled, and totally intrigued by the lonely child. They had been at a variety store, so she looked down at the plastic bag her husband was carrying. She turned to him and asked, "Darling, we bought some chocolates and cookies, let's give it to him. He needs it, we don't."

The two kneeled down, pulled the goodies out of their bag, and handed their purchase to him. Pebble's eyes opened wide. His stomach gurgled as he had been starving from days before. The lady gently wiped his face with a wet wipe. His face felt good, refreshed.

Pebble took one look at his goodies and couldn't wait to devour them.

The couple were tourists, from Miami, on a stopover from a cruise ship. They had needed some personal necessities and were walking the streets of Buenos Aires this early morning before their ship sailed off again. The lady straightened a lock of hair back from his forehead, gave him a warm caress with the back of her hand, and then sorrowfully moved on.

Pebble munched away, keeping watch on them as they distanced themselves. His heart lapsed back into the abyss of sorrow as the two people disappeared at the far end of the avenue. They had shown him kindness. Then a surge of energy zipped up and down his spine. He suddenly decided to follow them. He got to his feet and raced to the corner. There they were, way down. He ran faster. The couple walked slowly. It seemed the universe itself was cooperating in his favour; his task wasn't difficult. A force beyond his control kept his skinny legs and shoeless feet moving forward.

The lady seemed loving and genuine, if I could only be with her, he thought. He continued moving forward, watching them until they reached the port. Once they got on the gangway of a big luxurious ship, they disappeared from his sight.

He couldn't go any further. A shadow of loneliness and despair swept over him again. His heart sank further in sadness. But maybe he could sneak on board, but the gates and security guards barred his way.

He admired the big white ship, with blue wavy designs, a distinguished admirable logo. If I could only get in there, I could find my kind lady. She'll take care of me. Then he thought of his mommy. A pang of pain hit his heart; he felt she was gone forever. He would never see her again. In the past, she had disappeared a lot, but returned days later. Often, he had found himself alone in the squalor of that infested place they lived in. They had been moving from place to place; one worse than the other. Now, they had no more places to go and had resorted to living on the street. The landlord had thrown them out of the stinky dump, then she had bad mouthed them everywhere. That last time, she had grabbed him by the arm, shaking him from the entrance way, and had said to him, "Your mother is a filthy tramp and her tricks result in no money because she stinks. Both of you get out of my place before I get my goons after you."

After that, they had lived on the street. They would huddle together during the night. It didn't feel safe, but with his mommy at his side, he felt more protected. But no more. He had lost hope. The promise of Mommy to return with some cash had vanished.

The reality was Pebble was alone on the street, homeless. As young as he was, he knew this was his fate, he needed to accept it and move on.

Now, this marvelous ship gave him new dreams long after the nice couple boarded, the ship left. But Pebble kept returning to the port where there were always new ships. Some time passed, and the port had become Pebble's highlight. He stood there on the platform, wishing, planning, scheming to find a way to get on one of those ships. He was determined to make it happen.

One late afternoon, he was leaning on a wire fence, his fingers wrapped in the holes of it, daydreaming. He watched lots of children getting on board with their parents without any trouble. A little later, a group of youngsters arrived. Two girls were leading them. They were fretting, hurrying, trying to keep the gregarious bunch together. They all had name tags hanging around their necks. Pebble's brain leaped. Maybe the gods are working in my favor. He took a good look at the girls. The young girls were now trying hard to keep the undisciplined bunch together. "Sara, let's get them into a lined-up group of two or three; it's easier to head on board." He heard the dark-haired girl shout.

He figured this was his chance: sneak in among them, and once inside, he would find a hiding place. One girl with a dark complexion and jet-black fussy hair looked at him. The other was a more aloof blonde. He figured it was better to stick to the blonde girl's side, thinking, Once I sneak in, if get caught, I will deal with that later. Then he stepped back as the girl turned around to scrutinize him.

"Eh! You! How did you get here?" She whistled for one of the attendants and he was chased away.

Pebble would never pass as one of those tourist kids in his slimy condition. He was smelly, dirty, and barefoot. The dark-haired girl had given him one stern look and his heart sank. He turned around with his head down and returned to wander the streets, where he lived for a few more years. He learned survival, and how to be street smart. He met other homeless children; some older and some younger than him. Some were ruthless, some kinder, but they were all struggling to survive. Pebble wasn't counting his age or celebrating birthdays. A few years had passed since his mommy's disappearance and the ship discovery that had taken the kind lady away. Every now and then, he would go to the port to admire the ships arriving. He was hypnotized, watching and admiring the ships docking. A cloud of sadness would take him over, watching them sailing off without him. His body was growing despite the malnutrition. He was getting taller and turning into a handsome young boy. He was now ten. The desire to get away was getting stronger than ever. He would say to himself, I need to get on one of those luxury liners and get away from the misery of the streets of Buenos Aires. How am I going to do that? He had learned how to steal discreetly from the street vendors. There were plenty around the port. They were set up with their tables, with fancy tea shirts and all kinds of clothing and merchandise for the tourists. The area was usually crowded when the ships arrived. He had learned how to make his move at the right time, undetected by the vendors. He was a good kid with a conscience — didn't like to steal, but it was necessary. He had practised befriending the young attendant from the ship at the port, by offering some of his stolen goods. A guy named Fernando had become his friend. He was on duty by the far outer gate where people got in and out, heading to the plazas and coffee shops. He wore a name tag, scanning the passengers' cards as they came and left. He had gotten pretty friendly with him.

One day after delivering him a bunch of jewelry for gifts to take back, Pebble asked, "Fernando, I need to get out of here. Can you help me?"

"What do you mean, kid?"

"Is there any way you can help me get on that ship?"

"Buy yourself a ticket. You'll sail to Miami and won't have a problem getting on board. I'll show you South Beach."

"Money, where will I get the money? You have to get me in. I am willing to work, help out in any way I can."

"Eh! Sorry, you're too young. They don't hire kids to work here; lots of rules and regulations to follow. You can only come as a tourist."

"No chance for me to buy a ticket. I live on the streets here; I just want to get away."

"Sorry, pal, can't help you."

Fernando didn't seem the helping type. Disillusioned, Pebble gave up for a while.

The following season, he kept returning to the port, and as usual, admired the ships. Another fellow had taken Fernando's place. He accosted him, smiling, shy in a sweet docile manner. The new fellow's name was Oasé Rodrigas. He wore a tag on his shirt uniform with his name. He spoke with an accent. After befriending him, Pebble learned the young man was originally from Mexico, living in the US, and working mostly on the ship.

Oasé was a cheerful character. Not too tall, he looked distinguished in his crispy white shirt, the ship's logo in gold embroidery. He stood about five-feet-seven, black hair, and a mustache that suited him in a peculiar way. His eyes darted in kindness and mischief. Pebble wasn't sure how to take him. He seemed more promising than that Fernando guy that had brushed him off the year before. Now a season later, Pebble had also gained more confidence through his survival experiences.

"Oasé," he called out, bending his head and looking up at him sweetly, with begging eyes, "Please, help me, get me on that ship. I will do work for you. In some way, somehow, I know you can do it. I have no money. I am told how great Miami, South Beach is. I want to get there in the worst way. You must help me."

"Eh! Kid, are you joking? It takes a lot of red tape to come and work on board. You are way too young."

"No, I'm not; I'll do anything. Please, you must help me. I am sure you can find a way to get me on board."

"Are you crazy? You know how much red tape it takes to work on a cruise ship? Plus, all the legalities you need to go through?"

"I know, I know all that. There has to be a way you can sneak me in."

Oasé shook his head. "Do you want me to get in serious trouble? Get out of here!"

Pebble backed away and broke into sobs, disheartened and disillusioned. With his head down, distanced himself.

Oasé looked at him. A sorrowful twitch churned in his stomach. Pensive, he recalled, Wasn't I on the border of Mexico with the same desire to make it to the US at any cost? Just like that kid. I am an illegal immigrant. Why am I scorning him now instead of trying to help him? Shamed, he reconsidered.

"Eh! You. Pebble! Come back." As Pebble turned to look at him still tearing and wiping his cheeks, he slowly walked back toward him.

Oasé put an arm around his shoulder "You know, kid, I might reconsider. I'll see what I can do. You see, I understand. Myself, I got into the US illegally. It wasn't easy, I tell you. But with a lot of struggle, I survived. There are a lot of opportunities in the USA, especially if one is willing to work. Leave it with me, let me do some thinking. Don't get your hopes up, though. I will see what I can do."

Pebble's face lightened up. "Oasé, I'll be grateful if you do that for me. I will repay you back once I get a job. I will do anything. Wash dishes, sweep floors, as long as I can get away from here."

Oasé twitched his mustache and slapped a hand on his shoulder. "Okay, Pebble, let me talk to my superior. Be here on our next trip; we'll return in two weeks. I'll see if I can convince that Alonza guy in the kitchen."

Pebble gave him a big hug, elated with joy. "Oasé, you won't be sorry. My hard work will impress him. Can I start counting the days? When exactly will you get back?"

"Now, now, don't jump to any conclusions. I will try my best. Don't get your hopes up too high. It depends on the mood he is in."

Pebble was turning twelve and was totally unaware of why Oasé wanted to help him out.

He certainly mumbled under his breath, "This could be my opportunity to provide Alonza a new worker. Since he's been complaining lately, Pebble's offer might motivate him." Besides, Oasé was getting tired of him also. Alonza must realize I am getting sick and tired of being his pansy, in every which way.

Pebble, filled with hope, returned to the streets and roamed the city. Smiling to the homeless, he would cheerfully announce, "Soon, I will be taking off, across the ocean to a new horizon where I'll have lots of food."

He had become a professional thief over the past couple of years. Pebble walked around the market, eyeing the merchandise on display, analyzing the vendor. This was his homework time. Okay, observe, note, need, and when? After his mental calculation was complete. He would stride along nonchalantly with his hands in his pocket. If any of the vendors questioned him or greeted him, he innocently lowered his head and would respond, lying, "My mom's birthday is coming up. I am just looking to see what I can find for her." The vendors would usually be impressed at first.

"Nice kid," said Miguel, standing at the opposite side of the jewellery table, thinking he was a sincere young boy. But Pebble was in his research mode at that time, wondering what he could grab. He chose to strike when it got crowded and the vendor was too busy and distracted.

After a while, Pebble had learned to play his tricks well. The stealing and selling the goods had taught him entrepreneurship. But deep in his soul, he didn't like it. At night, fear and guilt would shake him. He didn't appreciate the dirty money stuffed in his shoes. The selling of the stolen goods was supposed to make him feel good. Instead, the guilt made him miserable. Often in the silence of the night, his tears would surge. Releasing his emotions in a good cry brought him relief.

He had met another homeless kid named Albert. He was a couple of years older. A chubby youngster that often bragged to him and the other homeless youngsters about how he managed to get his loot undetected. "Eh! Pebble, take a look at these goodies." With a big smirk on his face, he would recount and act up. "Old Samuel at the market didn't even blink an eye. I was talking to him, offering him a banana, while my back hand was doing the snatching."

Albert might have been older than Pebble, but he wasn't as caring. Pebble asked him, "Albert, doesn't the fear overpower you?"

"Eh! What fear! I was beaten a few times. Who cares? I got over it."

"One of these days, you will be caught for good and your fun will be over," warned Pebble.

"Ah, Pebble, you have to take chances. Do you want to dig in garbage bins the rest of your life?"

Pebble's recently stolen loot was highly guarded. It consisted of a new pair of shoes, new navy pants, a lighter blue shirt, and a white belt. That was what he needed, should he be able to get on that ship. He had it all planned. Pebble would wash up in the public washrooms by the port. He carried a small knapsack with his stolen toiletries and necessities. He lived on hope and waited. The ship was about to return in a day or two. Pebble walked up at dawn. He got himself freshly washed, dressed, and groomed. Please, God, help me get on that ship. If I could only board it, I will work so hard to make Oasé proud.

The sun was shining this particular morning and the sky was blue; light fluffy clouds were sparsely floating, but not menacing. A lovely day for the tourists to enjoy and explore this part of the world.

There stood Pebble, leaning by the outer fence wide-eyed, anxiously waiting for Oasé to appear. He stretched his neck hoping, looking. A lot of crew attendants. No sign of him in sight. Where is he? Then a tall fellow with a young woman walking beside him, chatting and smiling, both in uniform, were making their way over toward him by the exit gate. They positioned themselves to check out the passengers as they approached to get out of the gate and into the port's platform. An obscured sadness covered Pebble's heart. He had counted the days for the ship to return. Here he was now. But no Oasé in sight to deliver him the good news.

Chapter Two

Pebble's disappointment

Oasé had been assigned to a different maintenance service on the ship around the pool area today. His superior, Heinz, had gathered a few of the fellows and given his order the day before docking. "Look, guys, it will be quieter tomorrow as most of our passengers will be inland touring. It is a good time for us to spruce up around the pool area and prepare the ice sculptures."

Oasé thought of his young friend. But he had no choice but to follow orders.

Pebble waited and waited, fighting his emotions of disappointment.

A fellow and young lady slowly approached the gate together. The tall man with his broad shoulders, recessed hairline, protruding stomach, and sunken dark eyes looked unapproachable and intimidating compared to Oasé's small frame and smiley face.

Sorrowfully, Pebble leaned his head on the side and decided he rather go to the girl's side. He politely asked, "Excuse me, I have been waiting for Oasé. Do you know if he's coming ashore today?"

The young lady first looked at him up and down, hesitating for a moment before replying, "No. Oasé is on board duty today. I don't think he can."

Pitifully, Pebble responded, "Can you please tell him that Pebble is waiting for him if you see him?"

"Probably not until tonight. You see, I am on duty here and I cannot leave my post. Sorry."

"I see." Again, disappointed, he put his head down and turned to walk away.

The tall fellow had somewhat overheard his inquiry, but since he was engaged with some passengers couldn't intervene with Pebble.

Alonza turned to his assistant. "Elisa, excuse me for a minute. I need to talk to that young fellow. I have a message for him from Oasé." He hurried to reach Pebble's side with a voice as strong as his gigantic persona. "Hello! I am Alonza, Oasé's friend. You must be Pebble."

Pebble's spirit jolted joyfully. "Yes, I am."

"Oasé told me all about you. Okay, hang around when we are ready to depart. Oasé will try to be here if he can. Should he not be able to, I will work to get you on board."

"Are you serious?" He turned to stare at him. Alonza, having no time to continue talking, quickly turned around and dismissed him. "I must get back to my post. See you later." In no time at all, the lineup of passengers quickly increased, waiting to be scanned out.

At five o'clock, the ship's blaring horn signaled their departure. With Pebble on board. He had everything he owned with him: his stolen clothes, socks, and shoes that he was wearing, a small plastic bag clutched tight in his hand with ten dollars in US currency that he had picked from an unsuspecting tourist while standing in a crowded beer outlet, and the most valuable of all, his entrance card with his name and stateroom number.

He was the last to get in, following Alonza like a frightened kitten. This unknown was too much for him. Then Alonza turned to him with a stern look on his face. "Okay, you follow me. Once we reach the kitchen, you go to the dishes department. Oasé will take over from there." Pebble let out a sigh of relief. He felt much more at ease with the Mexican Oasé. His gut feeling wasn't right with Alonza. Why does this guy strike me the wrong way? He looks weird and severe? In the meantime, he was mesmerized by his surroundings. It took time to reach the set destination. Pebble didn't know where to look first: The immense luxurious lounges, or the sparkling brass iron railings complementing the beautiful stairways on the different levels. His eyes darted from the plush carpets to the luster of the walls. The spectacular staircases led to the fancy boutiques. The piazzas set up for the guests with coffee shops, treats. The music tunes in different melodies, coming from different directions. The openness of the glass windows let in the infinite blue sky and water as they touched each other on the far horizon. "If only Albert could see this. He will never believe it." Thinking he was dreaming, he continued following Alonza in a daze.

Chapter Three

The tour continues

They finally reached the kitchen department, where all the food preparation was taking place. It was another eye opener for young Pebble. He watched everything moving along like an assembly line. Finally, Oasé appeared from another department. "Eh! How are you, my friend?" As he greeted him cheerfully with a hand shake, Pebble's heart leaped. A familiar face. He considered Oasé his saviour. All smiles, he gave him a hug.

"Hola, Oasé, so nice to see you. ¿Cómo estás?"

"Muy bien. Lo siento, no pude estar afuera hoy."

He shrugged his shoulders, smiling. "Eh! Oasé, I made it. Estoy aqui."

"Good, Alonza took care of you. It wasn't easy Kiddo! But after much convincing, he finally promised me he would."

"Gracias, Oasé" As he looked at him with merciful eyes.

"Eh! You must be hungry. Why don't you make your way to the fifteenth floor? The buffet is on, go grab something to eat first."

Pebble looked around. It was easy for him to say it was beyond his imagination. "How do I get there? Am I allowed?"

"Look, Pebble, I cannot go with you as I am in charge to supervise the affair going on later. But I will walk you to the elevator. You push the button to fifteen. When you hear fifteen, the Hawaiian dining room, step out and just follow other passengers. Come back down when you are finished."

Fearing the unknown, he followed the instructions in doubt. Before he knew it, he found himself in line with other passengers. He was handed a plate and cutlery with no questions asked. A lovely hostess greeted everyone gracefully, including him. As he stepped forward, again he thought, I am dreaming. This cannot be real. Please, God, don't let me wake up from this spell. He ate to his heart's content. Then pensive with his full tummy, he thought, Now, how am I going to find my way back? A little lost, he slowly tried to find his way back to the lower floor, hoping to find Oasé.

Instead, Oasé had again disappeared. Alonza was around, busy checking things out. Pebble lifted his arm, waving to him, trying to get his attention as he was at a loss now on what to do next. Alonza, glanced at him and continued on his task at hand, totally ignoring him. Pebble quietly wished for his sweet Oasé to appear again since Alonza made him uncomfortable. After standing there being ignored, he mercifully walked over to Alonza. He stood aside, waiting for him to finish giving orders to some other crew members in a language foreign to him. His tone of voice sounded harsh and menacing. That scared Pebble even more while he stood, waiting for his turn. Finally, he glanced on his side. "Are you waiting for Oasé, kid?"

"Yes, he said he would see me later."

Irritated, Alonza growled, "I will try to page him for you. I knew he shouldn't have made any promises. He is responsible for the function up on deck. He will be tied up until late when everything is over."

Pebble didn't know how to respond. Shrinking in his own skin, he just waited. Alonza now was speaking to him in Spanish.

"Debería mostrarte a su cabaña. Okay." Alonza, impatiently turned to him and said, "segueme" Much disturbed, he turned to some other workers there and said, "Cover for me until I return."

He signaled Pebble, tilted his head, and grabbed a bunch of keys.

"Let's go, kid. I will show you your cabin."

The corridor was long and narrow and seemed to take forever.

Finally, he stopped in front of this door numbered 1911, opened the door with one of his keys, and let him in. "This is where you will sleep. Oasé will see you in the morning. Then you will be assigned to your duties. The morning duties start early here. You should be up at 5:00 am, and at the kitchen department by six."

Pebble listened to him attentively, but Alonza's demeanor was curt and cold. As Pebble entered the small room, he let out a deep sigh of relief since it had been a long anxious day for him. Once he noticed a real bed, his young body ached. He was so tired, he couldn't wait to throw himself on it in total abandon. Besides, he was only too glad to get rid of Alonza — the sooner the better. He nervously held the door open and said, "Thank you and good night."

As tired as he was, he couldn't stop taking in his surroundings. He said to himself, "A bed with pillows! A dresser with a mirror, a small desk, a bench, a real chair. A television. A washroom for myself. No windows." He was ever so grateful for whatever had placed this fortune in his life.

The morning arrived much too soon for him. Against his will, he forced himself to wash and dress like a normal human being now that all his necessities were at his disposal. He made his way to the kitchen department as he was told, hoping to reunite with his friend Oasé.

He approached two big heavy aluminum doors, which automatically opened, and there he spotted Oasé standing beside Alonza. Alonza seemed to be in charge of the kitchen staff. Oasé was to distribute and execute his orders. They were all in white uniforms. Everyone assigned at their stations worked like an assembly line. Others scurried about, carrying food to some of the workers. For a minute, Pebble watched, mesmerized. When he heard his name called, "Eh! Pebble, Good morning." Oasé slapped a hand on his shoulder to break his spell.

"Good morning, Oasé." Pebble smiled back.

"How are you? Are you ready for action? I hope you had a good night sleep. You sure have lots of dishes in that back room to sort out. We have a full house on this trip kiddo, plus you." He smirked with a wink.

"No problem, Oasé; anything you say. I am ready."

"First, we need to get you a white coat. I will show you only once what to do. You will be on your own from there on. Now, follow me."

They moved into the next big room, and their piles and piles of dirty dishes, with food and cutleries, were all stacked up over an immense counter. In a quick motion, Oasé showed him what to do. "Okay, amigo, first clear the food, then rinse the dishes, sort out the cutleries. Place everything in order and continue non-stop until the washer is completely full. Dispense the soap and turn on the lever. The cycle will complete itself. You continue."

He gave him another hand snap on his shoulder. "See you later! You will only be in trouble if the staff serving upstairs have no clean dishes." He winked, smiled, and disappeared behind the big double doors.

Pebble, once left alone, made some mental notes of his own and started to work. He was going to be twelve years old, mature for his age. The task at hand didn't scare him after the hardship he had endured in the slums of Buenos Aires. He thought, this is heaven for me. I must show him how capable I am. As long as I don't have to resort to that darn stealing ever again, he shook his head, pensive. That bothers me. I must confess the terrible sins I have committed someday. It had become a daily routine lately out of necessity. It instilled a tremendous fear in him of being caught beside remorse.

The ship had been at sea for two days. The demands from the passengers were greater than usual, the work load for the staff relentless. At the end of the shift, Pebble's body ached all over from the relentless motion of his steady movements. Once he reached his cabin, he dropped his exhausted body on the bed, surprisingly with no appetite, especially now that all that food was available to him. Sleep soon took him over in total abandon.

The following morning, Oasé peeked in at his dishwashing department to find Pebble fast at work. "Good job, amigo, you are doing great. Alonza is pleased. Keep up the good work." He slapped him on his shoulder and with a happy grin on his face left. Pebble smiled back, pleased for his acceptance. To his surprise, the double doors opened up again and Alonza appeared. He acknowledged him by nodding his chin.

He snooped around while Pebble held his breath, waiting for his comment while his uneasiness escalated. He tried hard to control his nerves. The aura Alonza carried wasn't pleasant. Pebble couldn't wait for him to leave. To his surprise, while he was bent over, totally taken with his work at hand, he turned to find Alonza right behind him. Pebble stepped aside to face him, giving himself a little more space for comfort. To his surprise, Alonza gave him a half-smile and said, "Good job, no complaints, keep up the good work. You are doing fine for a young fellow of your age."

Pebble's heart rejoiced. "Thank you," his voice squeaked, relieved. Alonza gave him a pat on his shoulder and proceeded to leave. Pebble felt encouraged and worked harder.

After work, he had gone to eat at the buffet. His eyes were bigger than his stomach, and he ate all his heart desired. It was Pebble's third night at sea on the ship. He didn't look for Oasé or bother with any of the crew members. He was tired with a full stomach, so he retired to his cabin. Once there, he kicked his shoes off and fell onto the bed. In no time, sleep took him, and his snoring could be heard from the hallway.

It was way after midnight and Pebble never heard the keys jingling or the door slowly opening with a slight squeak. When he felt heavy hands slowly feeling his body, a jolt of panic zipped through him as he didn't know where he was for a moment. As he opened his mouth to let out a scream, a big hand was placed over his lips, muffling his breathing.

He tried to clear his head from the wooziness and adjust his eye sight to the darkness around him. He was trying to make sense of what was happening to him when a voice startled him. "Eh! Pretty boy, what you say, sorry to wake you. I need a little treat."

Pebble's entire body shivered, petrified. He shook his head and tried hard to clear and adjust his vision. He slowly realized he wasn't on the street of Buenos Aires, but trapped in this cabin on the luxurious ship. I thought I was in heaven! He started to fight, punching and struggling with the big fellow that was pulling his clothes off. He kicked as hard as he could, but the intruder kept forcing himself on him. He was now wide awake. "Leave me alone, what do you want from me?" he cried out. He jumped up, threw his covers on the floor and tried to run. He reached the one and only door to escape. He was quickly grabbed by both arms and furiously thrown back on the bed.

"Look, pretty boy. You owe me. I pulled a lot of strings with my connections to get you on board. Now cooperate, and please don't make it hard for me. It's your choice. If you don't, I will throw you overboard to the sharks, and no one will miss you."

Suddenly, a big knife snapped open and there it was placed against his throat. "You know what we do with this? We slice the big fish in our kitchen. I warn you, be a good boy and I won't have to use it."

Pebble was crunched in a corner on the floor, shivering and trembling like a helpless puppy. "Where is Oasé? I trusted him; I thought he was a real friend!" OH! My God! What have I got myself into? he cried quietly, but the knife pierced his skin.

"Of course, I should have known better," he muttered. Now, through his vision obscured by tears, he could see his tormentor and recognized his voice.

Chapter Four

Tormented to the core

Like a bird in a cage, Pebble succumbed to his fate in the hands of the monster in disguise. His body ached to its core, along with his privates. His heart was broken and his soul tormented. Like a vicious wild animal, the perpetrator had his way with him without reservations. After he had his fill, he softly whispered in his ear. "This is our private affair, no mention to anyone. Okay, pretty boy. Eventually, it will be good for you too. In no time, you will look forward to my visits."

Pebble kept his eyes shut, holding his breath as he heard the shuffling of clothes. Then footsteps moving away from him, toward the door, and then quietly it clicked closed. "That son of a bitch, I will have to get out of this place as soon as I can. Nothing is worth the sexual abuse that monster is demanding. I'd rather starve on the streets with the homeless." Disheartened, the next morning got up and presented himself at his post, hurting but ready for his duty.

Oasé arrived and cheerfully placed an arm on his shoulder to greet him. "Eh! Amigo, you don't look too happy? What's wrong?" Pebble was unsure of himself. Should he respond? I don't trust anyone anymore. He gave him a smirk and remained taciturn, trying to control his raw emotions.

Oasé immediately got the hint by Pebble's sad eyes. My old buddy Alonza must have struck. . . he has been looking forward to his new treat. As much as he felt bad for Pebble, he knew life was cruel. He had been subjected to the same fate in order to get ahead. He figured in time, Pebble would understand and forgive him. The promise to fulfill his perverted sexual desire had been the only way to motivate Alonza to get young Pebble on board. How else could I do it?

A week had passed and Pebble's euphoric glamor had totally

disappeared. He dreaded returning to his cabin at night. As he fell asleep from exhaustion, the nightmares would return and the invasion continued. He would jump awake, shaking in fright. The ocean was rough that nigh; the wind blew furiously, rocking the ship pretty badly. Pebble's morale had reached its lowest. He broke down crying, begging for his mother or anybody to save him. He felt abandoned by the world itself. "God! Help me. I wish I was back on the streets with Albert," he said to himself, wiping away his eyes. Morning finally came. He had spent a sleepless night and dragged himself to his post. There waited his tormentor. Oasé popped in for a short time and then disappeared again. Alonza was snooping around, giving orders like an arrogant dictator. Pebble's stomach was filled with disgust and churning in turmoil. How am I going to get out of this trap? How am I going to do it? Who is going to help me? I need to get lost once we reach the port; out of site from that monstrous man.

When the double doors sprang open again, Oasé bounced in. He was loaded, carrying various boxes. "Eah! Pebble, help me with these boxes, will you?"

Pebble looked at him. Although he had lost trust in him — being so desperately in need of love and friendship — he wanted to believe that deep down, his Mexican friend's intentions had been genuine. He forced a smile and promptly offered a helping hand. "Oasé, the boxes are so heavy! What are you trying to do? You should have called me to help you unload."

Oasé tapped him on the shoulder, "Pebble," he said, smirking but with a serious look on his face. "You are still growing. I didn't want to hinder your body's growth by carrying this heavy stuff."

"OH!" he exclaimed, surprised as a pleasant feeling zipped through him. Maybe Oasé does care for me a little. Maybe I can trust him once more. I certainly need help to get out of this place he helped me get in. He shook his head, trying to control his mixed feelings. What choice do I have? I certainly cannot continue to stay here and cater to that brute and his nightly demands, he thought.

The ship was docking the next morning. Most of the passengers were getting off and the new ones would arrive for the repeated route. His intentions were to get out and disappear on this new land of sunshine and loose himself on the streets again. After all, he belonged to no one and no one would miss him. He doubted Alonza but trusted Oasé, and what had that gained him? Now, he felt stronger and determined to approach Oasé man to man. Later that evening, he knocked on Oasé's stateroom door.

Oasé made his way to the door, surprised to find Pebble standing there like a young soldier. "Eh! Pebble, come in, what's up?"

"What's up? Oasé, I thought you were a true friend; I trusted you. I thought you cared about me. You got me into this trap and you need to get me out of here. I need to get off this ship tomorrow; I promise you I will never bother you again."

"Kid, what are you saying? I thought you wanted to get in here in the worst way."

"Yes, I did, but not to be Alonza's toy, or be tortured for his pleasure every night."

"Sorry, Pebble, that part was part of his deal; I had no choice. It made me sad when I watched him make his way to your stateroom. I wanted to kill him. It made me sick to my stomach. But if I did that, we would both be in trouble."

"Oasé, if you have an ounce of decency in your being, you must get me a pass tomorrow and help me escape this nightmare."

Oasé placed a hand on his shoulder and looked him in the eyes, his expression was saddened. He took a deep breath and said, "I understand exactly how you feel. I will miss you, kiddo. But I'll see what I can do and check with you in the morning." He turned around, letting out an exasperated sigh. He did care for Pebble. Since the first time he had laid eyes on him, he had connected him to his deceased young brother. He had a strong resemblance to him. Suddenly, a flashback of that terrible afternoon on the beach sent shockwaves through his body. Yes, his young brother had lost his life by drowning in the Pacific Ocean. His conscience got the best of him. I must help Pebble at all cost. He brushed a hand through his hair and walked away. "I need to do what I can to help my young friend," he muttered to himself.

Later that morning, Pebble, assisted by Oasé with their passes, had no problem getting off the ship in Fort Lauderdale.

The port was crowded with all the passengers getting off. The traffic was horrendous from every direction. Anxious people waited gregarious to get on board; others left for their new destination.

Pebble didn't know which direction to go or where to look, as this part of the world was all new to him. His biggest desire was to distance himself from that ship and never look back. His past experience as a child growing in the slums of Buenos Aires had exposed him to misery and poverty, but nothing in comparison to what he had just endured.

He was excited to walk on this new soil. It was early morning; the air was crisp and the sun was shining. Oasé walking beside him gave him a sense of belonging. Oh, how he wished to have someone to love and him love back. It seemed he was destined to be alone on this world ever since he lost his mom. Oasé broke his gloomy thoughts just in time.

"Eh! Kiddo! Look at those palm trees. Look at those skyscrapers. In the future, you will grow up and reach out to the sky in infinity. I know you will. You are a smart kid." Smiling, he brushed his hand on the shoulder for encouragement. But Pebble's eyes were blurred from fighting tears, because he knew that he was soon going to lose his friend. He would again be alone in this unknown world.

"Oasé, can you stay? Please stay! I will resort to my old tricks and get stuff for both of us; we will get some money. Please stay with me." He hugged and tugged at his sleeve to hold on to him pleading.

"Pebble, come on now; be brave. I was lucky to have gotten you a pass. My heart ached for that son of bitch Alonza; that sex pervert. Sorry you had to submit to him. Try to forget about it; promise me you will. Eh! Bud, life is not easy. I will leave you by the beach. It is early and you have got all day ahead of you to explore. Look after yourself, and you know what to do to survive. I will have to get back on board. Now, my brave soldier, no feeling sorry for yourself, okay! Try to make your way to some restaurants. You got a little experience as a dishwasher and someone will hire you. Once you earn some money, you move on from there."

With a trembling voice, Pebble whispered, "Oasé can I get in touch with you? I would like to see you again. Don't you want to see me, also?"

"Of course, I do. I will have to be at sea for eight months. Occasionally, ashore from time to time, but I cannot make any commitment. My schedule is unpredictable."

Pebble's tears freely rolled down his cheeks.

They hugged each other, and with broken hearts, they parted.

Oasé could hear the sobs as he watched Pebble walk away, while a strong hatred toward Alonza grew in his heart. In his own pain, he turned around to make his way back on the ship.

Chapter 5

Pebble's New life

Here is where Pebble's new life began . . . in the south of Florida, USA.

At the young age of twelve years old. This new world was all his to explore. He walked everywhere, observing everything with a keen eye. His feet burned and ached; blisters broke and bled. He had to go on; courage and determination kept moving his feverish body, allowing him to explore his new surroundings until he could go on no more.

A child that had known nothing other than poverty, abuse, molestation, loneliness, and abandonment wandered the streets once more. He found a bench and sat on it, re-calculating his life experiences. The pain of endurance, the disappearance of his mother, the dealings with the multiple string of characters she would bring home at times. They had shared their dark, dingy residence for the night, leaving him in fear, always on guard. It had all been enough for a lifetime. As a child, he had no choice or control over their miserable existence. He went along as if this was the life for him and his mother, whom he loved unconditionally. Now that she was gone, life's misery had accumulated. Who could he trust? He believed Oasé was a caring soul, but Alonza's actions had stripped his dignity.

He fell asleep on the bench, thirsty, tired, and starving. When he woke up, his body seemed somewhat recharged. Pebble made a vow to put everything behind him and fend for himself. He had been forced to grow up at an accelerated speed in order to survive.

He was now in this new land thanks to Oasé. The sun was shining, the sky was emerald blue, the warm breeze pleasantly soothing, but his clammy skin felt dirty. He gazed at the palm trees, the low cedar green edges, the flowering shrubs, the manicured landscaping, the richness extending in front of the stately homes were much to admire. As he drifted along with no destination or direction, he landed in one of the main streets where the odor of food hit him.

There, the restaurants that were stretched out by the strip mall offered a variety of food and drinks. He couldn't read, but the pictures illustrated the plates of food. The offerings were enticing. He approached one of the hamburger outlets where the tables and chairs were sparse outdoors under the umbrellas. People seemed to leave a lot of food unfinished on their plates. He discretely helped himself to their leftovers. At these places, people seemed to be in a hurry. They were coming and going, therefore, no one noticed or paid attention to him eating the remaining food or retrieves from the garbage. He got up again and walked until his tired feet were bruised aching to the bare bones. Without realizing, he had found his way to the beach. There he stood, admiring the endless blue body of the Atlantic Ocean. The infinite stretch of beach with its lined-up high-rise reaching the sky. He moved forward toward the ocean. There, squishing his feet on the wet sand near the water where the waves gently soothed his worn-out feet. A peacefulness flowed through his entire body.

He looked up in the sky and made a wish. I have to survive here. This part of the world looks promising. As young as he was, Pebble knew to follow his instincts. He sat down on the sand to rest and contemplate. Before long, he let his tired body stretch on the warm sand and gave in to sleep once more. A short time later, with the sun beaming, he stood on his feet and continued his exploration. The seagulls were flying around endlessly. He stretched his arms out and amused himself by running among them, wishing he had wings like them. He related to them in freedom.

He soon learned the days on the streets here were easier than where he had come from. The days passed one after the other and he took to feeding himself and using the facilities at the public restaurants regularly. But he had to admit, the nights were scary and challenging. He was searching and worrying all day about where he would spend the night. He tried to stay away from public view by hiding in parks and dark places.

The time passed and his homeless life continued. Many months later, having become familiar with his area, he had gained some confidence and courage. His confidence was growing during the day, but remained scary at night. He had discovered the big food stores at the strip mall. He would amuse himself by watching people with the loaded buggies of food walking out. Crouched on the tiled brown brick cement floor by the side of the front entrance of Publix, he amused himself watching people going in and out of the store. When he saw the elderly people struggling, he felt sorry for them. He noticed some of them were having a hard time walking, and being able to place their purchases in the car or manoeuvring was hard. Deep down, he was a good-natured child. Therefore, his intentions for humanity were good. After holding back for fear, insecurity, and rejection, his instinct motivated his good intentions. He decided one afternoon to approach the shoppers and offer help. Especially, after noticing some elderly with walkers in distress. As he figured, some of them were reluctant to accept his good gesture. Some looked at him inquisitively, questioning him, "Where do you come from? Who are you? Are you from the store? You work here? Where are your parents, are you here alone?" as they grinned at him.

When he smiled with his innocent look on his face, some of them seemed reassured, but others were skeptical. Almost all of them questioned his effort. Pebble kept smiling in sincerity. This particular afternoon, a heavy-set lady he helped seemed to have a hard time walking. It was Melany Blair. She turned around and scrutinized the boy up and down. She placed a hand on her chin, thinking, there is honesty in this boy; the caring look on his face shows sincerity. She gladly accepted his gesture. After Pebble placed her bags in the trunk of her car and folded her walker and placed it neatly in her trunk and closed it, he said in Spanish, "Adiós." He moved to return to his post, waving his hand, but Melany grabbed his arm to stop him and said, "Young man, you deserve a tip for helping me." She opened her purse and handed the boy a green bill.

Pebble's eyes widened. Money! He had never had been handed this much money. He looked at it and said, "No, madam, you don't have to pay me."

"I insist you take this twenty dollar bill and buy something for yourself."

Shyly, he took the money. "Gracias." He stared at the bill in disbelief.

"What is your name?" the lady asked.

He gave her a faint smile, thinking for a second, and responded, "I don't have a name. I am a pebble on the beach."

"A pebble on the beach? What do you mean?"

"I was brought ashore on the beach. I consider myself a pebble on the beach. For whoever picks me up."

She gave him a big smile, thinking he had a good sense of humor. "I am glad the ocean waves brought you ashore. You are a mighty nice pebble on the beach, young man."

She got in her car and drove away. Pebble watched her leave, holding his fortune in his hand. I actually have money!

He walked back to his post to resume people watching. This is what he had been doing lately. That is how he amused himself daily. Every now and then, a dark cloud of fear and sadness would obscure his soul. The memory of his mommy tormented him. The fear of the night. . . All he wished was to wake up to daylight after a fearful night.

Every night as late as possible, he made his way to the far corner of the park. There on the bench in the dark, he stretched out, hoping to rest for the night. In the morning when the sun would rise on the horizon, bathing him with its warm rays, he would smile in gratefulness. "Thank God I have survived the night," he would say to himself. The new day would offer discovery and adventure with hardly any fear in sight. Time passed. He had encountered other homeless, some of them reeked of alcohol, used profane language, and were loaded with collected junk. He preferred to be alone.

He would usually find a public place to wash himself. In his wandering, he had stumbled onto a Jewish bazar outlet where people donated all kinds of merchandise. He had offered the sales girl half of his money and bought used clothing. He carried them neatly folded in a shopping bag. Since he had landed on this new place, he had not resorted to stealing lately. The tips had come in handy and that made him feel grateful. Every morning until his feet could take no more, he kept wandering to explore. By late afternoon, he would return to his favorite place by Publix. Once there, he would offer his services to whoever he felt was in need while not expecting anything in return. Most people, after some reluctance, accepted him and gave him tips for his gesture. It got to be his own created job, and more than that, it brought him joy to be helpful.

One day, a lovely lady with reddish hair, heavy set, and impeccably dressed was limping while pushing her buggy fully loaded with groceries.

"Hello, madam, can I be of any help to you?" With a sweet Spanish tone.

She turned around to face him without a word, creasing her forehead. "How can you help me? You are only a child yourself."

"I am fine. I can place your groceries in your trunk. Look," he said, and brought his arm up in a fold to show her his muscles. "I am strong."

She smiled and asked, "Are you here alone? Where are your parents?"

Again, Pebble thought, if I only knew. "OH! My mother died, I am okay. Here."

"Oh, my." She brought a hand on her mouth. "Are you sure you're fine, alone on the street?"

He nodded and looked up at her with his pitiful eyes.

The lady was Brenda Dolan, a widow. She had no children; married twice. Her husband had passed away two years ago. She lived alone with two cats, a bird, and a dog named Duke. The buggy contained a lot of bags to cater her beloved animals.

"Oh! You are sweet. Of course, you can help me."

Pebble, energized, walked with her to the car, and like a mature man, did his duty with her groceries and opened her car door for her like a gentleman.

Brenda looked at him and wished she could take him home to visit her animals. "You are adorable," she said while reaching in her purse. She handed him eighty dollars.

Pebble saw four green bills and again couldn't believe his eyes. "Thank you, thank you; I'd like to help you again."

"Yes, you may. Take care of yourself, now. I usually shop every Thursday. I might see you next week?" Off she went, checking the rear mirror and watching the boy walk back toward Publix. Shaking her head, she thought, I honestly believe the kid is a good kid, and he will use the money sensibly.

How right she was. Pebble was beside himself as he realized that was a lot of money. "What a nice lady," he muttered. "I hope I see her again."

Other people had walked out with groceries. When Pebble's offer of help was accepted, they would hand him a dollar or two. Pebble would stash his precious loot in the inside pocket of his pants, safeguarding the bills. They had been slowly accumulating. To his dismay, the money had become an added worry for him. He had encountered other homeless, some of them addicted to drugs or alcohol. If they got wind of his money, they would attack him, rob him, and it would be gone. He was so proud to be able to walk into any food store or outlet and treat himself and being able to pay. He possessed good senses and was a clean-cut child despite his erratic upbringing. He liked to be well groomed. He often made trips to the second-hand outlet for new clothing. The young lady, Claudette, had gotten used to his visits and often gave him additional items that they wanted to get rid of. Pebble kept his hopes up as he continued his journey on the street. Days passed and turned into months; the weather was warm and tolerable, and he was growing taller and stronger. He walked into restaurants, asking for work. When they asked him what he liked to do, he would shrug his shoulders, responding, "Anything." Most of them took one look at him and shook their head. "No. Sorry, not at this time. Check back when the season starts. By the way, how old are you?"

"Sixteen."

"You look much younger. Sorry, not now."

They all brushed him off with the same tune and answer.

Pebble didn't give up. One day, to his surprise, he stepped into this Italian restaurant. He couldn't read, but the pictures showing on the menu were enticing. His English was getting better as he tried hard to understand and put phrases together. Old Joe, another homeless, was coaching him as he spoke some Spanish also. They had made it a daily session. Pebble provided him with a juicy hamburger or a hotdog and a coke, and Old Joe loved to teach him to speak English.

This particular afternoon, he found himself in front of this restaurant with shimmering letter signs. La Scoglia Doro in gold. After scrutinizing the menu, he built enough courage to walk in. The place was empty except for few people sitting at the bar. The place was semi-formal with tables covered in white table cloths, fascinating paintings on the walls with lovely gardens and scenes of places he had never seen, nor would see. A magnificent grand piano sat in the far corner. To his amazement, it was bigger than he expected. Reluctantly, he made his way to the bar. A uniformed bar tender was busy mixing drinks. He waited to get his attention, then gently asked, "Is the owner here?"

"The owner? You mean Ugo? Yeah. He's in the kitchen."

"Can I talk to him?"

"Good luck. He's busy preparing for tonight's menu. A busy man, Ugo Perez. I will try, but don't count on it!."

Pebble nodded and waited patiently.

"Ugo, somebody here to see you! Can you come out?" He shouted with a raspy voice, probably from alcohol, or smoking cigarettes.

He winked at Pebble and said, "We'll see if he appears. He is the jack of all trades. After finishing his cooking, he goes for a nap. You see that piano there? He also entertains, playing and singing until late hours."

As soon as he said that the swinging doors of the kitchen opened a swift middle-aged man appeared. For a minute, Pebble's body shivered and his skin broke out in goose bumps. "Oh! My God! Is he Alonza's brother?" He wanted to run and disappear, his desire to talk to him gone. But he remained there, frozen. Just in time, the man spoke and broke his spell with a strong voice.

"Who wants me, Bruno?"

"This young man here."

He appraised Pebble with a serious look on his face. "What, this young man? You got me out of the kitchen for something you could have handled?"

"Ugo, he asked for you — the owner. I thought he's a relative of yours or something." He shook his head, disturbed.

In an abrupt way, he turned to look Pebble up and down. "Can . . . What can I do for you?"

Pebble shook in his pants. He wanted to say nothing and walk out that door as fast as he could. To his surprise, he heard himself say, "Sir, I am looking for a job."

Ugo sensed the young man's nervousness.

"Do you have something here for me to do?"

Ugo, having second thoughts, asked in a milder voice, "You seem young. What can you do? We like someone with experience in our kitchen."

"I have worked as a dishwasher in the kitchen on the luxurious ship, sir. I love to learn in the kitchen."

"You live here?"

"Yes."

"You speak Spanish?"

"Yes."

"Any other language?"

"Pochito Italian." He gestured with his hands. "From my friends on the street, sir; but I am willing to learn anything, sir."

Ugo smiled. "I'll tell you what. We are busy here. Give Bruno your name and phone number and we'll call you. We can use some help around this place, providing you are willing to adapt and apply at different tasks. We cannot pay much, as you will be assigned to odd jobs and be learning."

Pebble felt feint; was he hearing right? "Is this really happening?" he mumbled to himself. Before he knew it, Alonza's ghost walked away.

The bartender took a piece of paper and pen in hand. "What's your name and phone number, kid? He is a busy man — works day and night. I am glad he decided to get some help."

"I have no phone number. My name is Pebble. I will stop by every day and check with you, if and when I am needed."

"Okay, Pebble. Ugo is a good man, just overworked. You can learn a lot from him; especially, if you show a willingness to learn."

He smiled, elated. "I will come by tomorrow, and every day afterwards to check. Thanks, Bruno."

He shook hands, all excited and quickly left to go resume his post. He lowered his body on the stone bricks; looking up to heaven, he implored, "Please, God, let me get this job."

Chapter Six

Pebble's new adventure.

As promised, Pebble relentlessly checked in with Bruno every single day, plus checking other places for a job. Until one lucky afternoon, Bruno stretched his hand for a hand shake. "Eh! Welcome on board. I got good news. Ugo wants to see you and give you details of your job description. We are getting pretty busy around here. He decided to get some help. Good luck, buddy. I am glad you stopped by; he is waiting for you."

Although Ugo reminded him of the detested Alonza in his stature and serious expression, Pebble's gut feelings were kind of positive towards him. When he spoke, he sounded genuine. "Look, Pebble, you will start from the bottom here. You are young, and although you have not taken any culinary courses, I can teach you all I know in my specialties. You must apply and be willing to learn. For now, you can start washing and stacking dishes in the back room of the kitchen. You can clean tables and serve water. Show me how hard you can work. If all is promising, you will be the assistant chef to Mauro. I learned it all from a Sicilian grandmother and my Spanish father. Let's shake hands. Today is Wednesday; you can start on Monday if you like."

Pebble's heart rejoiced. He extended his hand to shake.

"Thank you, thank you. I will be here on Monday, sir."

"Call me Ugo, I'm looking forward to you joining our team." No mention of money was asked or given. Pebble was delighted to have a job for whatever Ugo was willing to pay for his work. It was all a plus and a refuge from the streets. Pebble's new career begins . . . At La Scoglia Doro.

Pebble took his job seriously. He was always early, waiting for the door to open until he was given a key. "A gift from heaven," he would mutter to himself. He stared at his first paycheck in disbelief. He needed guidance on what to do with it. He never knew about bank accounts or anything of that sort. How would an abandoned child know of such?

After a couple of weeks, Ugo had been watching him, and recognized Pebble was a good human being, willing to learn and eager to please. "Pebble, I suggest you slip into your uniform with our gold logo and work on tables two days a week; that will give you a little orientation, plus a feel of our clientele's demands."

"Yes, Ugo, anything you say. I'd love to do that."

It was around eleven o'clock in the morning. The bright sun rays were filtering through the windows, promising a lovely sunny day. The clear blue sky was a mix of amazing blue hues. Pebble felt lucky to be alive in this part of the world. He approached one table at the corner by the window to pour water. This lady startled him.

"Wait a minute, I know you!" Staring and bringing a hand on her chin, thinking. She tapped on his shoulder, and all smiles said, "Hi there! Do you remember me?"

Pebble lifted his head, not sure at first, but then a memory hit him. Yes, here she was. The red-headed lady that had given him the big tip of four green bills. "Of course! The lady from the food store." How could he forget? She had boosted his spirit and his life. With a big smile on his face, he offered his hand to greet her. "How are you, madam? Nice to see you again."

"Likewise, how are you? I see you got yourself a job."

"Yes, you could say that. It's whenever they need me."

"You have gotten taller. I had to look twice; I wasn't sure if you were the same. . . pebble on the beach, you said?"

He smiled. "Yes, my name is Pebble. I named myself that: a

pebble from the beach." Self-consciously, he turned his head to look at his boss standing by the counter, watching his time spent chatting while being paid. Then, encouraging her, asked, "Are you going to have lunch here? I will get someone to assist you."

"Yes, I am. I have asked a friend of mine to meet me here."

As they spoke, another lady walked in and headed toward them. Brenda introduced her as Susy Brown. After the introduction, Pebble excused himself and a server took over since he was only the water boy.

Time passed and Pebble had passionately been learning the restaurant business. Emilio Swartz, a man in his fifties, was the real owner of the restaurant. Since he had few other places in different locations, Ugo was his man in command. He depended on Ugo and his monthly statement reports to check the business success. Ugo, likewise, took his position seriously. Being the head fellow, his job was to reach every monthly quota and plus rate his employees' achievements. He had praised Pebble highly in his efforts as a good employee. He had worked hard to meet the demand of his customers; his duty was to oversee all over the places. He liked Pebble and his work ethic were admirable. By merit, he preferred him more than any other employee. His hours at work had doubled and he been learning more than expected. Most nights, they ended up working very late, especially on weekends. It was at one of those overwhelming evenings that, Pebble turned to Ugo and asked, "Boss, why don't you go home? I will clean up this mess if you'll allow me to stretch myself in the back room and spend the rest of the night here."

"Eh! Kid, what are you saying? Are you nuts or something? You can't sleep on that cement floor."

"You want to bet? You don't have to pay me the extra hours. It is in exchange for allowing me to sleep here the night, please."

"Eh! Be my guest, I have nothing to lose. One thing: make sure your bones wont ache in the morning. You need to be in good shape. The boat show is on and we will be busy tomorrow."

"Not to worry, I will be fine." Thankful, to have found himself a roof over his head for the night. He carried a small roll-up bag with his belongings, and after everyone was gone, it served him fine to rest on the floor by the corner in the back storage room.

One Saturday night, they had closed at three in the morning. Pebble had just stretched his tired body inside a zipped sleeping bag at the back of the kitchen. In no time he had slipped away from his exhaustion. When suddenly he was startled from his REM sleep by the sound of falling scattering glass hitting the floor somewhere, he jumped up, confused. He heard some whispering voices and footsteps. "God Almighty, somebody is in here?" He didn't know where to hide, run, or shrink into nothingness. If whoever it was discovered him, he was done in, they would hurt or kill him for sure. His heart pounded, as the door of the kitchen opened slowly and two hooded dudes, half-crouched, made their way forward. He quietly shriveled into a ball in his spot, breathless, motionless. This was worse than any nights he had spent on the streets. Covered, watching with one eye he observed . . . One of the two characters had a bag, and they opened the fridge door and grabbed the best sirloin steaks and threw them in the bag.

Pebble shrivelled deeper in his bag as the other was looking around. "What was that?"

One asked "did you hear a noise?"

"No, I must have hit something by the side. Let's hurry and get out of here."

"OH! Thank God." What seemed an eternity for Pebble, they finally exited the kitchen and proceeded to the other room. Silence returned, but Pebble was too terrified to move.

They were robbed, lucky for him, he wasn't discovered . . . Apparently, they only took food, and booze. But the place was in a chaotic state with broken windows. After that frightening incident, Pebble didn't feel secure sleeping at the back of the kitchen any more. Since he had some money now, he decided to find another refuge to spend the night. He would talk to Bruno and Ugo; maybe they would help him out.

The food was free for the employees, so Pebble didn't go hungry anymore. The money had accumulated, and he needed to figure out what to do with it. For now, he had stashed it in his underwear. He had found a pouch at the Jewish bazaar with an elastic string. He tied the loot on the loop of his pants, turning it on the inside. It was a bit of a nuisance, but by touching his flesh, it was secure at all times. The other workers talked about bank accounts and going to the bank to deposit their cheque or money. Bruno had exchanged his cheque from the register since he was ignorant about bank account. He was the bank. It was dangerous and it worried him. Listening to others, he thought, I need to do something with my illiteracy. He wanted to take some evening classes to learn how to read and write, but so far, he hadn't. His English had been picked up here and there through speaking. Since working, he hadn't seen Old Joe anymore, so he was getting by the best he could between Spanish and broken English. He was intelligent and young. He loved South Florida. His next plan was to enroll in evening classes.

His lady friend, Brenda, had become a regular at the place. She was well served, the food was great, and the attention made her feel special. The woman had become fond of Pebble. She could have been a good mother, but with her previous busy lifestyle, she had never had children. Later in life, she regretted the emptiness. It was Monday morning. She arrived at the restaurant earlier than usual, dishevelled, with her eyes bloodshot.

Pebble immediately knew something was wrong with his friend. He greeted her affectionately, rested his hands on her shoulders, and after taking a good look at her, asked in a melancholic tone, "Miss Brenda, what is wrong?"

Before answering him, she burst out crying. He embraced her tenderly, shocked.

"Come on, tell me what is wrong. What's happened? I am here to listen and help you if I can."

"My dog died. He was such a good, caring pet, waiting for me to return every time. He loved me to no end. Now he's gone. My cats, my Cherokee, none of them can replace my poor dog. They came and took him away this morning. I couldn't handle anything for his burial." She continued sobbing, broken-hearted.

"I am so sorry. I know how you feel; can I do something to alleviate your pain, Miss Brenda?" He kept rubbing her shoulders, trying to make her feel better. He wanted to pacify her; as she was drowning in sorrow.

"Miss Brenda, please tell me what I can do to make you feel better."

Then she looked up at him and between tears, asked, "Pebble, could you come over my place later when you are finished working? I cannot bear to be there alone, without my Duke. He was always at my side. I need someone with me at the house to help fill the void."

"Yes, of course, I will; don't you worry. You need to give me your address. I will be there right after work."

"What time do you finish working?"

"Usually late." Once he saw the despair on her face, he said, "On second thought, I will ask Ugo if I can sign off earlier, because you need me."

Brenda, with tears streaking down her cheeks, nodded in agreement and left shortly afterwards.

Pebble was sincerely affected by his lady friend's state of mind. He moved about, doing his chores like a robot and glancing at the clock for the time to pass all afternoon.

Ugo had granted his early leave. "You deserve it, my boy; go and help your lady friend," he had said, slapping his shoulder.

Pebble had money now, so he could afford to take a cab. At 6:30 pm, the taxi pulled up in front of the address he had been given by Miss Brenda. He paid his fair and tipped the driver. For a moment, he hesitated, not sure if he should go in or ask the taxi driver to wait for him. Or was he at the wrong place? While he was assessing the deluxe structure in front of him, he turned around to see the taxi driver speed away. Reluctantly, he made his way through the large black gate. The home was enormous. He knocked on the big double door and Brenda appeared in no time.

"Welcome, Pebble, come on in; glad to see you."

She looked pale and sorrowful, sniffing away while holding a tissue in her hands. As he stepped into the foyer, the overwhelming grandeur with the crystal chandelier surrounded by an opulent staircase leading to a second floor left a lot to his imagination. Pebble stood wide-eyed and breathless in admiration.

Where am I? Is this real? Brenda startled him from his thoughts

"Come, Pebble, we will sit in our family room. Come and meet my friends."

The entranceway led down a short, wide corridor to an open concept relaxing room, wall-to-wall windows covered the entire opening, lending to the intercoastal waterway. Pebble expected to see other people, as she had said: "my friends."

There, all together by the circular leather sofa, were two cats and a bird. Miss Brenda said, "Meet my companions. This is Lily, and this is Toky." They were both covered in fluffy white fur with a black streak on their heads and tails. They looked like twins. As they saw Pebble, they walked circles around him.

"They like you, Pebble. They haven't moved much from their spot since Duke died. I'm sure they are in pain."

"Amazing. Animals are so intelligent; they are beautiful." He bent over to pet them.

Miss Brenda took him over to the bird. He was in a colourful cage with all the trimmings: a miniature tree and other paraphernalia that a bird would enjoy. "Here is Sunshine."

He fluttered about with his wings, and looked strangely at his new visitor, showing off his yellow feathers with black and blue and orange stripe on his head. "He is incredible. I have never seen all those colours. He is stunning."

"He is from the Cardinal family. Sunshine was given to me by my husband two weeks before he died. Pebble, these are my babies, my life; I love them so. They all got along; Duke and the cats were best friends."

She broke down crying again, so Pebble walked over to console her.

"Now, now, Miss Brenda, we will work on getting you a replacement. I understand how you feel. It will be hard, but time heals. I will be here for you if you need me."

"Oh, Pebble, you are so sweet. The universe must have put you on my path. To think, there you were cuddled on the floor by Publix. When you offered to help me, I was impressed. I felt in my heart you were a good soul. Now, here you are in my home."

"Miss Brenda, I am the lucky one to have encountered you. You have no idea how much you inspired me. Your generous contribution gave me a lead in life."

***

From this day on, Pebble's life took a new turn. He had joined the rank of illegal residents in the USA. From that famous day he had escaped from the ship for the unknown, he had survived the homeless nights and the days. Now, here he was with this gracious kind person in this luxurious home. He didn't know what to think. In his own sincerity, he lifted his eyes in gratefulness for the bounty of life on his journey.

Brenda startled him from his thoughts, saying, "Pebble, I live here all alone. Come, look out here." She nodded for Pebble to follow, then walked toward the double sliding doors that opened out to a pool decked with palm trees and well-manicured flower beds and coloured shrubs in full bloom. Furnishings were delightfully coloured with turquoise blue and white. There it was, the intercoastal waterways with an illuminated yacht floating by. "Would you like to live here and give me a helping hand with the maintenance of this place? I could really use someone like you."

Pebble was breathless. Am I hearing right? Me, a homeless?

Although he had been contented sleeping in the back of the kitchen at the restaurant, this was beyond his imagination — A real house with such offerings! He turned to Brenda, and with an amazed look on his face, he said, "I thank you so much, Miss Brenda." But in doubt, he asked, "What did I do to deserve this? You don't know me well; you found me on the street and you are offering me to share your home?"

"Pebble, you impressed me with your first good deed. I could read honesty and kindness in your eyes. I know in my heart that you are a good soul."

"Thank you, thank you, Miss Brenda."

She touched his arm and said, "You think about it and let me know."

Months later, after more interaction, Pebble became Brenda's best friend. He assisted her and managed the house chores. She was an educator — well versed in her subjects. She guided him in his financial affairs. Taught him accounting, debit and credits, how to read financial statements. When Pebble revealed to her his life story and his illiteracy, she set up evening classes for him to learn to read and write as much as his heart desired. Brenda was delighted to be his tutor on night and weekends while he kept his daily job, where he was also learning all the fancy recipes from Ugo. The master chef had detected the goodness in Pebble, and it was a pleasure to share his knowledge and teach him.

***

Years later, Pebble became Pebble Dolan, a successful business man — all to be credited to his ambition and willingness. Most of all, his dedication to hard work and offerings to help others was repaid by the kindness of the people he encountered. Where they presented to him by God's will? Or by his mommy up above, looking out for him. He wondered . . .

Yes, in the worst time of his life, these people had given him hope. They believed in him. Brenda gained the son she never had, Pebble found the true mother he had lost and had never known. Ugo also had restored faith in Pebble's life.

Later with the blessings of his adopted mother, Brenda Dolan, Pebble fell in love and married his wife Rosalia Del Gatos, a Floridian spanish girl. They were blessed with two children, Ramos and Nicolas— a family of his own. They lived in a mansion on the shore of South Beach. Pebble rose from being a destitute homeless to a thriving entrepreneur in hotelier, and the owner of famous chains of restaurants. He often thought of his Osea' Rodrigas, his heart longed to find him. His many attempts brought loose ends with no results. Once he hired a private investigator to locate the man he had never forgotten. Unfortunately, the news wasn't pleasant. Oase' had passed away in Mexico City few years back with terminal cancer. Pebble was much saddened by the news. It was his adorable Rosalia and Brenda to help him lift his spirit. Pebble wanted to do something in memory of his kind friend. He instructed his office to contribute to Lung cancer research on a monthly bases.

Brenda and Pebble, with his wife and children had bonded immensely as a happy family. When that sorrowful day arrived . . . Pebble set, holding Brenda's hand by her death bed, spilling sorrowful tears of losing his true motherly love. She took her last breath and part of him went with her. Despite the pain of losing his dear beloved, a flame flickered in his soul, reminding him to: Rejoice, this human being has restored faith in you. He would never forget her kindness that had given him courage to keep going. OH! from homeless to the richness of terrestrial bounty.

Novel No. 28

OUR TERRESTRIAL JOURNEY

A seed is planted, derived from love.

A phenomenal transformation develops in the designated course of time.

A human life is born, to a mother's delight.

The development in its transformation in a year's time is amazing.

The time passes relentless out of control. From a new born, to childhood, to teen years, adulthood, creeping faster than we like in leaps and bounds old age.

From that long ago and our first step, we find ourselves running through life in an uncontrollable speed . We strive to achieve our goals with all our efforts. We ride the roller-coaster life presents us in sorrow , happiness, and challenges of endurance. We cry, we laugh, we find ourselves in sorrow and joy. We create, amalgamate, with much hard work. Our demands get greater as time moves on. The people we interact with, can be rewarding with love , support , disappointments or even grief. We must be able with grace to accept what comes our way. Some of it we can control, especially if it's our doing; others we cannot! Unfortunately we are not on this journey alone. When our life our actions are exposed to the world at large with its people; being family, friends , or all the rest of human beings. We must learn to exercise, patients and virtue , combined with potion of love and kindness . Only then the transformation might turn from sourness to sweetness. In the end is all about our reaction. If we can control our reaction; which its not what people do or say , or what life throughs at us ; It is how we react! In the end suffering in our calamities will only shorten our journey in misery. We must love unconditional. The legacy we leave is that of pleasant memories on our completed journey.

WE SEEK HAPPINESS

Happiness is an abstract feeling highly sought by any human being on this planet. Since the day we are born, we strive for happiness. We cry out from discomfort, hunger, pain, or any need of want. The demand continues as our life progresses. Our ego grows in leaps and bounds, full, out of control. We allow it and become it's server. Foolishly, we think once happiness fulfills our heart and soul, our humanly body should rejoice. Before we realize it, we are pushed back on the same path. What's next? More? Bigger, better. We must ask ourselves, "What makes us really happy?" How long will the jolt of happiness last in our sizeable existence? Are we willing to let go of our ego before it torments our spirit asking for more? If we humble ourselves in contentment, yes, happiness will find refuge in our inner self. Unfortunately, the majority of us humans always aspire for more. Which wouldn't be wrong if it's balanced with acceptance. Balance is the key. The majority of us, dominated by anxiety, will struggle to achieve what we have set up to accomplish. We have set goals that must be met.

Goals are rewarding if we appreciate it with gratitude. But in dissatisfaction and eagerness for bigger and better, negative thoughts will drive us. Because of that, we compromise our serenity.

Now What? One should measure his successes from where he started to where he has reached and appreciate it in gracefulness. Unfortunately, most human beings are driven by their demanding pounding of ego — a force beyond their control to conquer whatever their ego stirs their mind to feed. In moderation, we can still find some joy in our attainment. But the majority of us seem to fail, caught in a web of dissatisfaction. Our temporary fixation is unsettling, and our cycle continues, asking for more. Not necessarily because of greed— sometimes it's passion, pride, satisfaction, glory, either for oneself or to impress others. Also, for some caught in their obsession, it can become an addiction. Then, on the other hand, there are workaholics; they have a need for self-gain, to please themselves and impress the world. Fame. It all boils down to feeding the ego, and happiness is jeopardized.

Nothing in life is easy to achieve; there is always hard work involved. Hard work combined with eagerness in total dedication brings anger, fatigue, neglect of others and especially our loved family members. The chaos of withdrawals, resentments, absenteeism, distraction will affect our body and soul in unhappiness.

If we only could allow ourselves to step back and realize that our journey on this planet earth is remarkably short. Our body is temporarily on loan for us to take care of it. Our heart should be filled only with love for ourselves and spread out to others; the good deeds passed on in humility and sincerity. Our soul will reign in peace until the last day it leaves us. Once it expires with our last breath, it will continue its spiritual duty. As for ourselves, once we discipline our being to stay in spirituality instead of egotism, we shall find our much-sought happiness.

Novel No.29

MI AMOR JUST VANISHED
MY LOVE JUST VANISHED

Madrid, June 5, 1960. It was a splendid Sunday afternoon. The sun was shining and the sky a mantel of cloudless blue. A gentle breeze blew Dario's strands of hair, sprawling them loose on his damp forehead. It wasn't helping. As much as he tried to control his nervousness, it had gotten the best of him. Anxiously, he stared at his watch one more time. It was 1:45 p.m. "Where are you, Meera, mi amour?" he mumbled to himself. She was three quarters of an hour late. Furrowing his forehead, he strolled the path by the fountain once more. They had agreed to meet there the day before. Now, what could have happened to her? When she had been late in the past, obstacles had always been in her way. Maybe she had suffered another impediment. All Dario knew was that he loved her so and he couldn't give up on her no matter what.

The thought of her being unavailable for him was enough to drive him insane. He stood there, pensively watching the waterfall that cascaded, synchronized all around the large fountain. He shook his head. If only my love life could fall into place just like these crystallized drops of water in their endless cycle. He closed his eyes, wishing to appease his soul. As of late, worry had dominated, tormenting his entire being. Oh! How I wish Meera could belong to me and me only. Why is the world so cruel?

He was deep in thought when a familiar jostle of footsteps

made him turn. There she was, radiantly advancing toward him.

"Finally," he exclaimed. Opening his arms, ready to embrace her, his heart rejoiced and his soul erased all worry.

"Darling, perdón, I am sorry. I wasn't sure if I would still find you here," she said, trying to catch her breath. "Here we are, together again." She sealed his lips in a long lingering kiss before he could respond or ask questions. Dario held her close to feel her heart beat close to his.

She pulled away for a moment to let out a big sigh and gazed at his beloved face. He is so handsome, my Spanish amour, she thought. There he stood with his wide shoulders a tall slim body, with welcoming arms where she nestled in refuge. Their feelings were mutual and their hunger unfulfilled.

He let out a big sigh and pulled her back toward him. Oh! How his body needed her close to him. He was afraid to let go. When he held her in his arms, he needed no explanation. Their time together was precious with every minute counting.

Meera's tenderness suddenly seemed agitated as she tried to pull away. "Darling, the mist of the water falls is dampening my hair, spoiling it for you. Let's sit on the bench by the dwarf palmettos by the garden, for it is quieter and we can talk."

The public garden by the main square was a piece of heaven, the lush greenery with blooming gardenias, rose bushes in full bloom with their mixed colours, the erect sculptured monuments, testimonies in mute silence. Yes, the added roar of the fountains added music to their ears. They would usually find a secluded corner to hide in solitude.

"Mi Amour, I don't feel like talking. I just want to hold you as close to me as possible," said Dario, gazing at her with lucid eyes.

She looked at him pitifully. "Dario, my love, I need to apologize for my tardiness. I almost couldn't make it today."

"Fine, don't tell me. You are here now. That's what counts. My suffering erases the minute I see you, mi amour."

Meera tried to control the tears blurring her vision as she knew their future together was next to impossible. Yes, she felt Dario's body tremble in their embrace, as hers responded feverishly in love with the same emotions. But deep down, she knew their secret love would soon come to an end.

She couldn't break his heart, not now, not yet. Why had fate brought them together? she wondered.

***

Meera felt guilty being with Dario. A big sin as in disrespect for everyone concerned. She often searched deep in her soul for justifications. The Universe itself knew she couldn't control or dictate to her heart who to love, or when to love. It had all happened spontaneously, beyond her control, or Dario's, as a matter of fact.

Meera was a stunning brunette with long jet-black hair, big eyes, slim figure, and a sweet voice. An attractive young woman with a docile smile that melted anyone's heart. She was kind and caring; people gravitated toward her. Her obstacle in life was that she belonged to a loving and devoted Indian family of five. Her mom and dad, two older brothers — Hayshul was the oldest and Arnit the youngest. She was the only girl. Their family was extended with aunts and uncles and lots of cousins. Their families were well cultured, affectionate, loving people, following their custom.

***

Meera had no intentions of getting involved in an extra marital affair. The force of destiny had found its way into their hearts, which neither of them could control. She had met Dario Alvarez one afternoon at the library where she was doing some research, checking out the best way to learn and master her Spanish. He was the Chief Executive officer at the main branch. Her husband, Dr.

Zakir Nair, had gotten all the information for her. Dario Alvarez could inform her of their programs. They were newcomers to Madrid. He was not only flattered by her interest in his language, he sincerely had offered to help in any way he could. His recommendations were his duty and genuine.

Meera Nair was serious about learning the language. Her husband was an honorable medical research scientist and often travelled, giving lectures in his field and educating other doctors in his research venues. Occasionally, Meera accompanied him and stood at his side at conferences and wherever they were requested to spread his knowledge. Dr. Zakir Nair was well respected and admired by his collogues and successful with his hard work. The medical advances were continuing in the sixties with the first open heart surgery and the coronary angiography in 1960 The lab departments were honoured to have him and they often requested him to participate. They knew with his expertise he would be an asset to their complicated medical research. Dr. Zakir Nair had a reputation of brilliancy from past discoveries. The projects he had contributed to had been the most successful. This was the revelation, going on since the fifties by discovering birth control, the vaccine for yellow fever, first heart surgery, and lung machine.

Meera with her three-year-old daughter, and five-year-old son, Abdul, and Amrita the nanny had followed him on her parent's insistence.

"Your place, dear, is with your husband. You must, go with him," her mom, Anari Ishis, had said to her, holding her hand in such a caring manner. She loved her family and had been a good daughter. With their blessings, they had moved to Spain from Johannesburg. Dr. Zakir Nair also had insisted they follow him, as he felt duty-bound toward his wife and children. Although being a workaholic, he was highly regarded as a good person dedicated to his family when he had time. Meera often found herself at a loss to fulfill her time. She had dedicated herself to learning and mastering languages. When it came to Spanish, she had been struggling with putting phrases together, but vowed to herself she'd be fluent in this sweet language full of deep expressions. Especially when Dario spoke to her and the adoration she detected on his face from his vivid expressions. They were to be in Spain for three years, with a renewal contract of two consecutive ones.

Meera was twenty-eight years old. She was the daughter of Dishank Iahis, a pharmaceutical entrepreneur. They owned a chain in Johannesburg and the USA. Dr. Zakir Nair was fifty-two years old. Her marriage had been arranged by both their parents. She had no say. That was the norm those days, and that had been well accepted with everyone's consent.

"Dr. Zakir is a good suiter for marriage, Meera," her mom and dad had said. After the introduction in their living room, his parents had been present and they likewise were in full agreement.

When it came to romance and love, it would all follow later, her mom had said to her privately. Meera had been taught to be obedient. After all, her parents were looking after her well-being. Such feelings of love or attraction didn't count. A good match in social status, a reputable man to admire. But since she had met Dario, her discovery was shocking... her feverish body awakened by dopamine was driving her in his direction. Before they could control their emotions, they were in each other's arms, indulging in their longing for one another. Meera had never experienced such ecstasy and pleasure. She had a husband at home and here she was engaging in an illicit affair. This episode of love had surfaced beyond her imagination. She knew it was totally forbidden in her world. When it came to the material necessities and the abundance of wealth in life, she didn't lack anything. They lived in an opulent home in Johannesburg. A house keeper was in charge of their home. A cook in charge of their groceries and meals, groundkeepers to maintain their gardens and a fabulous designed pool extending around their two-story home with a large natural stone wall enclosed by iron gates. A chauffeur at their service, which she resented especially when craving some privacy.

Dr. Zakir, other than being absent a lot due to his work, was respectful and cordial toward her. But his mind was consumed by his research projects. He strived to discover new cures. He had married later in life, taking a wife and building a family had been done to appease his parents' insistence. He was married to his work. When he was introduced to Meera, he had gone along and Meera likewise. But now.... Meera kept questioning herself.

"Why doesn't my body tremble like it does when I am with Dario? I am so in love with him. If I could die in his arms It would be a blessing," she would mutter to herself while walking in a daze.

Dario, a thirty-year-old bachelor, lived in a two-story building on the second floor. The apartment had been gifted and provided to him by his parents. They occupied the first floor. He was the eldest of the three children. His brother and sister had left Madrid and settled on the island of Tenerife where the climate was more desirable. Dario's mother especially was always encouraging her son to get married. In the past, he had dated several Spanish girls, but his relationships always faded away and he would lose his desires after a short duration. The chemistry just isn't there anymore, he would say to himself. Since he had met Meera, his feelings were something never experienced before, his existence revolved around her. Unfortunately, she was married and belonged to another man. He knew they were both in a difficult situation. Their relationship had no future. Since they had met, their liaison encounters had caused raised blood flow to their starving hearts. Dario feared asking himself, "How long will I be able to indulge in this love of mine?"

He pulled Meera close to him once more. "Mi amour, tell me this love of ours will never be taken away from us?"

She fought back tears while burying her face on his shoulder, whispering, "My darling, only a miracle beyond my imagination can allow our meetings to continue."

He pulled her back and looked her in the eyes, shaking.

"Meera! Mi amour, what are you saying? My love for you is bigger than the universe. I cannot live without you. My biggest fear is to lose you."

"Dario, you know I am a married woman; it's been wrong from the beginning. We should have never given in to our feelings. There is no future for us. It is totally against our beliefs. If our love gets discovered, I hate to tell you the consequences."

"Come away with me. We will hide someplace in the world where no one can find us."

"Dario, my love, we need to be sensible. My heart longs for you, but I have a husband, a daughter, and a son. Oh! My family. Worst of all, my parents, my brothers. We must stop seeing each other. We must put an end to this love of ours with no hope."

"Meera, don't say such things. We deserve one another; we cannot deny our hearts what we are both craving."

Meera realized it had to be her decision to put an end to this fatal attraction between them, thinking, God, help me. Give me the strength before it's too late.

"Dario, I must go now." She untangled herself from his arms circled tight around her. Dario pulled her close to him once more, furiously.

"Meera! Mi amour por favor, let's meet tomorrow again, same time. A chi! Por favor, I implore you!"

She nodded without responding. She kissed him one last time and sadly walked away. She couldn't break his heart even more today. Hoping that a universal bliss would change the plans she had secretly overheard last night beyond closed doors from her husband's study before he left for the airport. He was to work at the laboratory in London, England on a month assignment. She didn't know who her husband was talking to, but she heard him mention her name several times to whoever he was having the conversation with. Therefore, her clandestine plans and meetings with Dario were questionable.

***

She arrived home to find the nanny in an uproar. Lolita, her daughter, had given her a hard time.

"Mrs. Nair! She has been difficult, crying all afternoon since her dad left. Then she started to cry out for you. All she did was ask for her daddy and mommy. I offered to read to her in bed. She just didn't want anything to do with me as much as I tried." The nanny had felt annoyed with Meera's absenteeism lately. She hadn't been there to offer emotional support to her daughter and son. She felt the children needed to be reassured of her affection. Her behaviour wasn't acceptable, dressing in Spanish attire in a provocative manner.

The nanny rolled her eyes behind her back. She is asking for trouble, that's for sure, she thought to herself, fearing for her.

Meera, oblivious in her fog, took a deep breath, made her way, tip-toeing toward her daughter's bedroom. There she was now, sound asleep. A pang of guilt hit her heart as she admired her daughter peacefully sleeping. "Yes, my child, Mommy has been neglecting you. I must put an end to this insanity of mine," she murmured to herself.

Meera had never suspected that Amrita, a mature woman in her mid-fifties from India, had been spying on her in bribing the chauffeur, Alaih, with her own rewards to discretely keep an eye on the goings on of Mrs. Zakir. She had a keen eye, and since the outings to the library studies, she had noticed the change in Mrs. Zakir. She had approached Alaih a while back while he was polishing the car. "Alaih, where are you to take Mrs. Zakir today?"

"At the library branch to study?"

"Alaih, can you keep an eye on her? I am worried. I am a woman, and I worry about her. You read me? You know what I mean? keep this confidential. Besides, you and I have it pretty good with our patrons here and wherever Dr. Zakir is sent. We don't want to jeopardize our future with them. I have a feeling that Mrs. Zakir is up to no good here in Spain; we must stop it, you and I! Before the doctor discovers her... whatever she is involved with." She scowled at him, putting a hand on his shoulder and a serious stern look on her face.

"What are you talking about, Amrita? I will do no such thing, spy on my boss. She is a good woman."

"Alaih! You men are all the same. Trust me.

There will be big trouble soon if you and I don't intervene."

"Amrita, I have no idea what you are talking about and will not engage in your malicious nonsense. Now, leave me alone as I need to finish my work and ready for my lady."

"Okay! Have it your way. I have warned you we will both lose our positions. God knows what will happen to her! Do me a favour, watch the way she dresses; her total appearance, as a matter of fact. That alone should open your eyes!" She stormed away.

Not much later, Mrs. Zakir appeared. Alaih, having been warned by Amrita, set his gaze on his boss. She is the picture perfect of a most beautiful Spanish lady, her auburn skin, her jet-black hair, tied in a knot falling on her shoulders. Her flared dress, with a shawl. She is desirable for any man to admire. I know she has never worn her Sari except at home for the doctor. He didn't say a word, it wasn't his place, but a cloud of doubt invaded his being. God help her and us, maybe Amrita is right...

He swallowed hard, but from that day on, he started spying on his lady boss. To his surprise, he too became troubled by his discoveries and had reported his findings to Amrita.

Meera, in her euphoric state, had no clue of the two culprits having her under their scrutiny. The euphoria when with Dario and pain when away from him consumed her. Alert, Amrita kept watching her every move at home and Alaih during her rendezvous. They waited for a while, praying for her affair to stop. Amrita confided in Alaih, "I hope she comes to her senses. Otherwise, if this relationship of hers keeps on going. . .We need to stop it."

They were both discretely vigilant like shadows in the dark. One evening after having had another stressful episode with the children crying for their mother, Amrita took it upon herself to place a phone call to her brother Harshul.

The decision was in their hands. Harshul didn't waste time to call a family meeting. The fate of Meera was to be decided. After they verified their daughter's and sister's affair, they advised Dr. Zakir of their intentions. Dr. Zakir on the phone had consented, "Yes, Mr. Dishank, if it is your desire to have Meera back with the children in Johannesburg, I will sacrifice myself for the duration of my contract and come back periodically whenever I can... Only to see the children."

Her brother, Harshul, her dad, and her younger brother, Arnit, arrived on an early morning private flight. And Meera with her two children were taken back to where she belonged. Her dad and brothers set her down, warning. "Daughter of my heart, you do not ever attempt to be in touch with your Spanish lover or any one leading to him. We will forget about this episode in your life and grant you forgiveness, only allowing you to stay alive. You have disgraced our family as you well know," continued her father with a menacing voice and tearing eyes. Then her brothers gave her the same ceremony, stating her fate in captivity and isolation.

Her despair in missing her Dario from that day forward tore her heart and destroyed her soul. She wished to die. Only God could help her; her life was over from every aspect. Days turned into nights, nights into days, months and years passed. Meera was kept against her will   prisoner in a secluded cottage   with double locked doors in solitude.

The sparkle in her eyes had faded, her life a total loss. As for her children, she was not allowed to see them nor them see her. She had been labelled a bad mother and an ungrateful wife, not to mention on how she had dishonoured her entire family.

The love and happiness in her heart and soul had totally been crushed, vanished.

***

Dario, in Madrid desolated, walked in a daze, looking, waiting, searching for her. But no, not a trace of her existence lightened his horizon. She had vanished from this earth without a trace. No one had seen her, no one knew of her or her whereabouts. His frantic search in vain, his heart was torn and his soul devastated in despair. Years passed with no sign of his beloved Meera.

Dario started to believe his search had no beginning and no end. As time passed, his broken heart relented.

"Meera! Mi amour, was your existence just a dream? You have vanished. Por qué, mi amour?" he would ask himself. No one was there to answer him. He sorrowfully continued to walk the park by the fountain, hoping for a miracle. No one ever appeared to console his bleeding heart. He shook his head. Yes, your existence must have been just a dream and I thought it was real, mi amour. He slowly dragged his feet, resigned in despair ,visualizing his beloved Meera, tears kept flowing down his cheeks. But the burning flicker of flame in his heart refused to give up. Someday, somewhere my beloved girl will reappear and will reunite for ever once again.

LET'S SPREAD OUR LOVE

Let's be thankful as we awaken each morning. We are granted the gift, to greet a new day on this planet earth.

Let's start by thanking our creator of its creation with the bounty around us.

Let's be grateful for the bliss of the universe.

Let's start our journey to observe only the beauty.

Let's concentrate only on our spiritual offerings that bring peace to our soul and joy to our hearts.

Let's give ourselves permission to indulge only in spreading our love to others in good deeds.

Let's block any negativity surfacing on our horizon today and every day.

Let's share our gifted fortunes with the less fortunate. It can be a smile, a simple touch, a hug, a phone call. Yes, a simple gesture of acknowledgement.

Let's make a vow to spread only kindness each and every new day. We will be surprised how we will find the light at the end of our dark tunnel.

A colourful rainbow on our horizon to path our way, for each and every day.

Let's spread our Love.

COME INTO MY WORLD

Come into my world, walk in stride with awareness, observe what's around you, take it all in without judging.

Engage your senses to choose only the pleasantness.

Yes, walk into my world with an aura of acceptance and admiration for beauty.

The strangers you encounter out there are connected to you spiritually by the universe.

Greet them with a simple hello, a smile, a nod.

Remember there is good in every human being.

Seek the goodness and you shall find.

Never build a fence around yourself, leave the boundaries open and the energy around you inviting.

Come into my world. Loneliness will never be part of you.

The joy you will give is the joy you will receive.

A heart full of love has no room for sadness.

While you come into my world, let's live together in harmony.

Only then loneliness removes its sadness.

Our journey on this blissful world is shorter than we realize, we must treasure every moment until our transit to infinity.

When we reach our spiritual dimension, we shall rejoice.
United, we shall share the bounty of our divine Creator.
Come into my world, to share peace and harmony.

www.ingramcontent.com/pod-product-compliance
Lightning Source LLC
Chambersburg PA
CBHW071805080526
44589CB00012B/694